# ZERO-BASE BUDGETING IN THE PUBLIC SECTOR

## A PRAGMATIC APPROACH

# ZERO-BASE BUDGETING IN THE PUBLIC SECTOR

## A PRAGMATIC APPROACH

**PETER C. SARANT**

Director of Management Analysis Training
U.S. Civil Service Commission

ADDISON-WESLEY PUBLISHING COMPANY
Reading, Massachusetts · Menlo Park, California
London · Amsterdam · Don Mills, Ontario · Sydney

ISBN 0-201-06869-9
BCDEFGHIJ-AL-798

This text is dedicated to President Jimmy Carter. It was written to assist him in his efforts toward improving efficiency and effectiveness in the Federal Government by using the zero-base budgeting process.

# FOREWORD

The Federal budget process is central to conducting the business of government. It is also a critical component in the political machinery of democracy. If there is any formalized planning in government, either economic or programmatic, it is articulated through the medium of the budget.

Any accomplished political or bureaucratic official understands and respects the influence embodied in the formulization of the budget. The political power of a purse grows ever stronger as governments consume larger shares of the gross national product. In order to partake of this power, it is obligatory that the aspirant know something of the techniques and methods by which public sector budgets are created.

The pervasive influence of the budget process is deeply appreciated by successful public officials and administrators. We have seen an ever-increasing use of this process as a means to redirect or control legislated programs. A parade of budgetary systems has marched by in just the past decade. State and local governments have followed the trend or initiated variations of their own. And the Congress itself has recently reorganized its own methods of budgeting. It is even now considering yet additional ways to exert greater fiscal control through its appropriation and program review processes.

Public officials, political scientists, students of public affairs, and all others who wish to be knowing observers or participants in the government milieu need to have a good grasp of the current rules by which the game is being played. This book addresses that need.

R. J. Borntraeger
Director, Management Sciences Training Center
U.S. Civil Service Commission
Washington, D.C.

# PREFACE

## WHY WRITE A TEXT ON ZBB?

In the academic world it's "publish or perish." Nowhere in the State or Federal Governments is this concept followed. Experienced public servants are not given the incentive to perpetuate Government efficiency and effectiveness through the documenting of their experiences, i.e., publishing of a text. These texts are left to be written by college professors, sometimes inexperienced, whose credentials are an academic degree. In our changing society, taxpayers are clamoring for improvements in the public sector. The only means to accomplish immediate and effective results is through "How-to" training. Publishers such as Addison-Wesley are beginning to realize the need and demand for texts that are written in a "real world" context.

Another reason for writing *ZBB in the Public Sector* was the lack of texts addressing zero-base budgeting in the public sector. Acceptable texts by Pete Pyhrr and Logan Cheek had been written, but those were primarily directed to private industry. Government officials needed a text applying the zero-base process to the public sector.

As demand grew for training services and implementing of the ZBB process, contractors appeared on the Government scene, taking almost one million dollars of the taxpayer's money through ineffective courses and consultant fees. It became so evident that in the Federal Government on April 27, 1977, President Jimmy Carter issued a memo to the heads of all the executive departments and agencies. He wrote, "Wherever possible, I want you to rely on the Office of Management and Budget for information about this system rather than turning to outside consultants . . . this approach will help ensure that Zero-Base Budgeting is applied uniformly throughout the Executive Branch and that we save the wasted effort and unnecessary cost of relying on consultants."

As officials in the Government were in need of an up-to-date and economical text to train their employees, educators were in need of a similar text to assist them in teaching the ZBB process. At the urging of my college students and colleagues, I have responded with this text, *ZBB in the Public Sector*. This text is written in a manner that makes it relatively easy for a reader to understand and apply the steps and concepts of the ZBB process. To make the ZBB process more comprehensive I have modified it and added a dash of "real world" flavor.

## HOW I WROTE THIS TEXT

The master plan was to write about each step in digestible pieces. Each bit of information was confirmed with Government officials who were currently implementing the ZBB process in a public sector. The Federal Government example was used mainly because it represented the biggest user of ZBB and State and local Governments would gain by these experiences.

Warnings on the improper use of the ZBB process are given to the reader throughout the text. The plans called for including in the text all the latest Federal directives and instructions such as OMB Bulletin 77-9 and revised Circular A-11. Illustrative exhibits and examples were drawn from actual Federal and State Government manuals and experiences. Many top officials and educators working closely with the ZBB process have contributed to this work.

The master writing plan was executed further by:

- Having knowledgeable and experienced practitioners review and contribute to the technical material

- Ensuring that technical material was timely and up to date

Complementing my own background and experience, I had the text reviewed by other professionals.

Whenever it was beneficial to my readers, I researched and excerpted from authorities in particular areas of zero-base budgeting. To interface the Management-by-Objectives (MBO) process with the ZBB concept, I excerpted from George Morrisey's, *Management by Objectives and Results in the Public Sector*. My search for *experienced* public workers in the automation of the ZBB process took me to Little Rock, Arkansas, where I contracted Fred Porter and Rita Henry. For the last chapter of the text, Mr. Porter and Ms. Henry wrote "Automating the Zero-Base Budget Concept."

Mr. Porter is the Budget Manager for the State of Arkansas and has been with the Arkansas Department of Budget since their initial utilization of an automated budget system in 1972. Over the past 5 years he has been a key figure in the operations and refinement of that system. When Governor David Pryor determined that a form of zero-base budgeting was needed in Arkansas, Mr. Porter assumed a paramount role in the redesign and development of their automated budget process for accommodation of the zero-base budget concept.

Ms. Henry is a computer application manager with the State of Arkansas's Department of Computer Services. Ms. Henry has been intricately involved in the development and refinement of Arkansas' automated budget system for the past 4 years. She functioned in various roles as chief programmer, system designer, and system analyst, in a number of major data process applications including state-wide accounting, and federal grants management and acquisition. The article that they co-authored is just as appropriate for the Federal Government as it is for a State Government.

Other contents have been taken from the States of Georgia, Texas, and Arkansas, from the U.S. Public Health Service, the U.S. Department of Labor, Department of Justice, the Environmental Protection Agency, and various agencies within the U.S. Department of Health, Education, and Welfare.

In this text, I have also shown the interrelationship with the proposed Sunset Legislation, the Reorganization Act, and Management-by-Objectives. To assist the reader I have printed in the Appendix a bibliography composed of 100 articles and books appropriate to the study of the ZBB process.

I have standardized the ZBB concepts for the public sector while still managing to keep the process flexible.

This book is the result of all these efforts. I hope that the effective implementation of ZBB is helped by this text. This is my contribution to the training profession.

*Washington, D.C.*                                                                  P.S.
*November 1977*

# ACKNOWLEDGMENTS

In January 1977, I taught the first accredited college course in zero-base budgeting (ZBB) for the U.S. Department of Agriculture Graduate School in Washington, D.C. Thirty-eight top Federal executives attended this class held at the Office of Education, U.S. Department of Health, Education, and Welfare.

My main objective of the ZBB course was to work "real world" ZBB problems that the executives would encounter at their agency. Attesting to the course's success, Senator Talmadge of Georgia wrote, "This was one of the most outstanding courses given on zero-base budgeting."

The credit goes to the academic insight of Dr. John Holden and Dr. Edmund Fulker, Director and Deputy Director of the U.S. Department of Agriculture Graduate School, who decided to conduct training for zero-base budgeting before President Carter issued his ZBB directive.

This text was the result of urging by my students and other colleagues for a book which would (1) ensure the successful implementation of ZBB, (2) enlighten and speed the educational process of learning ZBB, and (3) provide educators with an up-to-date "real world" text that would "walk" students through the ZBB process.

I also offer thanks to the men who methodically reviewed this text and whose suggestions greatly improved it — Mr. James Vincent, Assistant Director of the Interagency Auditor Training Institute of the Department of Commerce; and Mr. Jon Bellis, Associate Director of the Management Sciences Training Center of the U.S. Civil Service Commission.

I would like to give special thanks to Mr. Dave Winfield of the Office of Management and Budget, Executive Office of the President of the United States. His understanding of zero-base budgeting special techniques gained from experience in assisting in the implementation of ZBB both in Georgia and in the Federal Government was invaluable in his review of Chapters 1, 2, and 5.

I would like to acknowledge Raymond J. Borntraeger, Director of the Civil Service Commissions Management Sciences Training Center, for the confidence he has shown in me and the career-enhancing advice and assistance he has provided me with over the past years. He introduced me, as an accountant, to the field of training, developed me into a professional instructor, and gave me my opportunity as a manager. His inspiration and encouragement were the significant factors in my completion of this book and he deserves special recognition.

I appreciate my family's patience, confidence, and sacrifices while I was engaged in the writing of this book.

# CONTENTS

# CHAPTER 1
# INTRODUCTION TO ZERO-BASE BUDGETING

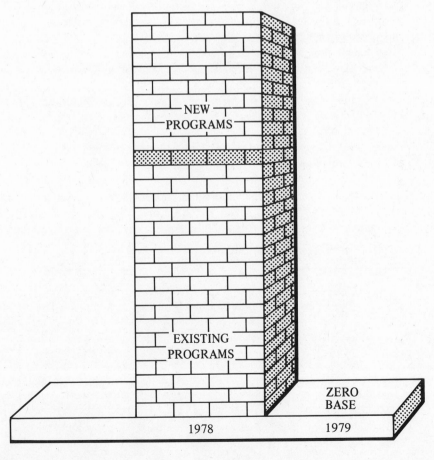

## WHAT IS ZBB?

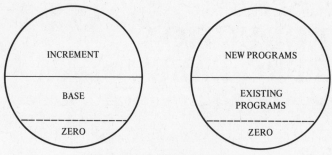

Model of traditional budget

Zero-Base Budgeting (ZBB) attempts to shift the traditional management approach of the Public Sector budget process towards a new mode of thinking and operation. Public budgets are traditionally prepared by taking the current level of funding for existing programs and increasing the expenditures to fund new programs, which are generally scrutinized closely. ZBB subjects existing, current programs and activities to the same kind of detailed analysis and justification usually reserved for new programs. Now, management will have to review selected ongoing programs vigorously and in detail.

Government programs may cross functional lines and be represented by an organizational unit that will be responsible for accomplishing the program objectives. It is the unit's manager who reviews and justifies the budget. In the Federal Government, the U.S. Office of Management and Budget has issued these instructions:

"Agencies should ensure that the basic decision units selected are not so low in the structure as to result in excessive paperwork and review."[1]

This can be interpreted to mean that all program elements within a program *are not* necessarily reviewed and justified under the ZBB process. The premise of zero-base budgeting is that agencies should review all programs at least once on a broad basis.

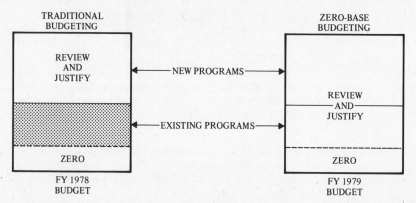

ZBB means "different things to different people." Some definitions are implying that zero-base budgeting is the act of starting budgets from "scratch" or requiring each program or activity to be justified from the "ground up." This is not true; the acronym, ZBB, is a misnomer.

ZBB refers to the review and justification of selected, not all, current program elements starting somewhere at a point *in* the base area and not necessarily *at* "zero base." (Refer to model of traditional budget.)

ZBB is a misnomer because in many large agencies a complete zero-base review of all program elements during one budget period is not feasible; it would result in excessive paperwork and be an almost impossible task if attempted.

## Definitions of ZBB

Since ZBB has not been fully established in the academic world as a major management approach, a number of definitions are presently in existence. Here are some of them:

> Zero-base budgeting is a management process that provides for systematic consideration of all programs and activities in conjunction with the formulation of budget requests and program planning.[2]

> ZBB is a system whereby each governmental program, regardless of whether it is a new or existing program, must be justified in its entirety each time a new budget is formulated.[3]

> Zero-base budgeting is a management tool . . . a method of more efficient use of limited resources in the pursuit of specified goals. The goal, as with any planning-budgeting process, is to identify the output desired, and the input resources required to obtain it. This need not involve a reduction of expenditures. An increase, if it efficiently contributed to the attainment of the desired goal, might be an alternative.[4]

> In the most literal sense, zero-base budgeting implies constructing a budget without any reference to what has gone before, based on a fundamental reappraisal of purposes, methods, and resources.[5]

The definition by the author, Pete Sarant, can be appropriately used in any environment, public or private:

> ZBB is a technique which complements and links the existing planning, budgeting, and review processes. It identifies alternative and efficient methods of utilizing limited resources in the effective attainment of selected benefits. It is a flexible management approach which provides a credible rationale for reallocating resources by focusing on the systematic review and justification of the funding and performance levels of current programs or activities.

## Concepts of Zero-Base Budgeting

ZBB is a management concept linking planning, budgeting, review, and operational decision making into a single process. Basic premises of ZBB in the private sector are that the budgets be justified from its "base upwards" and that new or existing programs and activities compete for resources annually by justifying current relevance, efficiency, and effectiveness. Terms defining ZBB in the public sector, such as justifying from its "ground up" or from "scratch" are erroneous and inappropriate. It is just as erroneous to mention that *all* programs and activities compete for resources in the "real world" of the public sector. There are public programs authorized by the legislature such as unemployment benefits or federal pensions for which it may be unsuitable to use the ZBB process.

ZBB is a flexible approach to budget formulation by which budget analysis and justification shifts away from *increments above* the baseline represented by existing programs to systematic review of *decrements below* that baseline; i.e., financial requirements for both *new* and *existing* programs or activities are justified and analyzed by the decision makers. The "thrust" of zero-base budgeting is:

- That it deals with practically all elements of the managers' budget requests, not just increments or changes over the previous year.

- That it examines ongoing activities just as closely as proposed activities.

- That it provides the managers a range of choices in setting priorities and funding levels.

Therefore, as stated in the Management Information Report on zero-base budgeting in Garland, Texas,

ZBB is a management tool which provides a systematic method for evaluating all operations and programs current or new, allows for budget reductions and expansions in a rational manner and allows the reallocation of resources from low to high priority programs.[6]

Traditionally, only *increments* such as increases to existing programs or new programs were subjected to detailed scrutiny and justification by managers. The other ongoing programs, the *base* programs, were not examined to determine if they effectively contributed to the agency's goals or objectives. Only periodic reviews of operational performance of program elements were made comparing budgeted with actual costs and outputs, and, of course, reviews were made whenever ongoing programs became subject to public attention. Under ZBB, examination and justification is made of both the base programs and the incremental programs. Under ZBB, managers can no longer take the current budget for granted and adjust only for new levels of effort for current programs or suggested new programs.

This new budgeting concept, ZBB, complements and allows the use of many current management techniques such as Management-By-Objective (MBO) and work measurement. ZBB is a complementary management tool that is flexible and can be adapted to meet the decisional needs of each agency. Finally, ZBB is a process by which (1) the goals and objectives of *decision units* at various levels in the organizational hierarchy are clearly identified; (2) appropriate alternative outputs to achieve those objectives are selected through analytical techniques such as marginal and cost-benefit analysis; and (3) means of efficiently using resource inputs can be identified and justified. It is a technique simple in concept but not necessarily easy to apply. This new technique adapts well to an agency's current budget process and can be a useful tool during the operating year.

## Characteristics of Zero-Base Budgeting

"The principal characteristics of zero-base budgeting are to:

- Involve managers (who have discretion over direction) at *all* levels in the budget and operational process;

- Justify the resource requirements for various levels of existing activities as well as for new activities;

- Focus the justification on the evaluation of discrete *programs, activities,* or other *function* of each *decision unit;*

- Establish for all managerial levels in an agency, objectives against which accomplishments can be identified and measured;

- Assess alternative methods of accomplishing objectives;

- Analyze the probable effects of different budget amounts or performance levels on the achievement of objectives;

- Use "decision packages" as the major tool for budgetary review, analysis, and decision making; and

- Rank program, activity, funding levels, and reallocate resources in order of priority."[7]

## Benefits of Zero-Base Budgeting

"This new system can provide significant benefits at all levels throughout the Federal Government. These benefits include:
- Focusing the budget process on a comprehensive analysis of objectives, and the development of plans to accomplish those objectives;

- Combining planning, evaluation, and budgeting into a single process;

- Expanding lower level management participation in planning, evaluation, and budgeting;

- Causing managers at all levels to evaluate in detail the cost effectiveness of their operations and specific activities — both new and old — all of which are clearly identified;

- Requiring that alternative ways to meet objectives are identified;

- Identifying trade-offs between and within programs; and

- Providing managers at all levels with better information on the relative priority associated with budget requests and decisions."[8]

Representative Charles H. Wilson of California, speaking before the House of Representatives, mentioned these additional benefits of ZBB:

- "It may eliminate duplicative and overlapping programs.

- An effective response to the problem of the erosion of public confidence in Government.

- It would permit Congress to better establish its priorities and allocate scarce resources.

- Efficiency in the legislative process might increase as ZBB would assist Congress to be more aware of what it is already doing."[9]

"Many agency management processes are aimed at providing some if not all of these same benefits. In many instances, however, such processes do not operate agency-wide and the information relevant to the processes is not gathered, analyzed, and reviewed in a systematic manner for all programs and activities. The value of zero-base budgeting is that it provides a process requiring systematic evaluation of the total budget request and all program objectives."[10]

## ZBB: A LINK TO A NEW PLANNING, BUDGETING, AND REVIEW (PBR) SYSTEM

After experiencing the demise of a program planning and budgeting (PPB) system which was to have revolutionized the budgeting world, the Government planners, budget analysts, and program analysts are hesitant about zealously supporting another fiasco.

They wish management would stop trying that "utopian link" ZBB would only threaten their independence and tranquility by requesting another "marriage" that would link the planning, budgeting, and review functions into a new system.

In formulating a budget using the zero-base budget process, an agency enters into three phases of management — planning, budgeting, and review. In the process of zero-base budgeting, all phases are linked into one system.

Zero-base budgeting is a technique; it becomes part of a system when the three stages of management — planning, budgeting, and review — are linked together. The ZBB technique is not the only management tool used in this PBR (Planning-Budgeting-Review) system. MBO, work measurement, cost benefit analysis, and program evaluation are some of the techniques that supplement the new Government *Planning-Budgeting-Review (PBR) System.* This ZBB technique should not replace a management system but build upon those already in existence. Graeme M. Taylor, one of the State and Federal Government's popular ZBB implementors, referring to this ZBB linkage to existing management systems, states:

> The budget, whether zero-based or not, will have to be capable of reconciliation with the Treasury's accounts. Various OMB reporting requirements, if maintained, will also have to be accommodated. However, unlike state and local governments, most of the federal government's management systems are not government-wide but are developed by each agency for its internal use. Since the most probable approach to ZBB in the federal government would be on a selective, agency by agency basis, the question of linkage to existing management systems arises primarily at the agency level. To the extent possible, the design of the ZBB approach in each agency should take account of and build upon management systems already in place, such as planning systems, manpower management systems, specialized information systems unique to each program, performance measurement systems, and cost-accounting and other financial management systems.[11]

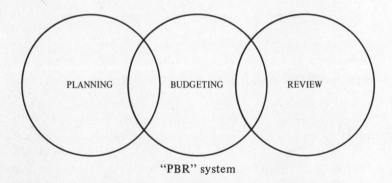

"PBR" system

President Carter's memo to all agencies states, "An effective zero-base budgeting system will benefit the Federal Government in several ways. It will combine planning and budgeting into a single process."[12]

## ZBB EXPERIENCES IN THE STATES

The spread of ZBB in the States was an indication of the continual search for improvements in the budgetary process. ZBB had been added to the many management approaches such as MBO and PPB used to manage and budget scarce resources in the States. Currently a dozen or more States have implemented ZBB or some components of the system. Among them are Arkansas, California, Idaho, Illinois, Missouri, Montana, New Jersey, Rhode Island, Tennessee, Texas, and Georgia.

State Governments took the lead in applying ZBB and became the "experi-
mental laboratory" of ZBB experiences by which the Federal Government has
benefited. The smart administrators who are interested in fashioning an appropriate
version of the ZBB process for their agencies are reviewing in detail these following
State experiences using the ZBB technique:[13]

- Idaho did not provide sufficient time for training and technical assistance.
  Not only didn't the agencies have an adequate understanding of the
  process but they failed to comply competently with the zero-base
  requirements.

- In Connecticut, zero-base review resulted in elimination of programs, but
  they ended up being retained because of "public appeal."

- In the State of New Jersey, ZBB met with staff resistance and the quality
  of information submitted was deficient due to their lack of fully understanding the basic system.

- In Tennessee, concern with the creating of large amounts of paperwork at
  lower levels, kept decision packages at the program level.

- Even in Georgia, the decision makers concentrated on a small number of
  issues and programs and "shortcutted" some recognized ZBB steps.


## ZERO-BASE BUDGETING AND OTHER PUBLIC SECTOR REFORMS

Three reform movements were emerging almost simultaneously in the public
sector. They were zero-base budgeting, sunset legislation, and reorganization. All
three reforms in the structure and processes of Government were at least in part a
response to the every increasing criticisms directed towards the public sector. Those
criticisms focused on the existence of a large number of ineffective or inefficiently
administered public programs; the seemingly eternal life of some programs and
agencies that have outlived their original usefulness; and the duplication and lack of
needed coordinates between the programs carried out by various governmental
levels and agencies. Since ZBB is but one of three current approaches to improving
the management of public sector agencies and programs, it is relevant to consider
its relationship to the other two approaches – sunset legislation and reorganization.

First, a description of sunset legislation is in order. The sunset concept began
in the State of Colorado and has been adopted by several other States. The sunset
legislation, if passed, would set an automatic expiration date not to exceed 5 years
for virtually every Federal program with the exception of such things as the interest
on the public debt, and self-financing programs like Social Security and Civil Service Retirement. This law would cause the "sun to set" on all programs – i.e.,
they would be automatically terminated unless reenacted by law. Virtually every
program would automatically have to be reviewed every 5 years or less. The idea is
to force the legislative branch to make the same kind of tough-minded, hard-nosed

evaluation of public programs that zero-based budgeting is designed to accomplish in the executive branch of Government. Under this system, compatible programs in a given area would simultaneously come up for reevaluation. After the reevaluation process, a program that is determined to have met its objectives and should be continued would be re-authorized by law.

Zero-base budgeting poses a challenge to Congress by increasing the imbalance of budgeting information between the executive and legislative branches of the Government. Zero-base budgeting is designed for use by the executive branch. If Congress wishes to review all of the alternative programs from which the President made his selection for inclusion in his budget, the congressional committees will have to obtain the information from the individual Government agencies. It is possible that the sunset legislation and zero-base budgeting could significantly alter the balance of power between Congress and the President since he will still have his veto and impoundment powers to restrict Congress from re-enacting many long-established programs that he considers nonproductive. Sunset legislation reached the Senate floor in the summer of 1977; and, if it passes, the public could see the greatest upheaval in governmental programs in its history.

At the time of the publishing of this book, witnesses before Senator Muskie's subcommittee raised more questions about the sunset legislative provisions than were answered. The Secretary of Health, Education, and Welfare, Joseph A. Califano, Jr., wondered if Congress could cope with "one thousand sunset reviews for HEW alone." Senator Henry M. Jackson, Democrat, of the State of Washington said, "the sunset legislation would overwhelm Congress with words."

## INTRODUCTION OF ZERO-BASE BUDGETING
## IN THE FEDERAL GOVERNMENT

Along with his other tools, President Carter has brought ZBB to the White House with him. Its successful use in Georgia and private industry had convinced the President to adapt it for the Federal Budget Process and so, on Valentine's Day, February 14, 1977 (Exhibit 1-1), President Carter issued an order establishing zero-base budgeting throughout the Federal Government and requested that each agency develop a zero-base budgeting system.

Following on the heels of this memo was Bulletin No. 77-9, Subject: Zero-Base Budgeting, issued by the Office of Management and Budget (OMB). This bulletin provided guidance to the agencies on the use of zero-base budgeting techniques for the preparation and justification of the agencies' 1979 budget requests. Separate instructions were also issued by the Office of Management and Budget in Circular No. A-11 in July 1977. This circular advised agencies how to submit budget materials to OMB. *All the ZBB information contained within OMB Bulletin No. 77-9 and Circular No. A-11 is quoted in appropriate chapters through the book.*

Now for an overview of the Zero-Base Budgeting process as implemented by the public sector.

THE WHITE HOUSE
WASHINGTON


February 14, 1977


MEMORANDUM FOR THE HEADS OF

    EXECUTIVE DEPARTMENTS AND AGENCIES


During the campaign, I pledged that immediately after the
inauguration I would issue an order establishing zero-base
budgeting throughout the Federal Government.  This pledge
was made because of the success of the zero-base budget
system adopted by the State of Georgia under my direction
as Governor.

A zero-base budgeting system permits a detailed analysis
and justification of budget requests by an evaluation of
the importance of each operation performed.

An effective zero-base budgeting system will benefit the
Federal Government in several ways.  It will

   .  Focus the budget process on a comprehensive analysis
      of objectives and needs.

   .  Combine planning and budgeting into a single process.

   .  Cause managers to evaluate in detail the cost-
      effectiveness of their operations.

   .  Expand management participation in planning and
      budgeting at all levels of the Federal Government.

The Director of the Office of Management and Budget will
review the Federal budget process for the preparation,
analysis, and justification of budget estimates and will
revise those procedures to incorporate the appropriate
techniques of the zero-base budgeting system.  He will
develop a plan for applying the zero-base budgeting concept to preparation, analysis, and justifications of the
budget estimates of each department and agency of the
Executive Branch.

I ask each of you to develop a zero-base system within
your agency in accordance with instructions to be issued
by the Office of Management and Budget.  The Fiscal
Year 1979 budget will be prepared using this system.

By working together under a zero-base budgeting system, we
can reduce costs and make the Federal Government more
efficient and effective.


                              Jimmy Carter

EXHIBIT 1.1

## AN OVERVIEW OF THE ZERO-BASE BUDGETING PROCESS

Many authors and contractors have written about zero-base budgeting without placing its process in some logical order for the public sector. Pete Pyhrr's process and order of ZBB applies to the private corporations, but leaves out important information when applying the process to the public sector. There is much more to be considered, such as the political process and its relationship with the bureaucracy, reorganization procedures, and the unique budget process of the United States.

The steps in the ZBB process explained in the rest of the text have been thought out logically and related to the "real world" of a Government agency. The various sections of this text are based on those specific steps necessary to introduce as well as continue the ZBB process within a typical Government agency.

Internal zero-base budgeting procedures are developed within an agency using the following steps in the ZBB process:

1. Identify an agency's organizational structure, management, decision units, and objectives

2. Develop decision packages

3. Review and rank decision packages

4. Prepare and submit the budget

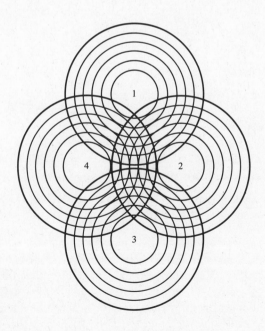

### Step 1: Identification of an Agency's Organizational Structure, Management, Decision Units, and Objectives

First, the identification of the interrelated hierarchical parts of an agency is necessary to determine an agency's suitability for the application of ZBB. Once we have determined that an organization is an acceptable candidate for the implementation of Zero-Base Budgeting, the next objective is to determine if an organization or program is being considered for reorganization. This can be accomplished by acquiring the *newest* organization chart and evaluating pending agency reorganization or program realignment, and then communicating this information up and down the various management levels before implementing or completing the ZBB process. In the event of a reorganization or program change, those agencies not properly informed may be wasting time and effort in preparing or reviewing budget requests for programs that possibly may be substantially adjusted. The message is quite clear — top management must communicate immediately any assumptions and changes in program direction to those at the subordinate level.

After determining the viability of the organizational structure the next stage would be to identify managers who would be developing the budget requests (decision packages). These two substeps only have to be done once, usually at the inception of the ZBB process in a Government agency. Improper identification of a manager could result in the unnecessary preparation of large volumes of decision packages and place an excessive burden on the budget staff.

The identification of the organizational entities (decision units) which will prepare budget requests for the agency are accomplished through selection by higher-level management. Selection of these decision units are based on relationship to:

- Organization

- Program structure

- Special analysis

- Reorganization, if applicable

Other selection factors are:

- That units are not too low nor too high in the organizational hierarchy to prevent meaningful review or analysis

- That managers of these units make significant decisions on the amount of spending and the scope, direction, or quality of work to be performed.[14]

It is these managers who will prepare the budget requests and justifications (decision packages) for this agency and will identify objectives for their organizational units. The objectives of an organizational unit must correspond with the goals, missions, and objectives of the higher-level organizational units. Many public agencies currently use the management-by-objective (MBO) technique, so this particular step should not be difficult. The determination of long- and short-term objectives is a necessary step in the development of a budget request. As objectives are identified, managers must simultaneously determine the key indicators by which efficient and effective performance are to be measured.

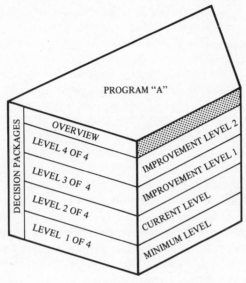

Decision package set

## Step 2: Development of the Decision Packages

Top-level management completes two functions in the zero-base budgeting process before decision packages (budget requests) are prepared. It decides what level of management develops the initial budget requests and gives the selected decision unit (organizational unit) the program and budget guidance it needs to prepare the requests (decision packages). These two functions illustrate why ZBB is first a "top-down" process before becoming a "bottom-up" management process. The guidance received from higher-level management before decision packages are developed includes items such as the specific services to be performed, personnel ceilings, estimated funding levels, and objectives to be accomplished. It should be noted that although the immediate program and budget guidance comes from the management tier above the decision unit, it usually represents an interpretation of the program and budget guidance that was given somewhere higher in the organization. This coordination of program and budget guidance "helps to insure that information provided in the decision package by a subordinate manager is broken down and arrayed in a manner conducive to higher level review of issues concerning the decision units."[15]

Having received the program and budget guidance, the organizational unit manager prepares a decision package set that includes decision packages reflecting incremental levels of funding and performance so that the cumulative amount of all packages represents the total budget request of the budget unit. Many different formats are used by the public sector for budget requests; however, most of the requests contain the same information. These budget request sets serve as the primary tool for budgetary review, analysis, and decision making.

An important stage in the development of decision packages is the performance of two types of analysis based on the program and budget guidance received from higher-level management. First, the decision unit manager examines alternative ways of accomplishing the major objectives. Management analysis, program analysis, and cost benefit analysis can be used for this examination. The best alternative is then selected and used as the basis for the second type of analysis, the identification of different levels of funding and performance.[16]

The manager prepares a set of budget requests that include incremental levels of funding, activity, and performance. This decision package set will include minimum, current, and incremental levels of funding and performance. The minimum level is that performance or funding level below which it is not feasible to continue a program, activity, or entity because it cannot fulfill its objective. The current level is the funding and performance level that would be reflected in the decision packages if the proposed budgeted activities will be carried on at the current operating level, without major policy changes. The minimum level of performance is identified below the current level, unless it is clearly not feasible to operate below the current level. The decision package set may also include. when appropriate, a level or levels between the minimum and current levels and any additional improvement increments above the current level. Each decision package displays different performance levels with associated funding requirements.[17]

There are many formats used in developing decision package .sets for the public sector. It should be noted that the decision package is a brief justification and request document that includes the key information necessary for managers to make judgments on program direction and resource requirements. Each level of a decision package, therefore, should contain at least information describing the activity, resource requirements, short-term objectives, and impact on major objectives.[18]

The decision package sets include an overview as well as the incremental "self-contained" decision packages. This overview is a "cover sheet" for the decision packages. It provides information necessary to evaluate and make decisions on each of the decision packages without the need to repeat information in each package. It usually contains such information as the long-range goals, major objectives, alternatives, and accomplishments of a program or an activity of an agency.[19]

Generally, decision package sets are prepared for all program and activities where there *is discretion* as to amount of funds to be spent, or the appropriate method or level of activity. In other instances where there is clearly *no discretion* in the amount of funds to be spent, or the appropriate method or level of activity, only one decision package should be prepared that summarizes the analysis and decision making that resulted in that request. It is sometimes appropriate that the lower-level managers support their initial decision packages by additional information or reports; however, discretion should be taken to avoid unnecessary and excessive paperwork. Also, top management may require other information to be included in the decision packages such as work measurement of man-power data statements, even though the data may not be required for budget submission to the Office of Management and Budget.[20]

## Step 3: Review and Rank Decision Packages

Once the decision packages (budget requests) are developed, they are ranked in order of priority by management. The ranking process provides management with a technique for allocating resources by focusing on the questions: "What goals or objectives should the agency be attempting to achieve first?" "How many resources should be allocated in attempting to achieve these objectives?" and "How many of the major goals should an agency attempt to accomplish at certain funding levels?" Thus, the ranking of the decision packages in order of priority allows managers at each level of the organization to determine which specific goals and objectives are more important than the others and to allocate limited resources to these important objectives.

The completed decision packages are ranked initially by the decision unit (budget unit) manager who has developed the decision packages. They are then sent upward through the management hierarchy whereby the decision packages are once again reviewed and ranked along with other "competing" decision unit packages. Each subordinate review level prepares a ranking sheet to submit to the next higher review level. This process can be repeated as many times as necessary; however, sooner or later a final consolidation and summarization of decision packages is prepared by a higher-level manager. Higher-level management's decision making needs may be met by recasting all or some of the initial decision packages into a lesser number of consolidated decision packages. The consolidated packages are based upon the more detailed information in the initial packages, but the information is recast or reinterpreted in a broader frame of reference to focus on significant program alternatives or issues.[21]

## Step 4: Preparation and Submission of the Budget

Once the decision package sets are accumulated from all programs or activities, consolidated, and ranked at highest possible agency level, the preparation of the detailed budget material begins. Some of the information for the budget estimates and justifications to be sumbitted to OMB are initially provided by the decision packages developed by the agency. After preparation of the budget estimates and supporting data for the budget year, the agency will submit these documents to OMB in the required format as prescribed by OMB Circular No. A-11. These requirements include a decision unit overview and set of decision packages or consolidated decision packages that are prepared and submitted to OMB for each decision unit identified by the agency in consultation with OMB. Agencies will also submit a ranking sheet that lists, in priority order, the decision packages that comprise the agency's budget request.

When the ZBB estimates are received in the Office of Management and Budget, they are referred to the examiner who is responsible for the program involved. This review of agency estimates at the OMB is a continuation of the ranking and review step of the ZBB process. This ranking process is heavily influenced by OMB's perspective, which may be different from the agency's. They identify significant program, budget, and management issues to be raised for discussion with agency representatives at hearings conducted in OMB during September and October. After the hearings are completed, the examiners prepare summaries of the issues and their recommendations for the Director's Review.[22]

The Director's Review provides an opportunity for the principal officials of OMB to obtain from the examiners an understanding of agency program aspirations and budget requests, an analysis of the significant issues involved, and the relationship of the agency requests to the planning targets recommended for the agency as a result of the Spring Planning Review. The review process is directed toward applying the President's policies to each agency's budget requests, identifying the aspects of the agency's budget that require specific Presidential attention, and developing OMB recommendations that the Director will make to the President regarding such items. Because of the size and complexity of the budget, the Director's recommendations together with those of the agency are placed before the President as portions of the review are completed. As soon as the President makes decisions on portions of the budget, agency heads are notified of the amounts that will be recommended to Congress for each agency's programs for the ensuing fiscal year.[23]

When the agency receives its budget allowance, the initial budget estimates are revised — in the conformity with the President's decisions — for inclusion in the printed budget documents. As soon as revisions of the individual budget schedules for each agency are completed, the figures are also consolidated to make up overall summary tables that present agency, functional, and various other tabulations. These summary tables together with final revenue estimates prepared by the Treasury Department, set forth the Government-wide budget totals. The President then transmits his recommended budget to the Congress.[24]

## NOTES

1.   Executive Office of the President, Office of Management and Budget, *Zero-Base Budgeting,* Bulletin 77-9, April 19, 1977

2.   Ibid.

3.   Pyhrr, Peter A., *Zero-Base Budgeting, A Practical Management Tool for Evaluating Expenses, 1973.* (John Wiley and Sons, Inc.)

4.   Wilson, Charles H., "Zero-Base Budgeting: Will it Work or is it Another Buzzword?", *Congressional Record – House,* January 31, 1977

5.   Taylor, Graeme M., "Introduction to Zero-Base Budgeting," *The Bureaucrat,* Spring 1977

6.   Lieninger, David L. and Wong, Ronald C., "Zero-Base Budgeting in Garland, Texas," *Management Information Report,* V. 8, No. 4a, April 1976

7.   Executive Office of the President, OMB Bulletin 77-9

8. Ibid.

9. Wilson, Charles H., *Congressional Record — House*

10. Executive Office of the President, OMB Bulletin 77-9

11. Taylor, Graeme M., "Introduction to Zero-Base Budgeting"

12. Executive Office of the President, OMB Bulletin 77-9

13. "U.S. Congress, Senate, Committee on Government Operations, Compendium of Materials on Zero-Base Budgeting in the States, January 1976," Government Printing Office

14. Executive Office of the President, OMB Bulletin 77-9

15. Ibid.

16. Ibid.

17. Ibid.

18. Ibid.

19. Ibid.

20. Ibid.

21. Executive Office of the President, Office of Managment and Budget, *Preparation and Execution of the Federal Budget,* 1977, p. 1-6

22. Ibid.

23. Ibid.

# CHAPTER 2
# STEP 1: IDENTIFICATION OF ORGANIZATIONAL STRUCTURE, MANAGEMENT, DECISION UNITS, AND OBJECTIVES

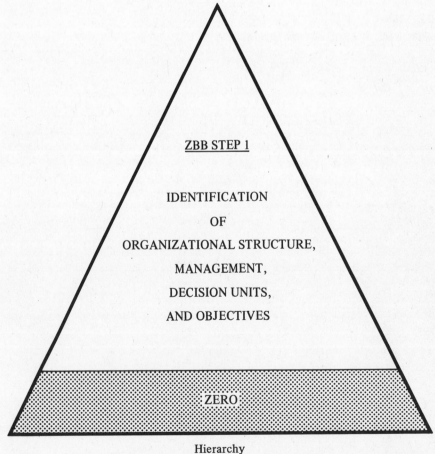

ZBB STEP 1

IDENTIFICATION

OF

ORGANIZATIONAL STRUCTURE,

MANAGEMENT,

DECISION UNITS,

AND OBJECTIVES

ZERO

Hierarchy

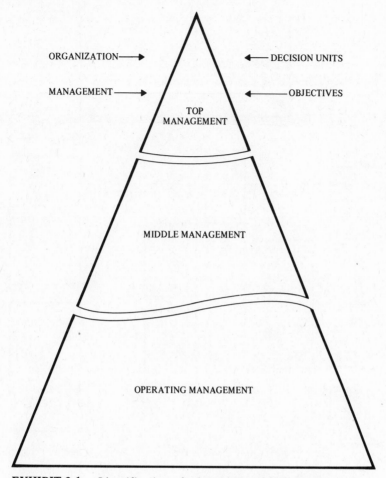

ORGANIZATION⟶          ⟵ DECISION UNITS

MANAGEMENT⟶          ⟵ OBJECTIVES

TOP
MANAGEMENT

MIDDLE MANAGEMENT

OPERATING MANAGEMENT

**EXHIBIT 2-1**     Identification of related hierarchical structures

One of the key characteristics of bureaucracy is hierarchy; hierarchy is needed to effect coordination of diverse activities by enabling superiors on successive levels to guide the performance of subordinates. An identification of the existing organizational structure must be made before we can identify the related hierarchy of decision units, managers, and objectives which will interact in the zero-base budgeting process (Exhibit 2-1).

## IDENTIFY THE AGENCY'S ORGANIZATIONAL STRUCTURE

Before management identifies the current organizational structure, these two determinations have to be made: Is the organization (agency) suitable for the application of ZBB? Is the organization or program being considered for reorganization now or in the future?

EXECUTIVE BRANCH AGENCIES

OTHER GOVERNMENTAL ORGANIZATIONS

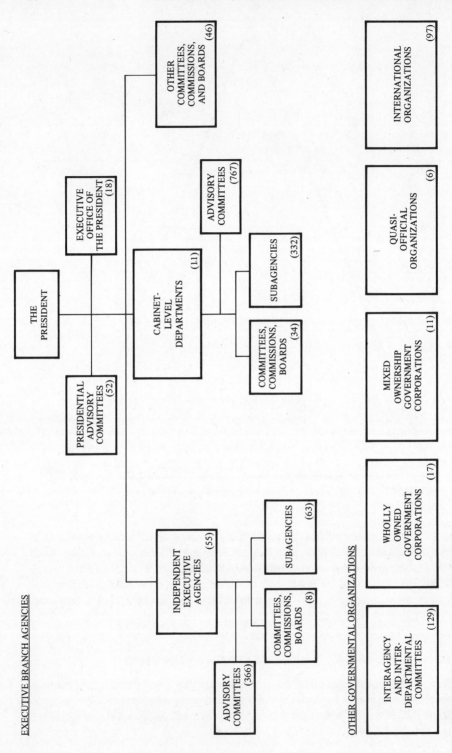

**EXHIBIT 2-2**   The executive branch

## The Executive Branch Agencies and Organizations

In the Federal Government the manager must determine that the organization is part of the Executive Branch and will be covered by the various directives or instructions concerning zero-base budgeting periodically handed down by the Office of the President. Recently, the Carter administration released a detailed categorization and accounting of Executive Branch agencies and organizations. It includes all Federal governmental nonjudicial and nonlegislative branch units.

It is important to note that this categorization of organizational elements is not an exhaustive accounting of the whole Federal Government. For this purpose, the Executive Branch is divided into categories of agencies reporting to the President and other governmental organizations. Examples of categories shown in Exhibit 2-2 (numbers on the exhibit represent total agencies):

- *Executive Branch Agencies*

  - *"Executive Office of the President,"* e.g., the Office of Management and Budget, the National Security Council, and the Council of Economic Advisors.
  - *"Cabinet-Level Departments,"* e.g., the U.S. Department of Agriculture, Department of State, and Department of Commerce.
  - *"Sub-Agencies"* of Cabinet Departments include such units as the Soil Conservation Service in Agriculture, the Agency for International Development within State, and the Census Bureau within Commerce.
  - *"Independent Executive Agencies"* include, for instance, the Veterans Administration, the Environmental Protection Agency, and regulatory commissions such as the Federal Trade Commission.
  - *"Sub-Agencies"* of independent Executive Agencies are the Department of Veterans Benefits in the Veterans Administration, the Office of Toxic Substances in the Environmental Protection Agency, and the Bureau of Consumer Protection in the Federal Trade Commission.
  - *"Other Committees, Commissions, and Boards"* include such independent entites as the Navajo and Hopi Relocation Commission, the National Capital Planning Commission, and the Marine Mammal Commission.
  - *"Presidential Advisory Committees"* include groups like the Presidential Council on Physical Fitness and Sports and the Federal Council on Aging.

Both Cabinet-level Departments and independent Executive Agencies also typically have multiple *Advisory Committees,* e.g., the Gila National Forest Grazing Advisory Board in the Department of Agriculture, and the National Drinking Water Advisory Council in the Environmental Protection Agency.

- *Other Governmental Organizations*
  - *"Interagency and Interdepartmental Committees,"* e.g., the Interagency Committee on Antarctica and the Interdepartmental Committee on the Status of Women.
  - *"Wholly-Owned Government Corporations,"* e.g., the Legal Services Corporation and the Tennessee Valley Authority.
  - *"Mixed Ownership Government Corporations,"* e.g., Consolidated Rail Corporation and the Rural Telephone Bank.
  - *"Quasi-Official Organizations,"* e.g., the U.S. Postal Service and the National Academy of Sciences.
  - *"International Organizations"* are both bilateral (e.g., the International Boundary Commission, with Canada) and multilateral (e.g., the Pan American Health Organization)."[1]

## REORGANIZATION IMPACT ON ZBB PROCESS

Next, it should be determined if an organization does, in fact, exist or a program is being considered for reorganization. Agencies periodically undergo "reorganizations" through the executive and congressional processes. It is extremely important that impending agency reorganization or program realignment be recognized and communicated up and down organizational and management levels before implementing or completing the ZBB process. A reorganization within an agency could affect the ZBB process if it occurs during the budget year. Do not continue the zero-base budgeting until full information is received about the new structure or program.

Reorganization and program changes resulting from new legislation sometimes occur simultaneously. In this event, the time invested in preparing and reviewing budget requests (decision packages) may be wasted if the manager does not consider new legislation when developing the decision package. Serious problems could occur if realignment occurs during the budget process or operating year. Reorganization may occur after budget requests and rankings have been completed, especially if the reorganization resulted from recommendations made by the agency.

*Example:*
In the Budget of the U.S. Government for FY 1978, there is a proposed reform of the Federal Nutrition Programs (Child Nutrition Reform — Exhibit 2-3) as follows:

The Administration is proposing a single, block grant to provide Federal funds to enable States to feed needy children. There are now 15 Federal programs which provide subsidies for 40 different types of meals. Programs at the Department of Health, Education, and Welfare and the Department of Agriculture will be affected.

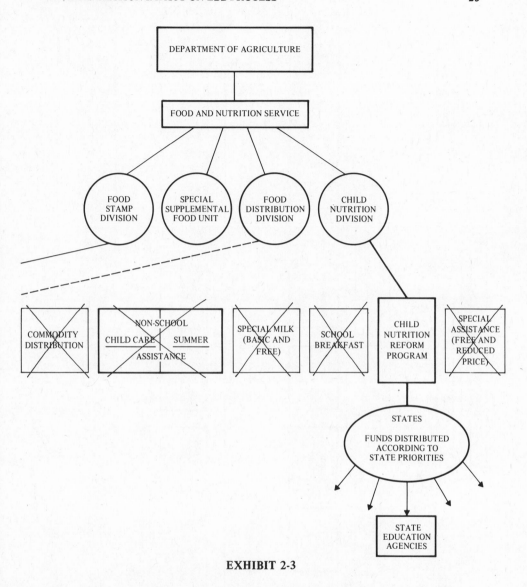

**EXHIBIT 2-3**

By eliminating unnecessary Federal programs and assistance to nonneedy children, this proposal is expected to save more than $1 billion in outlays in FY 1978.[2]

At one of my college sessions at the Department of Education, I showed this exhibit of the proposed reform of the Federal Nutrition Programs to managers who were in the process of developing budget requests (decision packages) for these programs. This proposed realignment came as a surprise; top management had kept them "in the dark" by not giving them any sufficient program guidelines.[3]

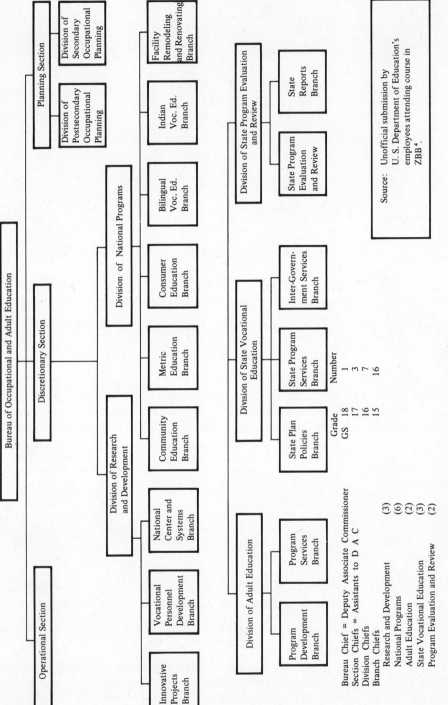

**EXHIBIT 2-4    Department of Health, Education, and Welfare**

Let us assume the managers of the Child Nutrition Programs, i.e., School Lunch and School Breakfast, continued to develop budget requests. Obviously they would have engaged in a great deal of wasted effort and expense (45 unnecessary budget requests). The message is clear; whenever possible, top management should communicate any assumptions and changes in program direction to those at a subordinate level (Exhibit 2-4). Possibly top-level managers should prepare the decision packages if a reorganization or elimination of a program is being considered.

## REORGANIZATION ACT OF 1977

A White House press release states, "In the Federal Government, President Carter has acquired more presidential authority over the Government structure through the Reorganization Act of 1977. Harrison Wellford of the Office of Management and Budget is spearheading the reorganization effort.

"President Carter signed into law on April 6, 1977, the Reorganization Act of 1977 and announced plans for a 'searching examination of the entire Government structure.' The Act gives the President authority to propose to Congress reorganization plans that will take effect 60 days later unless rejected by either the House or Senate. Congress, State, and local officials, and private citizens and groups will be involved at every stage of the reorganization process.

"The Office of Management and Budget will coordinate the effort. Reorganization recommendations are to be developed by special teams of Federal employees from OMB and agencies being reorganized, as well as experts from the private sector. *OMB is coordinating the effort to assure that budget and organization decisions are linked,* and to provide staying power for what will be a 4-year effort. 'Previous reorganizations have stressed moving agencies among Cabinet departments. Ours will take a bottom-up approach,' said Bert Lance, Director of the Office of Management and Budget, 'looking first at program and people's needs and reworking structure and process to meet those needs.'[4]

"The Carter administration's reorganization program is designed to make the Government more responsive, open, accountable, *and* efficient.

"Reorganization proposals will be developed and implemented over a 4-year period. Initial projects include creation of a Department of Energy, streamlining the Executive Office of the President and civil rights enforcement activities, and consolidation of consumer advocacy agencies. Later initiatives will be developed by functional area study teams which will do a comprehensive review of Government agencies and programs."[5]

## IDENTIFICATION OF THE EXISTING ORGANIZATION

After determining if a reorganization or program change is pending and that ZBB is applicable to their agency, top-level managers should identify and approve the newest organizational chart (Exhibits 2-5 and 2-6) and communicate them to the

DEPARTMENT OF HEALTH, EDUCATION, AND WELFARE

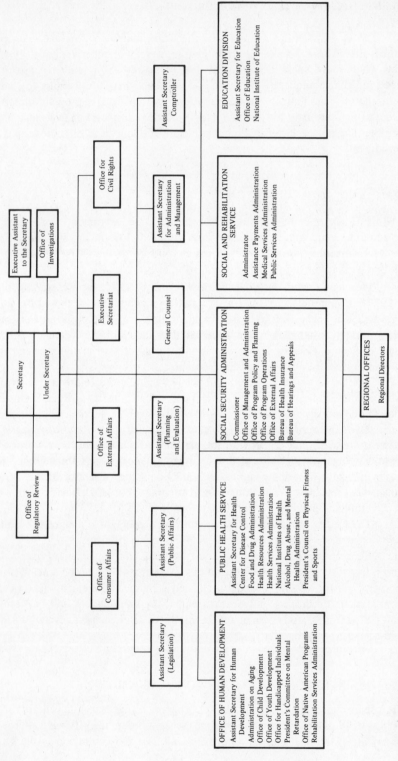

**EXHIBIT 2-5** Not adequate identification

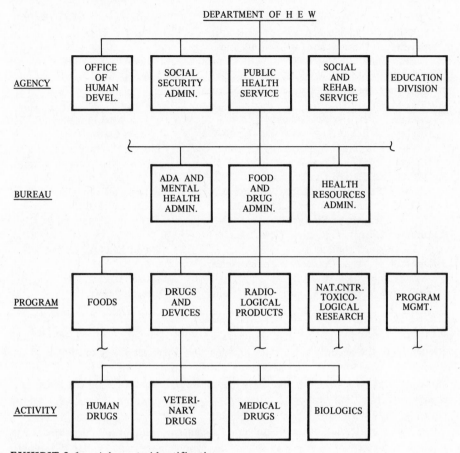

DEPARTMENT OF H E W

| AGENCY | OFFICE OF HUMAN DEVEL. | SOCIAL SECURITY ADMIN. | PUBLIC HEALTH SERVICE | SOCIAL AND REHAB. SERVICE | EDUCATION DIVISION |

| BUREAU | ADA AND MENTAL HEALTH ADMIN. | FOOD AND DRUG ADMIN. | HEALTH RESOURCES ADMIN. |

| PROGRAM | FOODS | DRUGS AND DEVICES | RADIO-LOGICAL PRODUCTS | NAT.CNTR. TOXICO-LOGICAL RESEARCH | PROGRAM MGMT. |

| ACTIVITY | HUMAN DRUGS | VETERI-NARY DRUGS | MEDICAL DRUGS | BIOLOGICS |

**EXHIBIT 2-6**    Adequate identification

lower levels of management. These charts will assist the managers in developing the budget requests. The organizational charts should show an organizational breakdown to the "zero" units, i.e., programs, activities, or program elements.

## IDENTIFY THE MANAGERS OF THE ORGANIZATIONAL UNITS

**Food and Drug Administration**

| Job Titles | Identified Manager |
| --- | --- |
| Commissioner of Food and Drugs | Alexander M. Schmidt, M.D. |
| Deputy Commissioner | Sherwin Gardner. |
| Associate Commissioner for Medical Affairs | John Jennings, M.D. |
| Associate Commissioner for Compliance | Sam D. Fine. |

| | |
|---|---|
| Associate Commissioner for Science | Mark Novitch, M.D., Acting. |
| Associate Commissioner for Administration | Gerald F. Meyer. |
| Assistant Commissioner for Planning and Evaluation | Gerald L. Barkdoll. |
| Assistant Commissioner for Public Affairs | John T. Walden. |
| Assistant Commissioner for Professional and Consumer Programs | William V. Whitehorn, M.D. |
| Director, Executive Secretariat | Curtis Neal, Acting. |
| Director, Office of Legislative Services | Robert C. Wetherell. |
| Equal Employment Opportunity Officer | Voyce P. Whitley. |
| Director, Bureau of Foods | Howard R. Roberts, Acting. |
| Director, Bureau of Drugs | J. Richard Crout, M.D. |
| Director, Bureau of Veterinary Medicine | C.D. Van Houweling, D.V.M. |
| Director, Bureau of Radiological Health | John C. Villforth. |
| Director, Bureau of Biologics | Harry M. Meyer, Jr., M.D. |
| Director, Bureau of Medical Devices and Diagnostic Products | David H. Link, Acting. |
| Director, National Center for Toxicological Research | Morris F. Cranmer. |
| Executive Director of Regional Operations | Joseph P. Hile. |

Managers must assure that resources are obtained and used effectively and efficiently in the accomplishment of an agency's objectives. They are heads of responsibility areas known as *decision units* which accomplish the agency's objectives. Managers that supervise discrete activities participate in the zero-base budgeting process because their responsibility areas require constant reassessment, careful planning, and tight budgeting by management.

The identification of the organization's managers is important because it assists top-level management to properly select the responsibility centers that will submit decision requests.

### Volume Problems

*The identification of a responsible manager who is not at too low a level in the hierarchy is important.*

*Example:*

The Food and Drug Administration, Public Health Service, identifies the team leaders of all the inspectors that determine if outside plants are maintaining standards for foods and drugs. They will be requested to develop budget requests (decision packages).

Obviously, the agency has made a mistake in judgment. The team leader of the inspectors is not only too low in the hierarchy of management and too small a position for important discretionary judgments, but also his supervisor makes all the important budgetary decisions.

*The improper identification of the level of management or the selection of the managers who will develop the budget requests could result in large amounts of decision packages being developed and place an unmanageable burden on the budget staff.* The number of managers identified to submit budget requests have an impact on the volume of packages developed.

*Example:*

After identifying the organizational units (Exhibit 2-6) the Food and Drug Administration (FDA), Public Health Service, has decided that five (levels) decision packages will be submitted by each manager. By counting from the top of the FDA management hierarchy to the "zero line," the agency has identified 200 managers that would submit budget requests. Two hundred managers times five decision packages each would result in 1000 budget requests being submitted for the new fiscal year by FDA.

By raising the hierarchy line of management identification from zero to the next highest level, 50 managers would be identified. This identification results in just 250 decision packages being developed and decreases the review burden during the priority ranking process.

## IDENTIFY THE DECISION UNITS OF THE AGENCY

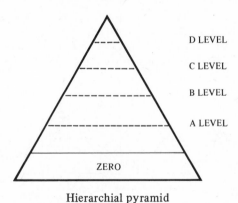

D LEVEL

C LEVEL

B LEVEL

A LEVEL

ZERO

Hierarchial pyramid

*THE "Z" RULE: The identification and selection of a decision unit close to the top of an organization's pyramid causes the area inside to constrict; thus, managers participating in the ZBB process and/or preparing budget requests (decision packages) become smaller in number. As these identifications are made closer to the point of the pyramid, a decline both in paperwork and time spent in preparing the budget becomes evident.*

## What Is a Decision Unit?

The Office of Management and Budget defines a decision unit as "the program or organizational entity for which budgets are prepared and for which a manager makes significant decisions on the amount of spending and the scope, direction, or quality of work to be performed."[6]

Entities that fit this criteria all have an equal chance at being the decision unit selected, i.e., Food and Drug Administration and Drugs and Devices as displayed in Exhibit 2-7. Many times the program structure or budget units are identified as a decision unit. An agency can be divided into entities (units) which could be responsibility centers, budget units, program elements, or other organizational units. Each one of these units could be identified as a potential decision unit whose manager would prepare the initial decision package. Another viewpoint is that an organization has a complete hierarchy of decision units — bureaus, programs, activities, etc. Thus, the objectives of the smaller decision units correspond with the high-level decision unit objectives.

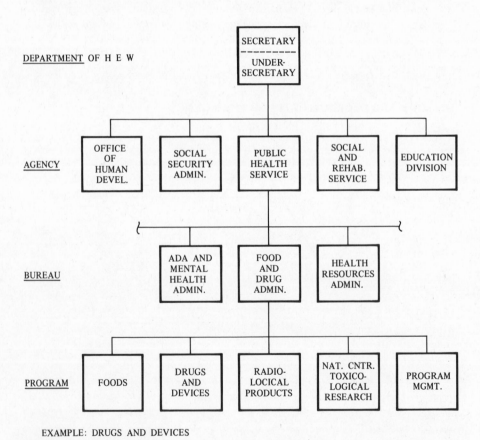

EXHIBIT 2-7    Decision units

## Method for Identifying Decision Units

The U.S. Office of Management and Budget Bulletin No. 77-9 states:

One of the first steps in zero-base budgeting is the identification of the *entities* in the program or organization structure whose *managers will prepare the initial decision packages.* In all instances, the identification of the decision units should be determined by the information needs of higher level management. *Agencies should ensure that the basic decision units selected are not so low in the structure as to result in excessive paperwork and review. On the other hand, the units selected should not be so high as to mask important considerations and prevent meaningful review of the work being performed.* A decision unit normally should be included within a single account, be classified in only one budget subfunction, and to the extent possible, reflect existing program and organizational structures that have accounting support.[7]

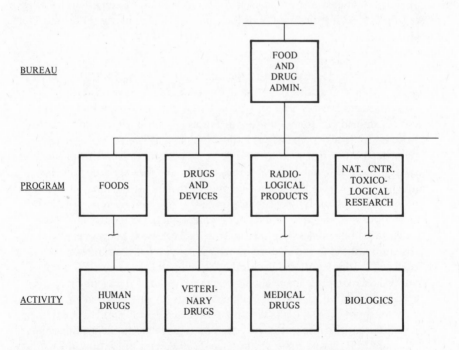

Lower levels of decision units at food and drug administration

Select the lowest decision unit which is not too low or not too high but which needs meaningful review and identify an entity whose manager will prepare the initial decision packages (budget requests).

*Example:*

The author has identified and is selecting the *program level* for the preparation of initial decision packages in the Food and Drug Administration, Public Health Service, because:

1. The selection of the activity level is too low and would result in excessive paperwork and review in the implementation year. The agency could strive to hit lower meaningful levels after the first year.

2. Meaningful review could be accomplished at this level containing much of the information that would have been obtained at the lower levels but more consolidated. Program managers should consult with the next lower decision unit levels for possible inputs.

3. The program level represents one budget subfunction and reflects existing budget and organizational structure having accounting support.

In April 1977, before guidelines were available from the OMB Bulletin 77-9, the Office of Administrative Management for the Public Health Service (PHS) delivered these ZBB instructions to all their bureaus including the Food and Drug Administration.

In determining its decision units, the Public Health Service (PHS) chose to work within the existing budget activity structure. The existing activities, i.e., Drugs and Devices, presently identified in the all-purpose budget tables, were examined and found in many instances to be too general, too inclusive to be useful to agency managers in decisionmaking. Therefore, they were subdivided into what were believed to be meaningful elements from which an agency manager could analyze various options and directly reflect his/her program priorities in the subsequent step of ranking decision packages in preparing the actual budget submission to the Assistant Secretary of Health (ASH). A list of the approved decision units is included (see Exhibit 2-6) by agency and includes their relationship to the present budget activity structure utilized in the all-purpose tables. Agencies or their bureaus may want to identify additional decision units below this level for their own internal use. However, these should be consolidated at the agency level. The agency submission to ASH should include decision packages and a ranking only for those decision units identified on the enclosed list. PHS believes it is necessary that the established decision units relate to the previous budget structure to facilitate implementation and subsequent utilization of ZBB.[8]

It should be noted that OMB Circular No. A-11 dated July 1977 states, "advance consultation is required from OMB for the decision units (program, activity, or organizational levels) that will form the basis of decision packages."[9]

In reviewing budget structures of other agencies there are differences in the nomenclature given each budget level. The relationship between the organizational structure, an agency's budget structure, or the uniform Federal budget structure has to be understood before ZBB is implemented. However, using the current agency's budget structure process makes sense.

*Example:*

At the National Science Foundation, the hierarchy of the budget structure is:

- Activity
- Subactivity
- Element
- Subelement
- Program

At the National Oceanic and Atmospheric Administration, budgeting estimates are broken down by:

- Bureau
- Appropriation
- Activity
- Subactivity
- Line item

The account identification structure for the United States includes:

- Agency code
- Appropriation symbol
- Fund type
- Function

Its budget schedules are presented by program and object classification.

The selection of the decision unit is usually made by identification of the organizational structure or of the budget structure.

All decision units should be identified, classified, and accounted for only once in a budget submission. Agencies are finding much difficulty in implementing ZBB so that duplication does not occur.

## IDENTIFY THE OBJECTIVES

### Planning – ZBB's Major Starting Point

Speaking for the private sector, Peter A. Pyhrr stated, "Planning establishes programs, sets goals and objectives and makes basic policy decisions for the organization as a whole."[10] For the public sector, Peter Sarant states, "Congress or other legislature bodies set missions by statute, then planning sets long-range goals and objectives, establishes programs, and makes policy in support of these goals." In the ZBB process, planning is the major starting point. Since Congress sets missions for the Government departments by statute, the identification of the long-range goals and major objectives for an agency starts at the top of the organizational hierarchy and ascends to lower levels, where short-term objectives are established consistent with the agency's missions or goals.

## ZBB – A Link to MBO

Hierarchy of objectives

Office of Management and Budget Circular No. A-11, dated July 1977, states that ZBB requires "establishment, for all managerial levels in an agency, of objectives related to *agency missions* against which accomplishments can be identified and measured. Program and organization objectives should be explicit statements of intended output, clearly related to the basic need for which the program or organization exists. Outputs or accomplishments expected from a program or organization (major objectives) and the services or products to be provided for a given level of funding during the budget year (short-term objectives) need to be identified."[11] In the ZBB process, missions, goals, and objectives should be identified by all managers.

    It should be noted that zero-base budgeting complements the Management-by-Objectives (MBO) system used by the public sector. Our first major step in ZBB, *identifying objectives,* links the ZBB process to the MBO system. Since many agencies have MBO solidly implanted in their planning, budgeting, and management process, the procedure of objective setting for ZBB should be familiar to operating agency managers.

## DEFINING MISSIONS

Before identifying objectives, a look at the following definition of missions, goals, and objectives would be informative. George Morrisey's book, *Management by Objectives and Results in the Public Sector,* published by the Addison-Wesley Publishing Company, has explained missions and objectives for the public sector precisely. The author, who is a widely recognized authority in the technique of Management-by-Objective (MBO), breaks the MBO definition into two parts, one for missions and the other for objectives. The missions describe the nature and scope of the work to be performed. They establish the reason for the organization or unit's existence. He regards the term *organization* as the description of the total body and the term *unit* (decision unit) as any smaller part of it.

The treatment of missions for the total organization is somewhat different than the treatment of objectives for a unit within it.

## What Are Missions?

"A statement of roles and missions — that is, a statement describing "the nature and scope of the work to be performed" — in effect describes the organization's or unit's reason for existence. The differences, as applied to the total organization or a smaller unit within it, are primarily ones of degree. For the total organization, the mission statement should include the broad identification of the type of operation for which it is responsible, its major areas of service, clientele or user groups, organizational approach, plus the philosophical basis for its operation. This statement provides a logical starting point for determining objectives and a means of testing their validity and establishing accountability for results."[12] Examples of mission statements are displayed in Exhibit 2-8.

## What Are Long-Range Goals?

The reader might think that government implementors might be in a bind trying to distinguish between missions and goals. As we stated previously, missions are set initially by Congress by statute and long-range goals are established through the planning process by a department or agency. These long-range goals are identified by the lower-level decision unit and "serve as a basis for determining the major objectives needed to work towards that goal."[13] These goals in effect are statements of long-range mission responsibilities and intended output.

A goal is a statement of intended output in the broadest terms. It is normally not related to a specific time period. Goals normally are not quantified, and hence cannot be used directly as a basis for a measurement system. The purpose of a statement of goals is to communicate top management's decisions about the aims and relative priorities of the organization and to provide general guidance as to the strategy that the organization is expected to follow."[14]

### Examples of Long-Range Goals

*Administrative Services Division, Office of Administration, Department of Commerce:*

- To provide and administer necessary procurement of property, supplies and services for the total function of the Department of Commerce.

*Drugs and Device Program, the identified decision unit of the Food and Drug Administration:*

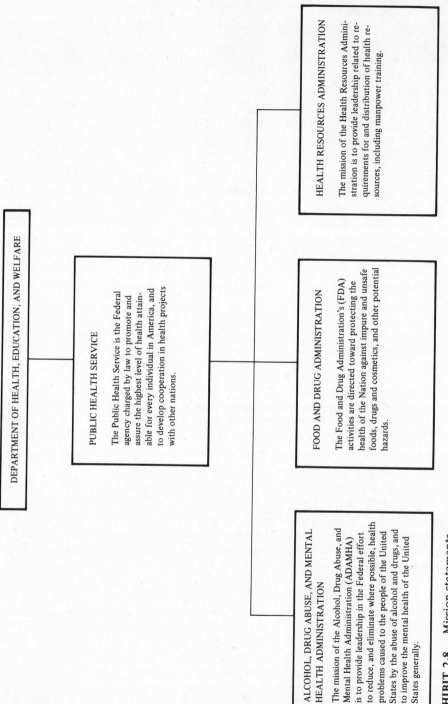

**DEPARTMENT OF HEALTH, EDUCATION, AND WELFARE**

PUBLIC HEALTH SERVICE

The Public Health Service is the Federal agency charged by law to promote and assure the highest level of health attainable for every individual in America, and to develop cooperation in health projects with other nations.

HEALTH RESOURCES ADMINISTRATION

The mission of the Health Resources Administration is to provide leadership related to requirements for and distribution of health resources, including manpower training.

FOOD AND DRUG ADMINISTRATION

The Food and Drug Administration's (FDA) activities are directed toward protecting the health of the Nation against impure and unsafe foods, drugs and cosmetics, and other potential hazards.

ALCOHOL, DRUG ABUSE, AND MENTAL HEALTH ADMINISTRATION

The mission of the Alcohol, Drug Abuse, and Mental Health Administration (ADAMHA) is to provide leadership in the Federal effort to reduce, and eliminate where possible, health problems caused to the people of the United States by the abuse of alcohol and drugs, and to improve the mental health of the United States generally.

**EXHIBIT 2-8    Mission statements**

- To develop FDA policy with regard to the safety, effectiveness, and labeling of all drugs for human use.
- To test, conduct research, and develop scientific standards and the composition, quality, safety, and efficiency of human drugs.

## WHAT IS AN OBJECTIVE?

Objectives are statements of *reasonable, measurable,* and *specific* results to be *achieved* within a certain period of *time.* They are "explicit statements of intended output related to the basic need for which the program exists."[15] In substance, these objectives should relate to the higher-level mission or goal statement of the agency. Mission or goal statements are continuing, nonspecific, and broad.

"Top level agency management should be involved in setting objectives for lower level agency managers to:

1. Help ensure that appropriate guidance is furnished to managers throughout the agency;

2. Aid managers preparing decision packages in defining, explaining, and justifying their work to be performed and the associated resources;

3. Aid intermediate level managers in understanding and evaluating the budget requests."[16]

Management should make sure when writing an objective statement that it includes these characteristics: reasonable, measurable, specific, achievable, and time-bounded.

The task of identifying objectives requires the participation by managers of all levels to determine the ultimate realistic outputs or accomplishments expected from a program or organization (major objectives) and the services or products to be provided for a given level of funding during the budget year (short-term objectives).[17]

This task of identifying objectives should be accomplished during the planning stage. Later, the decision unit managers use this identification in describing major and short-term objectives when preparing the unit's budget requests.

## WHAT ARE MAJOR AND SHORT-TERM OBJECTIVES?

Major objectives as used in the ZBB sense describe the major purpose of the decision unit. Short-term objectives describe the purpose of each increment (decision package) of funds requested.

### Characteristics of Major Objectives

- Relate to the needs to be met
- Identify the basic authorizing legislation

- Take long periods to accomplish

- Are measurable

- Are expressed in terms of explicit intended output

- Form the basis for determining and evaluating programs or activities[18]

*Example:*

*Federal Drug Administration*

To sample and test 90% of all drugs manufactured before 1951 for safety, effectiveness, and labeling by the year 1985.

## Characteristics of Short-Term Objectives

- Achievable during the budget year

- Show the expected results and benefits for the work or services performed

- Identified through quantitative measures

*Example:*

*Federal Drug Administration*

To sample and test 20% of all drugs manufactured before 1951. This is expected to reduce the illness rate caused by bad drugs 4% in the current year 1979.

## USE OF OBJECTIVES IN THE PREPARATION AND SUBMISSION OF BUDGET ESTIMATES

This process of identifying objectives is important not only because these objectives are described in each budget request increment but also because they are used in the preparation and submission of budget estimates.

Office of Management and Budget Circular No. A-11 establishes instructions for the preparation and submission of budget estimates each year for the Federal Government. Some of the requirements of OMB Circular No. A-11 that are related to the ZBB step, identification of objectives, are:

- *Basis for Agency Proposals.* "Agency proposals should . . . reflect missions, goals, and objectives of the agency, . . . and the judgment of the agency head with respect to the scope, content, pace, and quality of programs and activities that are being proposed to meet the agency's goals and objectives."[19]

- *Summary of Highlight Memorandum.* "This statement is usually in the form of a transmittal letter and leads off the budget submission of each agency. The narrative of the memorandum highlights the agency's budget, identifying the objectives, broad policies proposed, program plans, and amounts requested to achieve the resulting objectives."[20]

- *Narrative Statements on Program and Performance.* "The primary purpose of the narrative statement is to present briefly the objectives, the work program, and a measure of expected performance. These statements should set forth the significant long-range and short-range objectives of the activities financed by the account. Information should be provided on the impact of proposed budget year funding on the accomplishment of objectives. Such information should be derived from the zero-base justification materials, provided in the zero base budget justifications (decision package sets). Whenever possible, objectives should be stated in quantitative terms and performance measured in the same manner."[21]

### "IF MANAGERS CANNOT MEASURE IT, OR DESCRIBE IT, PERHAPS IT DOES NOT OR SHOULD NOT EXIST."

## MEASUREMENT OF OBJECTIVES

"As objectives are identified, managers must simultaneously determine the key indicators by which performance is to be measured." Major objectives of the *decision unit* should be measurable and "the expected results of the work performed or services provided (short-term objectives) should be identified to the maximum extent possible through the use of quantitative measures," in each *decision package*. In describing the accomplishments and impact of a decision unit toward meeting the major objectives, quantitative and/or qualitative measures of results should be used.[22]

For an objective to be effectively measured, there must be a clear indication of when it has or has not been achieved. Many types of services lend themselves to quantification while others do not, i.e., research and development, evaluation projects, etc. Management has to determine what measurable factors should be identified to serve as reliable indicators of both efficient and effective performance in achieving their responsibility area's (decision unit) objectives. Two types of measures of results could be used — quantitative and qualitative.

*"Qualitative* analysis is nonnumerical analysis where a manager attempts to describe relationships in a concise manner. The greatest weakness of qualitative analysis is that the analysis procedures are not explicit but often exist only in the mind of the evaluator. The principal advantage of qualitative analysis is that it provides useful and valuable information which would not result if only quantitative data analysis were applied. The zero-base budgeting system recognizes the desirability of providing such valuable information and provides appropriate opportunity for the provision of such information, both in the objective statement and the justification of the different levels of funding identified."[23]

OMB Bulletin 77-9 states, "if such [quantitative measurement] systems are not available; indirect or proxy indicators should be considered initially, while evaluation and workload systems are developed."[24]

A proxy indicator is called a surrogate; it is the closest way of measuring the accomplishment of an objective.

*Example:*

*Office of Education*
The objective — "to make certain underprivileged children eat nutritious breakfasts." A proxy measurement could be — the number of children eating breakfast at school.

Also, in most activities or programs, time at work could be identified as a measurement. An activity or program which is nonmeasurable can show at least these types of indicators:

|  | 19CY | 19BY |
|---|---|---|
| Agency total man-years | 4000 | 5000 |
| Man-years in activity | 400 | 250 |
| Ratio of activity man-years to total man-years | 1-10 | 1-20 |

"*Quantitative* analysis is numerical analysis, involving the use of numbers to describe trends or relationships. Most data analysis is quantitative to some degree. When objective statements are stated in a precise, quantitative manner, *performance and workload measures* can be derived from them as *indicators of achievement.* Whenever possible, objective statements should state quantitatively the desired condition to be brought about. Progress in achievement of the objective can then be more precisely measured,"[2 5] especially with the *use of performance measurements.*

### Performance Measurements — A Management Control Tool

The "thrust" of this section is to give the reader an overall insight into the use of measurements by the public sector and answer the question, "Why have performance measurements?"

The basic purpose of having performance measurements is their use in management control. Measurements assist managers in assuring that the resources

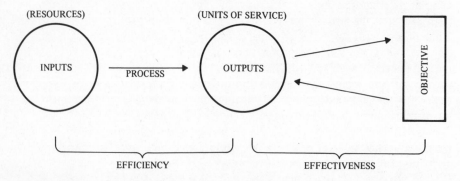

**EXHIBIT 2-9**    ZBB measurement systems model

obtained are used *efficiently* and *effectively* in the accomplishment of an organization's objectives. OMB Circular No. A-11 informs managers that, "The key indicators by which effectiveness, efficiency, and workload will be measured for each decision unit can often be obtained from existing evaluation and workload measurement (total measurement system) systems."[26]

## Total Measurement System

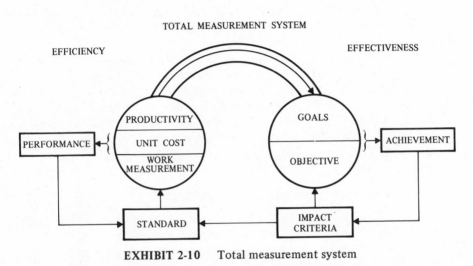

TOTAL MEASUREMENT SYSTEM

**EXHIBIT 2-10**    Total measurement system

"Efficiency is measured by comparing *operational performance* to some standard. Effectiveness is measured by comparing *program achievement* to impact criteria. If adjustments are necessary, the goals and objectives and operational procedures are changed. Feed back to the system is provided by a carefully planned management information system. The total system of measurement is illustrated above."

Source: Measuring and Enhancing Productivity in the Federal Sector – A Study for the Use of the Joint Economic Committee of the Congress of the U.S. – August 4, 1972

"The concept of a *total measurement system* can be viewed as two interrelated subsystems. The two subsystems are related by the measurement of cost-effectiveness which identifies the alternative that yields the greatest effectiveness for any given cost. The first subsystem is oriented to measurement of efficiency. Three of the measures – work, unit cost, and productivity – are concerned with the efficiency with which programs are being carried out. Each measure builds on the other.

"Work measurement, the lowest level of measurement, deals with man-hours per unit of output. Unit cost measurement deals with all costs required to produce the output and, therefore, is not limited to just manpower costs. However, unit cost measurement builds on work measurement in that work measurement is used to support the acceptability of manpower costs.

"Finally, productivity measurement deals with total outputs and total cost to provide an overall measure of efficiency. In addition, productivity measurement can be used to develop a measurement of total output per dollar cost. Since manpower is usually by far the most important resource in Government programs, indexes of output per man-hour are always computed and represent a partial measure of efficiency.

"The question of efficiency is relevant to the purpose of budget determination and manpower control and to the more general evaluation of how efficiently the Government's organizations are operating compared to their previous experiences, or compared to their counterparts elsewhere in the Government or in the private sector.

"The second subsystem (oriented to measurement of effectiveness) is related to the achievement of specified goals and objectives. While the first subsystem measures, for example, the efficiency of manpower training, this subsystem measures the numbers of jobs successfully filled by the trainees or the increment of the average income for the trainees. The purpose of this type of measurement is to help evaluate alternative approaches, alternative designs, and the need for the program itself."[27]

## The Concept of a Total Performance Measurement System

"Performance has two dimensions. One is the *dimension of efficiency* which involves the organization of manpower and equipment to perform certain jobs or carry on certain functions and is measured by such techniques as productivity rates, work measurement systems, and standards. The other is an *effectiveness dimension* dealing with the impact of those jobs or functions on the accomplishment of objectives, their contributions to public needs, and the levels of quality and service.

"The integration of attitudinal data with hard measurement data provides a powerful data base for assessing performance. Exhibit 2-11 depicts this integration model. As can be seen from the model, employee attitude data are related to both productivity and effectiveness, while customer attitudes relate to effectiveness. For example, employee attitudes will affect the final output in terms of quality and efficiency, while customer attitudes will reflect on the quality of the output or service provided. Attitude measurement, properly administered and used, gives an added dimensions to performance assessment and problem diagnosis that is powerful in identifying significant targets of opportunity for performance improvement"[28]

## Management's Performance Measurement Tools for Efficiency and Effectiveness

Measuring performance in the public sector is merely a matter of measuring *outputs of efficiency and effectiveness.* The measurement of efficiency is the ratio of outputs to inputs and the measurement of effectiveness represents the relationship of actual output to the organizational goals and objectives (Exhibit 2-9).

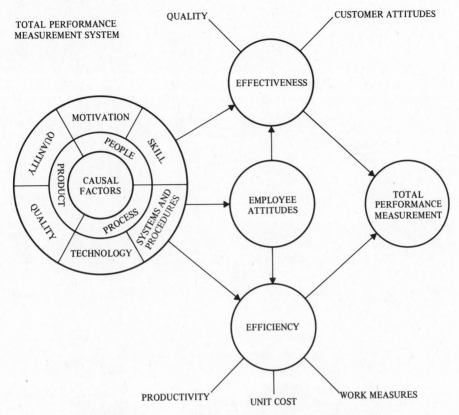

**EXHIBIT 2-11**    Total performance measurement system

Source: Annual Report to the President and the Congress, "Productivity Programs in the Federal Government FY 1974," Joint Financial Management Improvement Program, June 1975.

Effectiveness and efficiency measurements are used for evaluating the results of a program and for controlling the operations of a decision unit. An efficiency indicator such as the number of inoculations for the Public Health Service helps monitor a program's efficient use of resources but it does not necessarily contribute to the agency's objective. The Department of HEW's objective might be "reduce incidences of measles by 10%." An effectiveness indicator, number of incidences of measles, would assist in the evaluation of the achievement of this objective.

Efficient managers are considered to be those who have the lowest consumption of resources; however, they could also be *ineffective* managers if their unit's outputs do not contribute to the agency's goals. For example, a state agency could be processing welfare claims at a tremendous rate, but the agency failed to assist the clients in obtaining entitled services. As Peter Drucker said, "There is a sharp clash today between stress on efficiency of administration and stress of effectiveness."[29]

PERFORMANCE MEASUREMENT SYSTEM

Program Title Code ORGANIZED CRIME
Agency Dept. DEPARTMENT OF JUSTICE
Bureau Office CRIMINAL DIVISION
Program Mgr. J. Doe
Date Documented 10/4/74
Control Number 02     Budget Year 74

Exhibit B – Program Objectives/Performance Measure Relationships

| Broad Program Goals | 1.0 Eradicate Organized Criminal Activities and Influences in the United States | | | | | | | | | | |
| | 1.1 Eliminate Criminal Organizations and Operations | | | 1.2 Create and Maintain a Hostile Environment Toward Organized Criminal Activities and Influences | | | | | | | |
| Related Performance Measures | • Number of organized crime related homicides and missing persons reported<br>• Criminal organization profiles including:<br> – Number of known organizations<br> – Estimated number of members<br> – Estimated number of employees<br> – Estimated gross revenues (by type of operation)<br>• Rate of conviction/control to estimated number of members | | | • Gross assets and revenues of businesses suspected of being influenced (by industry and geographic area)<br>• Estimated revenues generated by type of illicit operations (gambling, narcotics, loan sharking, fencing, prostitution) by geographic area<br>• Cost to society of organized crime | | | | | | | |
| | **Direct** | | | | | | | **Support** | | | |
| Operating Program Objectives | 1.1.1 Eliminate membership in criminal organizations | 1.1.2 Disrupt criminal organizations | 1.1.3 Curtail criminal operations | 1.2.1 Create a public awareness of the influenced and effects of organized crime | 1.2.2 Create adverse societal and individual behavior and attitudes toward organized crime | 1.2.3 Reduce economic incentives for organized crime and provide legitimate | 1.2.4 Eliminate public corruption | 1.3.1 Obtain intelligence on organizations and operations of organized crime | 1.3.2 Improve legal sanctions against organized crime | 1.3.3 Improve administrative management | 1.3.4 Improve program management |
| Related Performance Measures | • Number of investigative cases opened, pending and closed<br>• Cases presented for prosecution as compared to cases investigated | • Number of violent deaths of organized crime members<br>• Number of informants | • Estimated losses of seized monies from gambling operation disruptions<br>• Bankruptcies attributed to organized crime | • Number of mass media campaigns<br>• Number and type of training programs | • State and local anticrime campaigns<br>• Investigative leads volunteered by public | • Illegitimate enterprises legalized<br>• Taxes collected from organized criminals, their organizations, and businesses | • Known or suspected collaborators<br>• Known or suspected corrupt public institutions | • Organized criminal systems identified<br>• Organized criminals identified | • Legislation enacted<br>• Regulations published | • Training program conducted<br>• New enforcement techniques developed and deployed | • Percentage of State and local agencies with crime squads |

**EXHIBIT 2-12**

"A major problem in progressing from *efficiency* to *effectiveness* measurement is that the latter involves establishment of complex external and internal cause-effect relationships with the external tending to be the more difficult to determine. For example, the goal of the National Highway Safety Bureau, Department of Transportation, is "to reduce the mounting number of deaths and injuries resulting from traffic accidents on the Nation's highways." Establishing a direct relationship between the outputs of the Bureau's three programs and the incidence of traffic deaths and injuries appears feasible, but not easy. Effectiveness measurement provides the means of determining whether the agency is proceeding on course and of establishing a relationship between management action and goal accomplishment. Both efficiency and effectiveness measurement are thus essential tools of managers in assessing true productivity, the former determining the cost of producing the agency's outputs and the latter the value of the agency's outputs to the recipient of its goods and services."[30]

*The "M.I." Rule: In preparing budget justifications using the zero-base budgeting process, both efficiency and effectiveness measurement indicators should be used in the decision packages, especially if a program element, i.e., activity, has been selected as the decision unit in which to prepare the initial packages.*

Both measurements are necessary because efficiency indicators measure operational performance and effectiveness indicators measure performance with respect to goals and objectives. The former is used for management control and the latter is used for management evaluation.

Note in Exhibit 2-13 that the efficiency measurements in both the program and activity unit can be the same. The efficiency measurement indicates the prudent use of resources by any organizational unit's manager. The effectiveness measurements assists management to evaluate the results of a unit in the accomplishment of its objective whether the unit is a program or activity.

## EFFECTIVENESS MEASURES

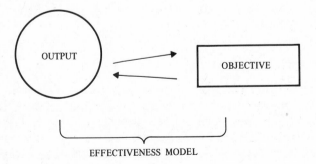

EFFECTIVENESS MODEL

Effectiveness measures are outputs expressed in terms related to an organization's objectives and are results or ends oriented. They express how well an organization

Functional Category: Health and Welfare
Program: Institutional Care of Youth

| Efficiency Measures | Effectiveness Measures |
| --- | --- |
| Pounds of laundry processed | Percent of parole violators |
| Numbers of meals served (see below | Percent of parolees without subsequent crime within 5 years |
| Cost per meal served (see below) | Average educational grade level improvement of inmates |
| Number of students counselled | Percent of inmates gaining employment skills |
| Number of attempted escapes | |
| Number of contact hours per student | |

Activity: Food Services

| Efficiency Measures | Effectiveness Measures |
| --- | --- |
| Number of meals served | Percent of underweight inmates that gained weight |
| Cost per meal served | Number of days of nutritional and well-balanced meals |

**EXHIBIT 2-13**    Output indicators

achieves its desired results. Some of the measurements used to assess the desired results are quality, response time, impact, and citizen reactions. Effectiveness measurements are shown by the relationship between a decision unit's outputs and its objectives. "Effectiveness measurement is the ratio between an achieved result and some end objective or goal. Thus, the output of programs is measured in terms of units of achievement of specified objectives and goals of those programs resulting in a measure of the degree of goal fulfillment."[31] Examples of effectiveness output indicators are in Exhibits 2-13 and 2-14.

## EFFICIENCY MEASURES

*Efficiency measures* are indicators of the output accomplishments or performance of a particular decision unit, i.e., program or program elements; it is process or means oriented. The main efficiency measurement's used by the Federal agencies are *productivity, unit cost,* and *work measurement.* All three measures are related and serve useful purposes. These three measures give the manager comprehensive information about the organizational unit in which he makes decisions.

Productivity measurements relate to efficiency and work measurements relate efficiency to a standard. Efficiency is expressed by the ratio of outputs to resource inputs used, i.e., amount of resources used to produce outputs.

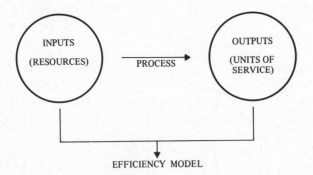

EFFICIENCY MODEL

Some States like Texas use effectiveness measurement only for programs and efficiency measurements (workload) for activities. This means that effective indicators in the State of Texas would only be used at the program level.[32] Effectiveness measures should be integrated with efficiency measures in order to highlight opportunities to improve performance in not only meeting the objectives but operating the decision unit prudently as well. In OMB Circular No. A-11, instructions are, "Agencies will extend the use of work measurement and unit cost analysis (efficiency measurements) to *both common service activities and program activities.* Usually, productivity indexes are based on organization-wide totals of both outputs and inputs, thus already covering both direct and indirect costs."[33]

### Justification of Amounts Requested

Agencies usually request funding for programs. Efficiency measurements are necessary in support of these requests. The Office of Management and Budget is requiring that agencies should base justifications on the following: "Detailed analyses of workload, employment requirements, productivity trends, the impact of capital investment proposals on productivity, and changes in quality of output. *Work measurement, unit costs,* and *productivity indexes* should be used to the maximum extent practicable in justifying staffing requirements for measurable workload."[34]

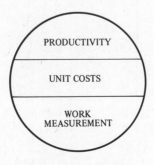

Efficiency indicators

EXHIBIT 2-14.    Measures of Effectiveness

| Long-Range Goals | Suggested Short-Term Objectives | Suggested Measures of Achievement |
|---|---|---|
| Reduce the rate of the Air Traffic Control, Air Navigation and Airport System induced restrictions, including weather delays, on the movement of aircraft. | Reduce the aircraft movement delay rate.<br><br>Lead Responsibility: AAT | The rate of delays per 1,000 aircraft operations at major hubs. |
| Increase the dollar value of exports of U.S. aviation products. | Increase the dollar value of aviation exports.<br><br>Lead Responsibility: AIA | The dollar value of the sale of U.S. aircraft and avionics equipment abroad. (The value is adjusted by the GNP deflator to constant 1971 dollars.) |
| Promote the increased efficiency of energy used in aviation and reduce energy consumption within the FAA. | a. To be established for the aviation industry.<br><br>Lead Responsibility: APD<br><br>b. Reduce the FAA energy usage rate.<br><br>Lead Responsibility: AAF/ALG | (To be developed)<br><br><br><br><br>The total kilowatt hours, fuel, oil, gas, and aviation fuel consumed by the FAA. |
| Increase the participation of minorities and females in the FAA and the aviation community. | a. Increase the level of minority employment in the FAA.*<br><br>b. Increase the level of female employment in the FAA.* | The net increase in the percent of minority employment in the permanent FAA work force.<br>The net increase in the percent of female employees in the permanent FAA work force. |

c. Increase the level of minority employees in the aviation industry.

The net increase in the percent of minority employees in the aviation industry work force.

d. Increase the level of female employees in the aviation industry.

The net increase in the percent of female employees in the aviation industry work force.

e. Increase the proportion of FAA contract dollars channeled to minority firms.

The dollar value of contracts awarded to minority firms (expressed as a percent of the dollar value of all contracts awarded for the year).

Lead Responsibility: ACR

*NOTE: Minimum levels of increase have already been set by OST.

Source: Federal Aviation Administration, Department of Transportation memo, "FAA Goals and Objectives," dated July 26, 1974, from Alexander P. Butterfield to regional directors.

## Unit Cost Measures

"Unit costs relate the volume of work to the funds required to produce the work. For example, the cost of producing 1,000 one-dollar bills is $7.69. The particular genius of unit costs is that they take out of the cost picture, fluctuations that occur because of differences in quantities. For example, if the total cost for producing a product were $10,000 in 1971 and $12,000 in 1972, it would look as if costs increased if only total cost is viewed. However, if 1,000 units were produced in 1971 and 1,500 units in 1972, the use of unit costs would show that, while costs in total dollars increased, the unit cost actually decreased, as shown below:

$$1971 = \frac{\$10,000}{1,000 \text{ units}} \text{ or } \$10 \text{ per unit}$$

$$1972 = \frac{\$12,000}{1,500 \text{ units}} \text{ or } \$8 \text{ per unit}"$$

"Unit costs relate the resource inputs required to produce the work outputs. These are obtained by relating physical work units produced to corresponding costs. Unit costs may include, in addition to personnel costs, the costs of supplies, travel, equipment, etc. Thus, unit costs reflect the ratio of personnel, materials, travel, and other costs to the output produced, and will be stated in the dollars (or cents) required to produce a unit of work. When unit costs include personnel costs, work measurement should be used to support the acceptability of this component."[35]

As far back as 1965, the Government has emphasized the unit cost measurement for accounting purposes and not just to justify the budget. GAO's pamphlet on "Accounting Principles and Standards for Federal Agencies" published in 1965 (with 1968 revisions) provided that:

> Cost accounting techniques should include, wherever appropriate and feasible, the production of quantity data relating to performance or output so as to make it possible to relate costs of performance with accomplishments and to disclose *unit cost* information.

## Disincentives to Greater Use of Unit Costs

Generally, the full use of unit cost was not being made by operating and top management in the Government. The agencies have indicated a concern in terms of who needs it and does value justify cost. "Many reasons are expressed or suggested as to why agencies do not use unit costs more widely in the preparation of their budget and in the management of their activities. In the following paragraphs we have attempted to interpret some of the disincentives which appeared to be the most real or are mentioned with the greatest frequency.

"Perhaps the primary disincentive is the fear that use of unit costs would tend to produce tighter budgets because it would make it easier for reviewers to understand the programs and to reduce budgets to minimum levels. Tighter budgets are not only more difficult for a manager to operate under but also produce other disincentives. In this respect, there is a prevailing belief that in Government the rewards in terms of prestige, promotions, and the ability to hire better people and to carry out more effective programs, are awarded to those who can justify the largest budgets. Officials are reluctant to expose their budgets to reductions by adopting unit costs without compensating incentives.

"A second factor of equal or greater significance is the belief among agencies that use of unit costs in the budget process would bring about lower quality program output and loss in program effectiveness. This fear seems to stem from the feeling that use of unit costs would cause reviewing authorities to become overly concerned with efficiency to the detriment or disregard of program effectiveness, and that the unit costs would be used to effect unjustified budget reductions. The officials also fear that the unit cost measures may not be realistic and, thus, could be improperly used to justify budget cuts which would reduce program effectiveness.

"A third and related factor is the belief that the use of unit costs in its budget would build rigidity into agency programs and its management would make it more difficult for the agency to respond to unforeseen changes in situations and to congressional or public wishes for program changes.

"A fourth disincentive concerns the question of cost versus benefits. The establishment and maintenance of a cost accounting system needed to develop good unit costs is not without a cost of its own. Many agencies feel that it is not worth the added benefits or information that unit costs would provide. In particular, many agencies with well developed work measurement systems believe that unit costs measures would not provide them with sufficient additional information to warrant the added costs.[37]

## Productivity Measurement

Another important efficiency measurement to draw attention in recent years is the productivity measurement. It was this tool, a productivity index, that was used extensively in the study done by the Joint Financial Management Improvement Program in "Measuring and Enhancing Productivity in the Federal Sector." The States also had a study made by the Urban Institute culminating in the publication of *The Status of Productivity Measurement in State Government: An Initial Examination* in September 1975.

The development of productivity indices (measurements) has provided the Federal managers with a means of measuring the overall impact of productivity of capital investment, technology, and other factors. These data not only are useful in justifying the budget but provide productivity data to national planners and economists and provide managers with displays of overall efficiency trends.

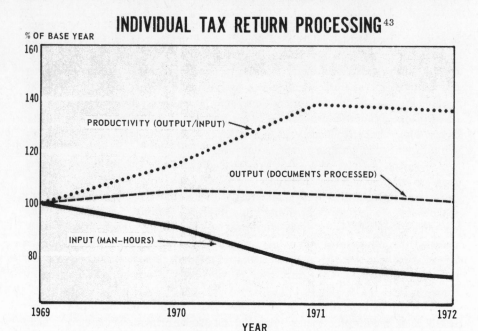

Individual tax return processing

## What Are Productivity Indexes?

"Productivity indexes are based on the ratio of total output to resource input. Output measures are based on the volume of product or services produced for use outside the organization, with due allowance for differences in the nature of individual products or services. Measures of input may be based on the amount of personnel alone, on personnel costs, or on a more comprehensive measure of resource inputs that includes nonlabor costs."[38]

"Overall productivity indexes are measures of the *final* physical outputs of an entire organization (or component, subcomponent, etc.) divided by the physical inputs, in order to produce a productivity index which can be consistently computed from year to year in real terms (i.e., in constant dollars). Labor inputs will be used in all cases. Capital and other cost inputs will be included where significant to the activity (as in the case of industrial facilities and costly data processing installations)."[39]

## What Are the Uses of Overall Productivity Measures?

"Such measures serve an entirely different purpose from those concerned with current performance. In the Federal setting, we found that, when applicable, they can offer four values:

1. First, they enable the manager to review trends in overall productivity from year to year on a consistent basis.

2. Second, they reveal the results of all past actions to improve productivity, including investments in labor-saving equipment, changes in organization and systems, upgrading of employee skills through training, etc. Thus, the measures provide a *scorekeeping technique* which managers would otherwise lack.

3. Third, they reveal emerging trends and permit managers, where possible, to take steps to influence those trends. If workload is increasing more rapidly than the manpower applied then the productivity per man-year will increase. Conversely, if workload is dropping while manning remains fixed, productivity per man-year will decline.

4. Fourth, productivity data may be used effectively at the various stages of the budget process: (1) by providing a vehicle for systematic projection of resource needs based on outputs, (2) by providing better information on the unit cost trends of alternative services, (3) by making possible a rational selection of improvement goals, and (4) by providing a progress report on how the goals are being achieved."[40]

## WORK MEASUREMENT (WORKLOAD INDICATORS)

OMB Bulletin A-11 states, "Properly developed work measurement procedures should be used to produce estimates of the staff-hours per unit of workload, such as:

1. Staff-hours per claim adjudicated
2. Staff-hours per staff maintained in the field
3. Staff-hours per infested acre of pest control

These estimates should represent an acceptable level of performance based on current realistic time standards. If the agency does not have a work measurement system that provides this type of information, the use of statistical techniques based on historical employment input and work outputs may be used."[41]

### What Is Work Measurement?

"The conversion of a quantitative statement of workload to a quantitative statement of the manpower to produce that workload. Work measurement data consists of stating quantities of work performed in terms of hours consumed as compared to a standard. For instance, if the standard for reproducing pages of photo copy is 50 per hour and the operator produces only 47 per hour, he is working at 94 percent of standard."

There are, basically, two major categories of work measurement techniques available:

- Engineered work measurement techniques set a specific amount of time per resource for a specific job, considering method, working conditions, and a designated degree of expected worker diligence and utilization necessary to achieve such a performance. Specific techniques include time study, work sampling and predetermined time systems.

- Historical work measurement techniques attempt to establish a relationship between past performance and time usage. Statistical analyses and estimates based on technical judgment are the basic techniques used for estimating this relationship.

**Work Measurement Systems (See Exhibit 2-15)**

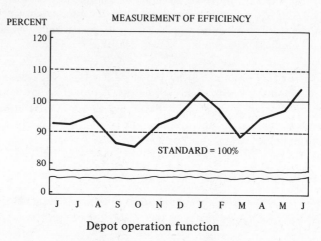

PERCENT               MEASUREMENT OF EFFICIENCY

Depot operation function

This chart is an example of how the overall efficiency of a major function is reported to top management. Ranges (acceptable tolerances shown by the dotted lines) provide a basis for evaluation of the function's performance.

"Work measurement systems can contribute to effective management decision making by providing information on how much time is actually spent to perform certain tasks as compared to a standard. With this information managers can decide such things as how many men will be needed to perform predicted future workloads and whether work performed has been accomplished efficiently. To be useful such systems must be soundly conceived and accurately maintained and the results must be effectively used.

*Example:*

Some of the data we obtained at one installation we visited illustrates how such data can be used. At that installation daily reports are produced on such functions as loading items to be shipped on railroad cars. Actual time spent is compared to the standards established for the steps involved, such as loading containers on pallets, to determine the degree of efficiency achieved in performing the work.

These data are summarized into broader categories as they go up the line. For instance, they are summarized by branch and reported weekly to the division level.

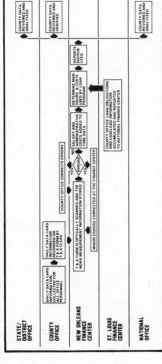

# How the System Works

## PROCESS OVERVIEW

The FmHA Work Measurement System is designed so that minimal time will be required by personnel to record and transmit data. At the same time the system provides sufficient information to meet the agency's planning needs. The flow diagram describes the new system from initial collection of the work measurement data to the distribution of the final reports.

## OBJECTIVES AND GOALS

Provide Information for Decisions at County, District, State, and National Offices for:

A. Establishment of Realistic:
1. Manpower planning
2. Workload planning
3. Budget planning

B. The Agency to Justify Manpower Levels.

C. Determining Possible Improvements in Program and Administrative Areas.

D. Determining Manpower Costs for Carrying Out Each Loan Program.

E. Establishing State Time Estimates for All Loan Programs. (State data can not be compared without evaluating the variables (i.e. socio-economic) that affect each state).

## THE SYSTEM IS NOT DESIGNED TO:

A. Make Comparisions Between County or District Offices.

B. Evaluate Individual County Offices. However, County Data Can Be Compared to State Estimates.

## DAILY DATA CARD FmHA FORM 026-1

The numbers shown in the Key, 1 through 9, 0 and X, will be used to record the time spent in hour increments for each loan type. Across the top of the data card are columns numbered 1 through 10 with each column representing an hour of work. The first column (1) is for the first hour of work, the second column (2) is for the second hour of work, etc., regardless of whether you begin at 8:00 A.M. or 12:00. For a given hour of the day, the greatest amount of time spent on a particular loan type and phase of the loan process will be coded on the data card for that hour of work during the day.

## EXHIBIT 2-15

NOTE: Sample of work day shown in red.

At the division level they are summarized monthly and reported to the directorate level. An example follows:

1. Actual man-hours for the month                                    2,551
2. Standard hours for work accomplished                        2,025
3. Percentage of efficiency (line 2 divided by line 1)       79%
4. Actual man-months required for work accomplished     15.1
5. Man-months required for work at standard                 12.0

The agency's Director gets information or problems within any of the agency's functional areas in a monthly formal briefing. These briefings involve comprehensive performance appraisals which examine the status of each major program in terms of relative indicators of progress. The briefings include assessment of the performance of individual installations as well as organization-wide accomplishments. Data are presented on (1) current trends in workload and performance efficiency, (2) status in meeting key program objectives, (3) qualitative indicators of mission performance, and (4) status of progress in special interest areas."[4 2]

In preparing the justification for the manager's budget, work measurement is useful to determine, evaluate, and justify program costs and personnel requirements. Responsible managers can use the work measurement system to estimate future personnel and financing requirements, to estimate time of completion of workload, and evaluate the effect of management decisions on policy, procedures, and equipment, etc.

## NOTES

1.   Office of the President, *Reorganization Act of 1977*, White House press release of April 6, 1977

2.   U.S. Budget – 1978

3.   U.S. Department of Agriculture Graduate School's initial 10 week course in ZBB, January-March 1977, taught by adjunct professor, Pete Sarant. (The first college course in ZBB taught in the U.S.)

4.   Ibid.

5.   Office of President – Reorganization Act

6.   Executive Office of the President, Office of Management and Budget, *Zero-Base Budgeting*, Bulletin 77-9, April 19, 1977

7.   Ibid.

8.   Public Health Service, U.S. Department of Health, Education, and Welfare, Office of Administrative Management's manual, *ZBB for the Public Health Service*, April 1977

9.   Executive Office of the President, Office of Management and Budget, "Preparation and Submission of Budget Estimates," OMB Circular A-11, July 1977

10.  Pyhrr, Peter A., *Zero-base Budgeting, A Practical Management Tool for Evaluating Expenses,* 1973 (John Wiley and Sons, Inc.)

11.  Executive Office of the President, OMB Circular A-11

12.  Morrisey, George L., *Management by Objectives and Results in the Public Sector,* 1976 (Addison-Wesley Publishing Company, Reading, Massachusetts)

13.  Executive Office of the President, OMB Circular A-11

14.  Anthony, Robert N., *Management Control in Nonprofit Organizations,* 1975 (Richard D. Irwin, Inc.)

15.  Executive Office of the President, OMB Circular A-11

16.  Executive Office of the President, OMB Bulletin 77-9

17.  Ibid.

18.  Office of the President, OMB Circular A-11

19.  Ibid.

20.  Ibid.

21.  Ibid.

22.  Ibid.

23.  State of Texas, Governor's Budget and Planning Office, *Budget Manual – Needs, Objectives and Measures for the 1978-1979 Biennium*

24.  Executive Office of the President, OMB Bulletin 77-9

25.  State of Texas, Budget Manual

26.  Executive Office of the President, OMB Circular A-11

27.  U.S. Congress, Joint Economic Committee, "A Study of Measuring and Enhancing Productivity in the Federal Sector," by Representatives of the Civil Service Commission, General AO and OMB, August 4, 1972

28.  Joint Financial Management Improvement Program, "Productivity Programs in the Federal Government FY 1974," annual report to the President and the Congress, June 1975

29.  U.S. Congress, A Study on Measuring and Enhancing Productivity in the Federal Sector

30.  Ibid.

31.  Ibid.

32.  State of Texas, Budget Manual

33.  Executive Office of the President, OMB Circular A-11

34.  Ibid.

35.  U.S. Congress, Study on Measuring and Enhancing Productivity in the Federal Sector

36.  Executive Office of the President, OMB Circular A-11

37.  U.S. Congress, Study on Measuring and Enhancing Productivity in the Federal Sector

38.  Joint Project on Measuring and Enhancing Productivity in the Federal Government, "Case Studies in Federal Productivity Charge FY 1967-1972," jointly by Civil Service Commission, General Accounting Office, and Office of Management and Budget

39.   Executive Office of the President, OMB Circular A-11

40.   U.S. Congress, Study on Measuring and Enhancing Productivity in the Federal Sector

41.   Ibid.

42.   Executive Office of the President, OMB Circular A-11

# CHAPTER 3
# STEP 2: DEVELOPMENT OF DECISION PACKAGES

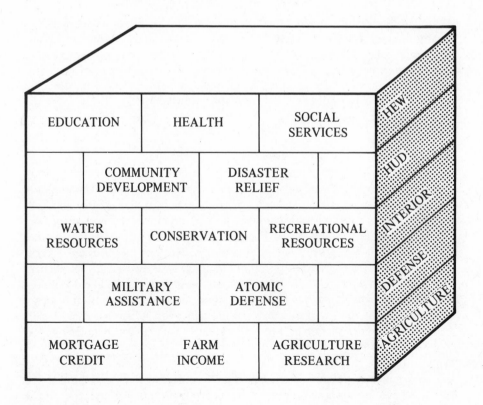

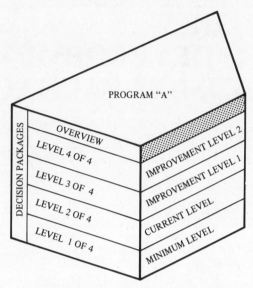

Decision package set — "building blocks" of the budget

## PROGRAM AND BUDGET GUIDANCE FROM HIGHER-LEVEL MANAGEMENT

Before a decision unit manager can be expected to develop decision packages competently, the manager has to receive program and budget guidance from the higher-level management. The information included in the guidance is usually generated during the planning stage. Also, a bottom-level manager would unnecessarily "spin wheels" if changes in the political arena such as potential reorganizations or *program deletions* were not conveyed to him on a timely basis.

*Example* (Message prepared for U.S. Budget):

> *Reorganization Proposal — Department of Energy*
> The current Federal organizations for developing and carrying out energy policy have been created by a series of independent actions taken primarily during a period of crisis. Improved coordination of energy programs calls for changes in the present structure. A Presidential report prepared for Congress that is required in the Energy Conservation and Production Act has recommended improvements in the organization and coordination of these programs. It has proposed that the functions of the Federal Energy Administration, the Energy Resources Council, the Energy Research and Development Administration, the Bureau of Mines and Power Administrations (Department of the Interior), the Rural Electrification Administration (Department of Agriculture), and the Federal Power Commission be joined within a single cabinet level Department of Energy.

The guidance received from higher-level management may determine the specific service, performance, output, or funding levels and the objectives to be

**EXHIBIT 3-1**    Planning assumptions and expenditure guidelines for HEW

*Planning Assumptions*

A. The budget mark for Fiscal Year 1979 allows for a net increase in obligational authority of 8% over Fiscal Year 1978 and is composed of the following assumptions:
  1. An inflation factor of 10% is expected.
  2. An average of 2% for each agency, in total, must be absorbed to reduce the budget deficit.
     a. Programs involved in the care and protection of life and property are exempted.
     b. Mandatory benefit program obligations (uncontrollable) are exempted.
  3. No new initiatives shall be included unless they can be achieved within the agency target.
  4. Personnel ceilings are reduced by 15% from the FY 1978 ceilings.

*Expenditure Guidelines*

A. Expenditure ceilings should be set at 15% above the FY 1978 level to the extent practicable. This Federal stimulus is needed to spur the economy and reduce the unemployment rate.
  1. Discretionary grant awards should be made earlier in the year so that more funds may be spent during the current year.
  2. Programmatic obstacles to early starts of awards should be removed.
     a. Step up submission of application due dates.
     b. Step up review council and field reader schedules.

Source: ZBB Manual Conceptualized for the U.S. Department of Health, Education, and Welfare developed as a project for ZBB course taught by Pete Sarant.

discussed. This helps to insure that information provided in the decision package is broken down and arrayed in a manner conducive to higher-level review of issues concerning the decision units (see Exhibit 3-1).

*Example:*

  *Guidance from the President of the U.S.*
  Major longer run actions to be taken include policies and programs to:

  · Increase the use of coal, nuclear power, and renewable power resources;

  · Accelerate development of federally owned domestic coal, oil, and gas resources;

  · Reduce the rate of growth of energy consumption;

  · Develop breeder reactor, solar, fusion and other energy technologies that could meet our energy needs at the end of this century and beyond; and

  · Establish FEA, ERDA, and the ERC to provide basic capability within the Federal Government to plan and execute national energy policies and programs.

  Budget outlays for these programs to carry forward overall national energy policies are to increase from $4.1 billion in 1977 to $6.1 billion in 1978 and $6.9

billion in 1979. Total outlays, including off-budget Federal entities, are to rise from $4.6 billion in 1977 to $6.7 billion in 1978 and $8.3 billion in 1979.

Guidelines should provide a common basis or direction from which managers can begin their analysis and preparation of budget requests. "Top level managers should prepare planning guidelines to be utilized by all levels of management in the formulation of requests for appropriations. These guidelines should generally reflect agency policy with regard to individual program needs and objectives; projected work load and performance levels; alternative methods of delivery to be evaluated; and, any other considerations that impact the planning and budgeting process such as number of personnel, changes in staffing patterns, or new services to be considered."[1]

*Example:*

*Guidance to U.S. Department of Transportation*

"Outlays for *railroad* programs should increase from $1.1 billion in 1976 to $1.7 billion in 1979. Comprehensive rail legislation, enacted in 1976, forms the basis for temporary Federal support of the Nation's rail freight system. In addition, freight railroads are expected to receive direct and guaranteed loans totaling $970 million through 1978, of which at least $170 million is to aid necessary mergers and consolidations of the Nation's rail network.

"Construction is scheduled to start in 1978 along the 457-mile rail corridor from Washington to Boston. This project will rehabilitate track that was allowed to deteriorate by the bankrupt railroads along the Northeast corridor. Your 1979 request for the corridor should be $400 million; some 123% higher than in 1977."

*Example:*

*Overhead Guidance by U.S. Department of Health, Education, and Welfare*

"Charges for FTS usage must be budgeted for as in past years. At this time the structure of the service and rate system is being renegotiated by GSA. However, we anticipate that FTS charges are likely to increase by about 20% over the current level."

*Example:*

*Costing Guidance by Environmental Protection Agency*

"It is suggested that costs be developed by reviewing past cost for ADP systems services and extrapolating proposed costs for various levels of service."

Under traditional budgeting, budget requests were submitted reflecting one total amount, such as $170,000 as shown in Exhibit 3-2, representing all levels of funding and performance in just one package. Using the zero-base budgeting

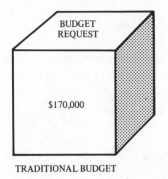

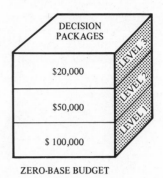

TRADITIONAL BUDGET                                    ZERO-BASE BUDGET

**EXHIBIT 3-2**    Development of decision packages

process, the decision unit manager prepares a decision package set that includes decision packages reflecting incremental levels of funding and performance, so that the cumulative amount of all packages represents the total potential budget request ($170,000) of the decision unit (see Exhibit 3-2). Therefore, instead of a manager submitting one budget request for program funding which possibly could be rejected in its entirety, the decision unit manager gives top level decision makers an option to at least keep certain incremental levels of a program or activity.

## WHAT IS A DECISION PACKAGE SET?

A decision package set (Exhibit 3-3) includes a decision unit overview (cover page) and various decision packages reflecting incremental levels of funding and performance for the selected decision unit, i.e., programs, activities, etc.

The decision unit manager prepares a decision package set that includes decision packages that will cumulatively amount to the total potential budget request of the decision unit (Exhibit 3-3 shows $160,000 cumulative amount). "Each package shows the effect of that funding and performance level on meeting

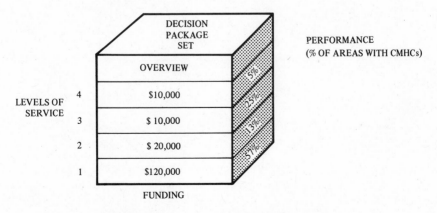

**EXHIBIT 3-3**    Mental health administration

## DECISION UNIT OVERVIEW

A-11-24A

The decision unit overview
will contain the information
required by section 24.1 (a) (1).

DECISION UNIT OVERVIEW

Department of Government, Office of the Secretary
Salaries and expenses: 16-1166-0-1-755
Budgetary and financial administration and service (Decision Unit #1234)

The heading should specify
organizational entity, account
title and code, and decision
unit title and identification
code.

Long-range goal.

To operate an effective and efficient financial management and budgetary program that is responsive
to management's needs and meets the requirements of OMB, GAO, Treasury, and the Department.

Major objectives.

1. To formulate and execute the budget and operate the accounting system in accordance with applicable standards
   and to perform the following ongoing activities:

   -- To prepare annual budget estimates for submission to OMB and budget justifications to Congress.

   -- To record financial transactions accurately, promptly, and completely to ensure that funds are not
      overobligated or overexpended.

   -- To prepare the financial information and reports needed by management officials.

   -- To process vouchers on a timely basis; to have 97% of all vouchers processed for payment by the due
      date with an error rate below 3%. (This was formerly 99% and 1% respectively; see discussion under
      "Accomplishments.")

2. To improve the budgeting and accounting systems by:

   -- Automating the accounting system by BY+3 (approval for this project was obtained previously).

   -- Designing and installing a cost reporting system that will permit compilation of unit cost data by BY+1.

3. To obtain GAO approval of the accounting system by BY+2.

4. To operate a Department-wide reports control system that measures and allows evaluation of reporting workload
   to keep such workload to a specified yearly minimum. Initial target is to reduce by BY+1, total number of
   reports and pages each by 15% of the PY level. (This is discussed further below.)

EXHIBIT 3-4A

PREPARATION AND SUBMISSION
OF BUDGET ESTIMATES (1977)

## DECISION UNIT OVERVIEW—Continued

A-11-24A (Cont.)

Overview (Cont.)

Alternatives.

1.  Currently, it is anticipated that planning and development for automation of the accounting system will be accomplished by an outside firm. Although systems design and development could be conducted in-house, contractor's staff and support capabilities would permit more timely completion of the project (3 versus 5 years). Moreover, the results of a study conducted in accordance with OMB Circular No. A-76 indicate that an in-house effort would be 15% more expensive in the long run.

2.  The departmental Information Systems Office could assume the reports control function. Many of the reports are computer generated and Information Systems already maintains a control system for them. The broad knowledge of departmental operations available in the Office of the Secretary was particularly useful for the first two phases of the comprehensive review of report requirements. However, the remaining portion of that study is ideally suited to the capabilities and resources of the Information Systems Office. It was decided to accept this alternative (see decision unit 8225) and to transfer one person from this office to maintain continuity on the study.

Accomplishments.

General: Ongoing objectives related to budget formulation and execution and operation of an accounting system were satisfied this year. 99% of all invoices were paid by the due date and the error rate was below 1%. This was consistent with the previous objective. However, this objective has changed as a result of a benefit-cost analysis that indicated that satisfaction of that objective is only marginally cost effective.

Automation: A statement of work suitable for contracting out a feasibility study will be drawn up during the current year.

Cost reporting system: An analyst has been working with a cost accountant from the departmental accounting office. Systems development is proceeding on schedule; the basic units for which data will be collected have been identified, and report formats have been developed.

Accounting system approval: Two staff members have been developing instructions and control systems and establishing reporting requirements. Principles and standards have been approved for all subsystems, and designs will be completed for 8 of the 12 subsystems at the end of the current year.

Reports control: 50% of the departmental requests for new reports have been denied. In addition, a comprehensive review of existing reporting requirements has been conducted and some were terminated. The net effect will be a 10% reduction of PY report volume for the current year.

**EXHIBIT 3-4B**

the assigned objectives. The decision packages serve as the primary tool for budgetary review, analysis, and decision making, although additional materials may also be made available or requested for review."[2]

"However, amounts proposed for supplementals and for rescissions are shown separately for the current year and reflected in the amounts for the budget year in the respective decision packages. For the purposes of justification and review, a separate decision package set are prepared for each proposed program supplemental. New programs or activities (e.g., those resulting from proposed legislation or a new major objective) are presented in a separate decision package set. Proposals for abolition of current programs or activities or parts thereof also be reflected in a decision package and are discussed in a summary and highlight memorandum."[3]

## WHAT IS A DECISION UNIT OVERVIEW? (EXHIBIT 3-4)

A decision unit overview is a cover sheet for the decision packages. It provides information necessary to evaluate and make decisions on each of the decision requests without the need to repeat that information in each package. It should be at most two pages long and contain the following information to be explained later:
  1. Identifying information
  2. Long-range goals
  3. Major objectives
  4. Alternatives
  5. Accomplishments

## WHAT IS A DECISION PACKAGE? (EXHIBIT 3-5A-F)

It is a brief justification and request document that includes the information necessary for managers to make judgments on program direction and resource requirements. It is the primary tool for budgeting review, analysis, and decision making.

There are many formats used in developing decision packages (see Appendix) in the public sector. The author has designed a decision package using the format recommended by the U.S. Government's Office of Management and Budget (OMB) (see Appendix).

OMB suggests that each decision package should be no more than two pages long and contain the following information:
  1. Identifying information
  2. Activity description
  3. Resource requirements
  4. Short-term objectives
  5. Impact on major objectives
  6. Other information
These contents will be explained later in the chapter.

PREPARATION AND SUBMISSION
OF BUDGET ESTIMATES (1977)

# DECISION PACKAGE SET
## Minimum Level

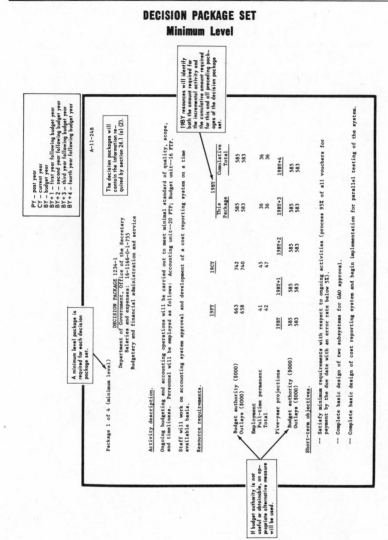

PY — past year
CY — current year
BY — budget year
BY+1 — first year following budget year
BY+2 — second year following budget year
BY+3 — third year following budget year
BY+4 — fourth year following budget year

A-11-24B

The decision packages will contain the information required by section 24.1 (a) (2).

A minimum level package is required for each decision package set.

19BY resources will identify both the amount required for the incremental activity and the cumulative amount required for this and all preceding packages of the decision package set.

Package 1 of 4 (minimum level)

DECISION PACKAGE 1234-1
Department of Government, Office of the Secretary
Salaries and expenses; 16-1166-0-1-755
Budgetary and financial administration and service

Activity description.

Ongoing budgeting and accounting operations will be carried out to meet minimal standard of quality, scope, and timeliness. Personnel will be employed as follows: Accounting unit—20 FTP; Budget unit—16 FTP.

Staff will work on accounting system approval and development of a cost reporting system on a time available basis.

Resource requirements.

|                              | 19PY | 19CY | 19BY | 19BY+1 | 19BY+2 | This Package | Cumulative Total |
|------------------------------|------|------|------|--------|--------|--------------|------------------|
| Budget authority ($000)      | 663  | 742  |      |        |        | 585          | 585              |
| Outlays ($000)               | 658  | 740  |      |        |        | 583          | 583              |
| Employment                   |      |      |      |        |        |              |                  |
| Full-time permanent          | 41   | 45   |      |        |        | 36           | 36               |
| Total                        | 42   | 47   |      |        |        | 36           | 36               |

Five-year projections

|                              | 19BY | 19BY+1 | 19BY+2 | 19BY+3 | 19BY+4 |
|------------------------------|------|--------|--------|--------|--------|
| Budget authority ($000)      | 585  | 585    | 585    | 585    | 585    |
| Outlays ($000)              | 583  | 583    | 583    | 583    | 583    |

Short-term objectives.

-- Satisfy minimum requirements with respect to ongoing activities (process 95% of all vouchers for payment by the due date with an error rate below 5%).

-- Complete basic design of two subsystems for GAO approval.

-- Complete basic design of cost reporting system and begin implementation for parallel testing of the system.

If budget authority is not useful or obtainable, an appropriate alternative measure will be used.

EXHIBIT 3-5A

PREPARATION AND SUBMISSION
OF BUDGET ESTIMATES (1977)

## DECISION PACKAGE SET—Continued
### Minimum Level

A-11-24B (Cont.)

Package 1 of 4 (Cont.)

Impact on major objectives.

-- Voucher processing will not meet major objective during the budget year. (See "Other information" below.)

-- Installation of cost reporting system will be delayed one year.

-- No progress will be made toward automating the accounting system.

-- Objective of obtaining GAO approval by BY+2 will be missed by one and a half years.

Other information.

-- At this level of funding, fewer staff members would be involved in the development of the accounting and cost reporting systems. The resulting lack of understanding of these systems would reduce our ability to work with them and make later modifications.

-- This level of funding will satisfy the major objective with respect to voucher processing after the budget year because of increased productivity.

-- Review of fund utilization and control will occur when time is available.

-- Financial statements, including the reconciliations, previously prepared on a monthly basis, will be prepared on a quarterly basis.

-- Cash window hours will be reduced to 4 hours a day. There will be no back-up capability for the cashier and congestion will occur.

-- Preparation of management reports will be delayed; backlogs will probably increase and an additional 10 hours per pay period of overtime effort will be required.

EXHIBIT 3-5B

## DECISION PACKAGE SET—Continued

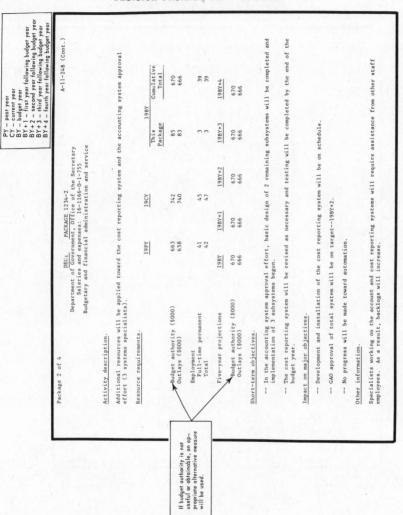

PY – past year
CY – current year
BY – budget year
BY+1 – first year following budget year
BY+2 – second year following budget year
BY+3 – third year following budget year
BY+4 – fourth year following budget year

Package 2 of 4                                                      A-11-24B (Cont.)

DEC1      PACKAGE 1234-2
Department of Government, Office of the Secretary
Salaries and expenses: 16-1166-0-1-755
Budgetary and financial administration and service

Activity description.

Additional resources will be applied toward the cost reporting system and the accounting system approval
effort (3 systems specialists).

Resource requirements.

| | 19PY | 19CY | 19BY+1 | 19BY | This Package | Cumulative Total |
|---|---|---|---|---|---|---|
| Budget authority ($000) | 663 | 742 | | | 85 | 670 |
| Outlays ($000) | 658 | 740 | | | 83 | 666 |
| | | | | 19BY | 19BY+3 | 19BY+4 |
| Employment | | | | | | |
| Full-time permanent | 41 | 45 | | | 3 | 39 |
| Total | 42 | 47 | | | 3 | 39 |

Five-year projections

| | 19BY | 19BY+1 | 19BY+2 | 19BY+3 | 19BY+4 |
|---|---|---|---|---|---|
| Budget authority ($000) | 670 | 670 | 670 | 670 | 670 |
| Outlays ($000) | 666 | 666 | 666 | 666 | 666 |

Short-term objectives.

-- In the accounting system approval effort, basic design of 2 remaining subsystems will be completed and
   implementation of 3 subsystems begun.

-- The cost reporting system will be revised as necessary and testing will be completed by the end of the
   budget year.

Impact on major objectives.

-- Development and installation of the cost reporting system will be on schedule.

-- GAO approval of total system will be on target--19BY+2.

-- No progress will be made toward automation.

Other information.

Specialists working on the account and cost reporting systems will require assistance from other staff
employees. As a result, backlogs will increase.

If budget authority is not
useful or obtainable, an appropriate alternative measure
will be used.

**EXHIBIT 3-5C**

PREPARATION AND SUBMISSION
OF BUDGET ESTIMATES (1977)

## DECISION PACKAGE SET—Continued
### Current Level

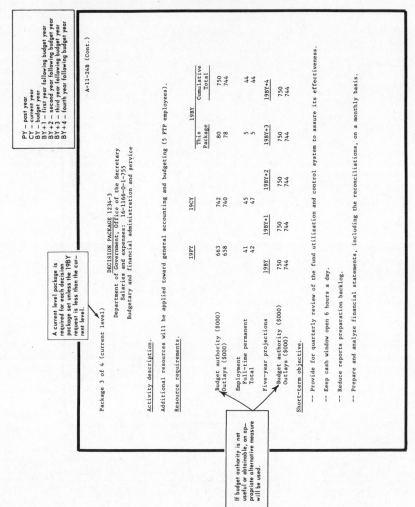

EXHIBIT 3-5D

PREPARATION AND SUBMISSION
OF BUDGET ESTIMATES (1977)

## DECISION PACKAGE SET—Continued
### Current Level

A-11-24B (Cont.)

Package 3 of 4 (Cont.)

Impact on major objective.

-- Budgeting and accounting operations will function more effectively and efficiently:

    Response time for financial reports requested by management will average 2 days (a reduction of 1 day from the minimum level).

    Frequent on-site reviews of the use of funds in comparison with the budget plan can be accomplished.

-- No progress will be made toward automation.

Other information.

-- Turn-around time on typing work will be reduced by one day.

-- Overtime will not be required at this level.

-- Backup capability for the cash window operation will be available.

EXHIBIT 3-5E

PREPARATION AND SUBMISSION
OF BUDGET ESTIMATES (1977)

## DECISION PACKAGE SET—Continued

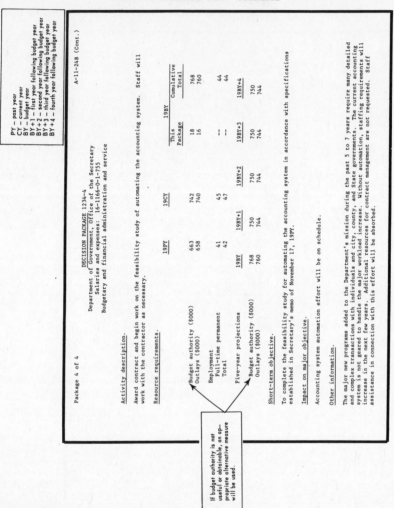

A-11-24B (Cont.)

PY — past year
CY — current year
BY — budget year
BY+1 — first year following budget year
BY+2 — second year following budget year
BY+3 — third year following budget year
BY+4 — fourth year following budget year

Package 4 of 4

DECISION PACKAGE 1234-4
Department of Government, Office of the Secretary
Salaries and expenses: 16-1166-0-1-755
Budgetary and financial administration and service

Activity description.

Award contract and begin work on the feasibility study of automating the accounting system. Staff will work with the contractor as necessary.

Resource requirements.

|  | 19PY | 19CY | 19BY This Package | 19BY Cumulative Total |
|---|---|---|---|---|
| Budget authority ($000) | 663 | 742 | 18 | 768 |
| Outlays ($000) | 658 | 740 | 16 | 760 |
| Employment |  |  |  |  |
| Full-time permanent | 41 | 45 | -- | 44 |
| Total | 42 | 47 | -- | 44 |

Five-year projections

|  | 19BY | 19BY+1 | 19BY+2 | 19BY+3 | 19BY+4 |
|---|---|---|---|---|---|
| Budget authority ($000) | 768 | 750 | 750 | 750 | 750 |
| Outlays ($000) | 760 | 744 | 744 | 744 | 744 |

Short-term objective.

To complete the feasibility study for automating the accounting system in accordance with specifications established in Secretary's memo of November 17, 19PY.

Impact on major objective.

Accounting system automation effort will be on schedule.

Other information.

The major new programs added to the Department's mission during the past 5 to 7 years require many detailed and complex transactions with individuals and city, county, and State governments. The current accounting system is not geared to handle the major workload increase. Without automation, staffing requirements will increase in the next few years. Additional resources for contract management are not requested. Staff assistance in connection with this effort will be absorbed.

If budget authority is not useful or obtainable, an appropriate alternative measure will be used.

**EXHIBIT 3-5F**

## PREPARATION OF DECISION PACKAGES

### Zero-Basis Analysis

Before preparing the packages, "The decision unit manager performs two types of analysis based on the program and budget guidance received from higher level management:

1. *The manager examines alternative ways of accomplishing the major objectives.* Such alternatives may require legislation and may have been identified and developed as a result of a major reexamination of the program or activity. In other instances the alternatives identified may not be fully developed, but will serve as a basis for reexamining the program at a later date. In still other instances, the alternatives identified may be the first steps toward more significant changes that will take longer than 1 year to accomplish. Normally, the best alternative is then selected and used as the basis for the second type of analysis.
2. *The manager identifies different levels of funding, activity, or performance.* The purpose of identifying these different levels is to provide information on:
   a. Where reductions from the total request may be made.
   b. The increased benefits that can be achieved through additional or alternative spending plans.
   c. The effect of such additions and reductions."[4]

### Different Levels of Funding and Performance (Service or Effort)

The decision unit manager prepares a set that includes decision packages reflecting incremental levels of funding and performance (service or effort). The cumulative amount of all packages represents the total potential budget request of the decision unit.

A set of decision packages according to the U.S. Government's Office of Management and Budget should include a minimum, current, and incremental levels of funding and performance.

### Minimum Level

A minimum level is actually the "grass roots" funding level necessary to keep a program alive. Any level below this will cause the program to terminate and "zero out" of existence. Therefore, the minimum level is the "performance or funding level below which it is not feasible to continue a program, activity, or entity because no constructive contribution can be made toward fulfilling its objective. The minimum level:

- May not be a fully acceptable level from the program manager's perspective or
- May not completely achieve the desired objectives of the decision unit."[5]

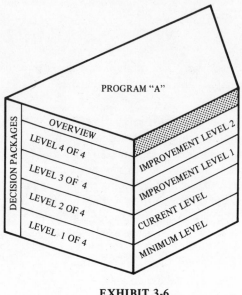

**EXHIBIT 3-6**

*Example:*

Bureau of Adult Education, HEW, Bilingual Vocational Education — This program's minimum objective is to provide $13,000,000 in grants for vocational training, and $2,000,000 in procurement contract for development of instructional materials for bilingual vocational education for persons of limited English-speaking ability.

If the Office of Education does not continue at this minimum level then they would not be able to obligate appropriated funds and will be in violation of the Impoundment Control Act of 1974.

This level is not fully acceptable from the program manager's perspective because the program could not monitor the contracts and grants nor establish program priorities at this level.

**Current Level**

A current level of service is the top of the "base level" which would be reflected in the decision packages if the proposed budget programs or activities will be carried on at the current operating level without major policy changes. Other nomenclatures used in the public sector for this performance and funding level are *maintenance, workload,* or *current operations* level. In all instances, the minimum level should be below the current level unless it is clearly not feasible to operate below the current level.

*Example:*

> At this level the Office of Education will be able to monitor the contracts and grants and establish program priorities for the next year. The resources required and the services given will be the same as the current year.

## Incremental Level

"The decision package set may also include, when appropriate: (1) a level or levels between the minimum and current levels, and (2) any additional increments desired above the current level."[6] Some managers could "hedge" against a favorite program going out of existence by preparing decision packages at levels between the minimum and current level. Agencies using additional increments above the current level sometimes call these the *improvement levels.*

*Example:*

> A decision package is prepared at an incremental level for the Bilingual Vocational Education program. At this incremental level the program can provide a higher level of performance or service.

> The program would be able to provide technical assistance to applicants, evaluate the program, and provide national leadership to bilingual vocation education if this request for additional resources is funded.

## Various Levels of Funding or Performance

It would be appropriate at this point to mention that decision packages are "self-contained" budget requests. Under ZBB, the decision maker is prohibited from denying funds to any incremental level of performance because of the total amount of funds requested. Various levels of decision packages produce different performance outputs and have separate funding requirements.

*Example:*

> Community Mental Health Centers are needed to control mental health in the community. Below is an incremental table for different levels of effort:

| Level of Service | Outputs Indicators Number of CMHC's | Staff Requirements (Employees) | Fund Requirement |
|---|---|---|---|
| 4 | 25 | 10 | $ 10,000 |
| 3 | 25 | 10 | 10,000 |
| 2 | 30 | 20 | 20,000 |
| 1 | 720 | 200 | 120,000 |
| Totals | 800 | 240 | $160,000 |

**Preparing Decision Packages for Mandatory (Noncontrollable) Programs**

The decision packages serve as the primary tool for budgetary review, analysis, and decision making. Normally each package shows the effect of that funding and performance level on meeting the assigned objectives. "Generally, a *series of packages should be prepared* for all programs and activities where there is *discretion* as to the amount of funds to be spent, or the appropriate method or level of activity. In any instance where there is clearly *no discretion* in the amounts of funds to be spent or the appropriate method, or level of activity, *at least one decision package* should be *prepared* that summarizes the analysis and decision making that resulted in that request."[7] This decision package should support the conclusion that only one funding or activity level can be considered. It will be, at the least, a documented budget request for the agency's information system.

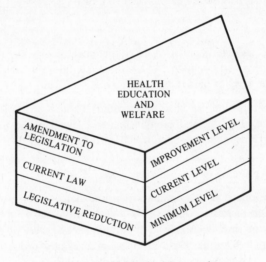

Noncontrollable decision packages

"*This does not mean that where a spending level is mandatory under existing substantive law, only one level will be identified.* There are many instances in which the decision on whether to propose legislative changes is made during the preparation of the budget. There are also instances in which changes in regulations or program administration can affect the amount of resources needed to carry out a mandatory program. In these instances, packages should be prepared that analyze the effects of different funding or performance levels or alternative methods of accomplishing the objectives."[8]

*Example:*

*Department of Health, Education, and Welfare*

The instructions for submitting 1979 POC budget requests identified these noncontrollable programs:

Social Security Administration:
    Old-age and Survivors insurance
    Disability insurance
    Supplemental Security income

Health Care Financing Administration:
    Medical assistance (Medicaid)

Public Health Service:
    Health resources — loan repayment

Office of Education:
    Guaranteed student loan program


For these programs it was suggested that the initial (current level) decision package start from current law using the latest economic assumptions and State estimates, where appropriate. The minimum level would then be reached by legislative proposals or new regulations which would reduce spending. Similarly, any "program improved" package would take the form of amendments to the authorizing legislation.[9]

"Sometimes legislation may be required to put into effect some level of funding or performance. However, nothing in the ZBB process should inhibit or prohibit any decision maker from submitting, requesting, or reviewing any information needed for analysis and decision making. For example, separate decision package sets may be prepared to examine the impact to different alternatives. Also, packages reflecting increased performance or funding levels may introduce alternative methods of accomplishment that were not feasible at a lower level."[10]


## Preparation of Decision Unit Overview

The overview provides information necessary to evaluate and make decisions on each of the decision packages without the need to repeat that information in each package. It contains the following information:

1. "Identifying Information — Includes sufficient information to identify the decision unit, and the organizational and budgetary structure within which that decision unit is located. A unique four-digit code will be assigned to each decision unit by the agencies. Each package should include the title of the appropriation or fund account that finances the decision unit, the account identification code and the agency's four-digit decision unit code."[11]

*Example:*

*"DECISION UNIT OVERVIEW*
Department of Health, Education, and Welfare
Mental Health Administration
Federal Support of Community Mental Health Services
Mental Health: 75-0001-0-1-551"[12]

ACCOUNT IDENTIFICATION CODE

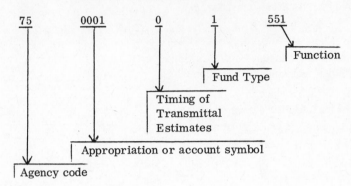

In addition to the account identification code, each decision unit has a four-digit code identification code.

*Example:*

Grants for construction of mental hospitals (4321). By adding additional codes at the end of the number, i.e., 4321-3, an agency could identify the decision package number. The number "3" would represent decision package number 3 of 4 decision packages. Not only will this coding assist in tracking decision units internally but it will also show the relationship between the budget account structure (account identification code) and the decision units identified in the agency submission of justification materials. This relationship is explained in the chapter on budget submission.

2.   Long-Range Goal — "When appropriate, identify the long-range goal of the decision unit. Goals should be directed toward general needs, to serve as the basis for determining the major objective(s) undertaken to work towards that goal."[13] In Chapter 2, missions and goals were defined as a statement describing the nature and scope of work to be performed and in effect describing an organization's or unit's reason for existence. It provides a logical starting point for determining objectives and a means of testing their validity and establishing accountability for results.

*Example:*

"To ensure needy citizens access to community based mental health services, regardless of ability to pay. Services should be of high quality, provided in the least restrictive environment, and in a manner ensuring patients' rights and dignity."[14]

3.   Major Objective(s) — "Describe the major objectives of the decision unit, the requirements these objectives are intended to satisfy and the basic authorizing legislation. Major objectives normally are of a continuing nature or take relatively long periods to accomplish. Objectives should be measurable and should be those that program managers employ; they should form the basis for first determining and subsequently evaluating the accomplishments of programs or activities.

*Example:*

> To assist in the establishment and operation of a nation-wide network of 1,200 qualified community mental health centers (CMHCs) by 1984 to ensure availability and accessibility of services to residents of each mental health catchment area."[15]

An important early step in zero-base budgeting is the identification of objectives for all managers preparing and reviewing decision packages, as discussed in Chapter 2. "Program and organization objectives should be explicit statements of intended output, clearly related to the basic need for which the program or organization exists. The task of identifying objectives requires the participation by managers at all levels to determine the ultimate realistic outputs or accomplishments expected from a program or organization (major objectives)."[16]

4. Current Method of Accomplishing the Major Objectives — This is a statement or description of the methods, actions, or operations necessary to accomplish the major objectives of the decision unit (i.e., What will be done? How will it be done?).

*Example:*

> "Grants are made to public and nonprofit entities to plan and operate community mental health center programs. The planning grants are one-time grants, not to exceed $75,000 each. The operating grants are for eight-year periods with a declining Federal matching rate."[17]

5. Alternatives — The first step in preparing a decision package is that the manager examines alternative ways of accomplishing the major objectives. "Describe the feasible alternative ways to accomplish the major objectives. *Identify which of the alternatives represents the best method proposed for the budget year.* Briefly explain how the approach selected contributes to satisfying the major objectives and the rationale for not pursuing other alternatives. This may include a discussion of organization structure and delivery systems; longer-range cost factors; and when applicable, the unique aspects and need for the program that cannot be filled by State or local governments or the private sector. (See Zero-Base Analysis described previously in the chapter.)

*Example:*

1. Consolidate Federal funding for community mental health services and other categorical health service programs into a single formula grant to the States.

2. Consolidate Federal funding for community mental health services and other community-based inpatient and outpatient services — as well as institutionally based short-term acute and long-term care services — for the mentally ill and mentally retarded.

These alternatives are not being pursued because the States thus far have not been able to ensure that funds will be targeted into high priority areas. The Secretary believes the Federal Government must have the ability to control the funding.

3. Provide for mental health services coverage through the national health insurance proposal. This alternative is not presently viable because passage of the national health insurance act is not near. Intensive study is now being directed toward this alternative for possible consideration next year.

6. Accomplishments — Describe the progress of the decision unit toward meeting the major objectives. This section should include both quantitative and qualitative measures of results.

*Example:*

Since the establishment of the CMHC program in the mid-1960's, 670 CMHC's have received Federal funding of nearly $2.0 billion. In 1977, nearly 600 centers were operational, covering 45% of the population (90 million people), and providing treatment services to 2 million individuals annually."[18]

## Development of Decision Packages (Documenting Different Levels of Service)

After the manager examines alternative ways of accomplishing the major objectives, the best alternative is then selected and used as the basis for the second type of zero-base analysis — the identification of different levels of funding, activity, or performance.

This analysis is accomplished through the preparation of decision packages for each level of funding, activity, or performance. Each package should contain the following information:

1. Identifying Information — This information is the same included in the decision unit overview plus the package number. If four packages exist then the first package would be designated 1 of 4, the second package would be 2 of 4, etc. Also, indicate if package is minimum or current level.

*Example:*

DECISION PACKAGE — 4321-1
Department of Health, Education, and Welfare
Mental Health Administration
Federal Support of Community Mental Health Services
Mental Health: 75-0001-0-1-550
(Package 1 of 4 (minimum level))

2. "Activity Description — Describe the work to be performed or services provided with the incremental resources specified in the package. This section should

include a discussion and evaluation of significant accomplishments planned and the *results* of benefit/cost and other analyses and evaluations that will contribute to the justification of that level.

*Example:*

> *Level 1 of 4 (minimum level)*
> Continue grants only to the 450 CMHC's currently receiving Federal support, until each CMHC's eight-year grant cycle is completed.
>
> *Level 3 of 4 (current level)*
> Fund 50% more newly qualifying CMHC's. That is, for every two CMHC's whose eight-year eligibility period ends, fund three newly qualifying CMHC's.

3.     Short-Term Objective — State the short-term objectives (usually achievable within 1 year) that will be accomplished and the benefits that will result with the increment specified and the cumulative resources shown in the package. The expected results of the work performed or services provided should be identified to the maximum extent possible through the use of quantitative measures.

*Example:*

> *Level 3 of 4 (current level)*
> To ensure in 1979 access to qualified comprehensive mental health services to *51%* of the population (this results in treatment of about 2.2 million patients).
>
> *Level 4 of 4*
> To ensure in 1979 access to qualified comprehensive mental health services to *53%* of the population (this results in treatment of about 2.3 million patients)."[19]

Notice that each level shows an increment of performance. If top management accepts level 4 of 4 objective, 2% more of the population will have access to qualified comprehensive mental health services.

The information for this item in the decision package is obtained at the time the ZBB step "Identifying Objectives" (Chapter 2) is accomplished. Goals, major objectives, and short-term objectives are agreed to initially by top and lower levels of management. Most agencies are required to have a management-by-objective (MBO) system which will now complement the ZBB system in regards to setting objectives and preparing decision packages. "However, lack of precise identification and quantification of such objectives does not preclude the development and implementation of zero-base budgeting procedures.

4.     Impact on Major Objective(s) — Describe the impact on the major objective(s) or goals of both the incremental and the cumulative resources shown in the package.

*Example:*

### Level 1 of 4 (minimum level)

The major objective of 1200 qualified CMHC's by 1988 would not be met if this short-term objective were continued. It is unlikely that *any* net increase in qualified CMHC's would result at this level because few communities have the resources to develop a qualified program.

It is estimated that for each community that would develop a qualified CMHC, an existing qualified CMHC would cease to qualify because of cutbacks in service provided due to tight funds. The impact of continuing this level objective follows:

|                                           | 1977 | 1978 | 1979 | 1980 | 1981 |
|-------------------------------------------|------|------|------|------|------|
| Number of public and nonprofit CMHC's     | 700  | 710  | 720  | 730  | 740  |
| Number of CMHC's receiving grants         | 400  | 450  | 400  | 350  | 300  |
| Percent of population covered             | 43   | 45   | 45   | 45   | 45   |
| Percent of probable patients covered      | 45   | 50   | 50   | 50   | 50   |

### Level 2 of 4

Even without the planning grants, many communities will be encouraged to develop CMHC's because of the possibility of receiving the operating grants. However, the major objective would not be met at this level of funding. It would take until about 1990 to establish 1200 qualified CMHC's. The impact of continuing this level follows:

|                                         |      |      | 1979 This Package | 1979 Cumulative | 1980 | 1981 |
|-----------------------------------------|------|------|-------------------|-----------------|------|------|
|                                         | 1977 | 1978 |                   |                 |      |      |
| Number of public and nonprofit CMHC's   | 700  | 710  | 40                | 750             | 800  | 850  |
| Number of CMHC's receiving grants       | 400  | 450  | 50                | 450             | 450  | 450  |
| Percent of population covered           | 43   | 45   | 4                 | 49              | 58   | 65   |
| Percent of probable patients covered    | 45   | 50   | 4                 | 54              | 64   | 69   |

5.   Other Information — Include other information that aids in evaluating the decision package. This should include:

  •  Explanations of any legislation needed in connection with the package.

  •  The impact or consequences of not approving the package.

  •  For the minimum level package, the effects of zero-funding for the decision unit.

  •  For packages below the current level, an explanation of what now is being accomplished that will not be accomplished at the lower level.

  ◦  The relationship of the decision unit to other decision units, including the coordination that is required.

*Example:*

*Level 1 of 4 (minimum level)*
Continuing grants to the 450 CMHC's currently receiving Federal support until each CMHC's eight-year cycle is completed is the minimum level because (a) the Government has an eight-year contract with each CMHC, and (b) no new CMHC's will receive any grants. If zero-funded, the Government would be subject to legal action brought by CHMC's.

This level would cease to encourage communities to develop CMHC's because of the (a) lack of planning grant funds and (b) lack of operational grant funds, thus negating the potential growth in the number of qualified CMHC's.

Only 57% of the high priority catchment areas would receive qualified CMHC coverage.

*Level 2 of 4*
By 1982, 70% of the high priority catchment areas will have a qualified CMHC. Assuming the objective of CMHC's is desirable even by 1990, stretching out the program past the major objective date of 1984 will increase total program costs from $3.6 billion to $4.3 billion due to estimated increases in service costs."[20]

6.   Resource Requirements — At this point, a zero-base analysis begins which requires all the discipline at management's command. After the manager justifies the decision unit's budget requests by evaluating in detail the cost effectiveness of the unit's operations, the manager is ready to estimate the amounts of funds and personnel needed to accomplish the decision unit's objectives. The manager must review his current expenditures and revise his material, labor, and overhead, expense figures for the budget year for all levels of performance. Then a breakdown is make of total obligations, budget authority, outlays, and personnel requirements needed *for each level of performance* by the decision unit to assist in this evaluation.

## Contents of Resource Requirement Section

"OMB Circular 77-9 states that the resource requirement section include appropriate information, such as obligations, offsetting collections, budget authority or outlays, and employment (full-time permanent and total), for the past, current, and budget years for the upcoming budget. The increment associated with each package should be listed, along with the cumulative totals for each measure used in that package, plus all higher ranked packages for that decision unit. At an appropriate level in the process, budget authority and outlay amounts for the 4 years beyond the budget year should also be included, in accordance with criteria in OMB Circular No. A-11.

*Example:*

*Level 1 of 4 (minimum level)*

| | Dollars (in thousands) | | | |
| --- | --- | --- | --- | --- |
| | | | 1979 | |
| Funds Required | 1977 | 1978 | This Package | Cumulative Total |
| Planning grants ($) | 1,000 | 1,000 | 0 | 0 |
| Operating grants ($) | 97,000 | 147,000 | 120,000 | 120,000 |
| Total obligations | 98,000 | 148,000 | 120,000 | 120,000 |
| Budget authority | 98,000 | 148,000 | 120,000 | 120,000 |
| Outlays | 97,000 | 145,000 | 119,000 | 119,000 |
| Five-year estimates | 1979 | 1980 | 1981 | 1982 | 1983 |
| Budget authority | 120,000 | 100,000 | 80,000 | 60,000 | 40,000 |
| Outlays | 119,000 | 98,000 | 79,000 | 59,000 | 40,000 |

| | | | 1979 | |
| --- | --- | --- | --- | --- |
| Personnel Summary | 1977 | 1978 | This Package | Cumulative Total |
| Total number of permanent positions | 98 | 148 | 120 | 120 |
| Full-time equivalent of other positions | 2 | 2 | 2 | 2 |

*Example:*

*Level 2 of 4*

| | Dollars (in thousands) | | | |
| | | | 1979 | |
| Funds Required | 1977 | 1978 | This Package | Cumulative Total |
| --- | --- | --- | --- | --- |
| Planning grants ($) | 1,000 | 1,000 | 0 | 0 |
| Operating grants ($) | 97,000 | 147,000 | 20,000 | 140,000 |
| Total Obligations | 98,000 | 148,000 | 20,000 | 140,000 |
| Budget authority | 98,000 | 148,000 | 20,000 | 140,000 |
| Outlays | 97,000 | 145,000 | 19,000 | 138,000 |
| Five-year estimates | 1979 | 1980 | 1981 | 1982 | 1983 |
| Budget authority | 140,000 | 142,000 | 143,000 | 145,000 | 146,000 |
| Outlays | 138,000 | 141,000 | 142,000 | 144,000 | 145,000 |

| | | | 1979 | |
| Personnel Summary | 1977 | 1978 | This Package | Cumulative Total |
| --- | --- | --- | --- | --- |
| Total number of permanent positions | 98 | 148 | 20 | 140 |
| Full time equivalent to other positions[21] | 0 | 2 | 0 | 2 |

## Be Cautious in Preparing Service Level Estimates

Pressed for time, a manager who wants a stated amount of funding for a program, might just "plug" the resource figures for each service level as long as the packages total to the figure he has in mind. If top management disallows two levels of decision packages, the manager could be caught short of funds in order to perform at the remaining levels.

*Example:*

The manager of the Healthy State Environment unit has a total budget of $600,000 for FY 1978 for a program which inspects 95% of the factories which cause smoke. In submitting his FY 1979 budget request, the manager determined his objectives at each of the three incremental levels to be 70%, 15%, and 10%. He then circumvented the zero base analysis, by dividing his total resource requirements by three and requested $200,000 for each level of performance. As the result of ranking, top management accepted only the minimum level and the manager now has an objective to inspect 75% of the factories at a cost of only $200,000. The realistic amount that should have been requested for this level of performance would be $450,000.


## Definition of Budget Authority, Obligations, and Outlays

Before continuing, there are several budget concepts that a manager needs to know before estimating resource requirements. *Budget authority* is the authorization by the legislative body, Congress, usually taking the form of appropriations which permit obligations to be incurred and payments to be made by an agency. *Obligations* incurred by Government agencies include accruing liabilities for salaries and wages and entering into contract for purchases. This obligation which is generally liquidated by the issuance of checks or the disbursement of cash are called *outlays*.

"Government agencies are permitted to enter into obligations requiring either immediate or future payment of money only when they have been granted authority to do so by law. The amounts thus authorized by the Congress are called *budget authority*. Budget authority permits *obligations* to be incurred, and for most accounts the amount of the authority is related to the obligations expected to be incurred during the year. In some cases — especially construction, research, and procurement — budget authority is requested and provided to finance the full cost of each project at the time it is started, regardless of when obligations are expected to be incurred and the expected time of completion. Budget authority usually takes the form of *appropriations,* which permit obligations to be incurred and payments to be made. When budget authority is made available by the Congress for a specific period of time any part that is not used for obligations during that period lapses and cannot be used later.

"A *rescission* is a legislative action that cancels budget authority or unobligated balances of budget authority prior to the time the authority would otherwise have lapsed. Rescissions are offset against new budget authority in arriving at the total of budget authority for each year. Obligations generally are liquidated by the issuance of checks or the disbursement of cash; such payments are called *outlays*. Outlays during a fiscal year may be payments of obligations incurred in prior years or in the same year. Such outlays, therefore, flow in part from unexpended balances of prior year budget authority and in part from budget authority provided for the year in which the money is spent."[22]


## Object Classification

OMB did not include instructions regarding the inclusion of the "object classification" in the decision package. However, the author did include it (see Exhibit 3-7). This inclusion of the object classification (elements of expense) schedule in the decision package or as a supplement to the package is necessary and important for three reasons:

**Object Classification** (in thousands of dollars)

| Identification code 75-0600-0-1-553 | 1976 act. | TQ act. | 1977 est. | 1978 est. |
|---|---|---|---|---|
| Direct obligations: | | | | |
| Personnel compensation: | | | | |
| 11.1    Permanent positions | 110, 041 | 29, 364 | 133, 782 | 145, 937 |
| 11.3    Positions other than permanent | 4, 854 | 1, 308 | 7, 350 | 8, 089 |
| 11.5    Other personnel compensation | 1, 535 | 405 | 2, 070 | 2, 237 |
| Total personnel compensation | 116, 430 | 31, 077 | 143, 202 | 156, 263 |
| 12.1   Personnel benefits: Civilian | 12, 187 | 3, 408 | 14, 493 | 15, 833 |
| 21.0   Travel and transportation of persons | 6, 281 | 1, 444 | 7, 142 | 8, 203 |
| 22.0   Transportation of things | 514 | 142 | 643 | 667 |
| Rent, communications, and utilities: | | | | |
| 23.1    Standard level user charges | 9, 937 | 5, 541 | 11, 511 | 15, 886 |
| 23.2    Other rent, communications, and utilities | 8, 855 | 2, 024 | 10, 939 | 11, 186 |
| 24.0   Printing and reproduction | 1, 804 | 391 | 2, 223 | 2, 473 |
| 25.0   Other services | 33, 716 | 6, 443 | 41, 856 | 46, 873 |
| 26.0   Supplies and materials | 7, 619 | 1, 863 | 9, 741 | 10, 048 |
| 31.0   Equipment | 5, 103 | 2, 585 | 6, 631 | 6, 673 |
| 32.0   Lands and structures | 3 | 3 | | |
| 41.0   Grants, subsidies, and contributions | 2, 721 | 781 | 1, 521 | 1, 521 |
| 42.0   Insurance claims and indemnities | 94 | 41 | 117 | 117 |
| Total direct obligations | 205, 264 | 55, 743 | 250, 019 | 275, 743 |
| Reimbursable obligations: | | | | |
| 11.1   Personnel compensation: Permanent positions | 193 | 74 | 618 | 172 |
| 12.1   Personnel benefits: Civilian | 16 | 6 | 52 | 14 |
| 21.0   Travel and transportation of persons | 14 | 5 | 79 | 5 |
| 22.0   Transportation of things | 3 | 1 | 8 | |
| 23.2   Rent, communications, and utilities: Other rent, communications, and utilities | 2 | 1 | 8 | |
| 24.0   Printing and reproduction | 1 | 1 | 3 | 1 |
| 25.0   Other services | 667 | 244 | 2, 092 | 346 |
| 26.0   Supplies and materials | 164 | 60 | 523 | 127 |
| 31.0   Equipment | 193 | 70 | 617 | |
| 32.0   Lands and structures | 15 | 3 | | |
| Total reimbursable obligations | 1, 268 | 465 | 4, 000 | 665 |
| 99.0   Total obligations | 206, 532 | 56, 208 | 254, 019 | 276, 408 |

**Personnel Summary**

| | | | | |
|---|---|---|---|---|
| Total number of permanent positions | 6, 362 | | 7, 339 | 7, 491 |
| Full-time equivalent of other positions | 316 | | 542 | 542 |
| Average paid employment | 6, 675 | | 7, 475 | 8, 033 |
| Average GS grade | 9. 39 | | 9. 31 | 9. 31 |
| Average GS salary | $14, 829 | | $15, 570 | $16, 349 |

Source: U.S. Budget of U.S. for FY 1978

**EXHIBIT 3-7**    Food and Drug Administration

1.   Object classification schedules that "crosswalk" approved programs are printed in the U.S. Budget (Exhibit 3-7). There must be some source available to top management to supply these details to OMB.

2.   Without the availability of the object classification schedule, top management may be tempted to "pull figures out of the air."

3.   Lower-level managers have to analyze these expenditures for each budget request. Some documentation or vehicle should be required for reviewing and justifying each element of cost.

An "object classification" schedule (Exhibit 3-7) can be prepared for each level of service. The last package will show the cumulative totals for the set. If the entire package is accepted, it is these totals that can be posted onto a work sheet.

## Additional Schedules

It is sometimes appropriate that the lower-level managers support their initial decision packages by additional information or reports, however, discretion should be taken so as to avoid unnecessary paperwork. Top management may require other inclusions and justifications for budget requests based on such items as work measurement or manpower data.

*Example:*

> "The Public Health Service requires that the man-power justification be prepared with data produced under each agencys' Manpower Management Program (MMP) where possible. This man-power justification requires data by budget activity, by decision unit, by division."[23]

Once the managers have developed a decision package set (Exhibits 3-8 to 3-13) for each program they begin to rank them in order of priority."[24]

## NOTES

1.   State of Texas, *Budget Manual, Needs, Objectives and Measures for the 1978-1979 Biennium,* Governor's Budget and Planning Office, 1977, 49 pp.

2.   Executive Office of the President, Office of Management and Budget, *Zero-Base Budgeting,* OMB Bulletin 77-9, April 19, 1977.

3.   Executive Office of the President, Office of Management and Budget, "Preparation and Submission of Budget Estimates," OMB Circular A-11.

4.   Executive Office of the President, OMB Bulletin 77-9

5.   Ibid.

6.   Ibid.

7.   Ibid.

8.   Ibid.

9.   U.S. Department of Health, Education, and Welfare, *Instructions for Submitting 1979 P.O.C. Budget Requests,* Washington, D.C.

10.   Executive Office of the President, OMB Bulletin 7709

11.   Ibid.

12.   Ibid.

13.   Ibid.

14.   Ibid.

15.   Ibid.

16.   Ibid.

17.   Ibid.

18.   Ibid.

19.   Ibid.

(EXAMPLE)

CONSOLIDATED PROGRAM SUMMARY

U.S. DEPARTMENT OF LABOR

Appropriation

Account I.D. No. 16-0105-0-1-505

Agency     ESA

Title Office of Workers Compensation Claims

PAS   990.00

Long Range Goals:

To protect American workers from undergoing undue hardship as a result of incurring a work-related disease or injury.

Major Objectives:   Legislation: Workers' Compensation Act of 1972

1. Assure that workers receive appropriate benefits, in a timely manner.
2. Return as many workers as possible to a normal life and to the labor force.
3. Assure complete and sufficient insurance coverage in workplaces.
4. Evaluate the efficiency and the effectiveness of the program in order to make such changes as are necessary to meet the needs of the employed.

Current methods of accomplishing the major objectives:

1. Claims are processed within 30 days of filing to assure that benefits are available when they are needed.
2. Medical treatment is monitored and physical and vocational rehabilitation is provided.
3. The performance of insurance carriers is monitored and evalutaed.  Insurance coverage and self-insurance programs of employers are monitored, with advice and assistance in obtaining proper coverage given when necessary.
4. Managers routinely assess program efficiency using data from the management information system and other  sources.

EXHIBIT 3-8A

Office of Workers' Compensation Claims

## Alternative Methods:

Two alternative approaches were considered: administration by the States, and combination with other workers' compensation programs in a single organization. The first alternative was rejected because the Act was written specifically to provide coverage for employes not covered by State laws due to traditional division of Federal/State jurisdiction. The second approach was rejected due to essential differences in the intent, employers and employees included, and methods of coverage which were determined to be irreconcilable. However, ESA plans to investigate the possibility of consolidating rehabilitation programs, since the differences between them are not so great.

## Accomplishments:

Average processing time for new claims has been reduced to 24.2 days, which is near the theoretical minimum time of 23 days.

Thus far in FY 1977, 317 workers have completed rehabilitation programs and found employment. There are currently 377 enrollees in medical rehabilitation, and 749 in vocational rehabilitation.

Numerous instances of employers without adequate insurence coverage have been encountered, most of which have been corrected through negotiation and assistance. Several insurance companies have been found which, for various reasons, have not provided adequate benefits the employees covered under their policies. Current statute and regulations do not provide the Department the power to compel employers and insurers to follow Departmental coverage guidelines.

Numerous changes in processes, ogranization, and resource use have been made in order to improve the services which the Department provides employees.

**EXHIBIT 3-8B**

EXAMPLE

CONSOLIDATED DECISION PACKAGE
(Agency) ESA
(Title) Office of Workers' Compensation Claims

PAS CODE 990.00
Account I.D. No. 16-0105-01-505
Program Manager (Signature)

Package 1 of 4
Level Minimum

Activity Description:

Process workers' compensation claims in the maximum time allowed by statute.

| | 1977 | 1978 This Package | 1978 Cumulative Total | 1979 This Package | 1979 Cumulative Total |
|---|---|---|---|---|---|
| **Resource Requirements:** | | | | | |
| Budgeted Positions: FTP | 397 | | 447 | 360 | 360 |
| Other | 25 | | 25 | --- | --- |
| Staff Years | 411 | | 461 | 349 | 349 |
| | | | | | |
| Personnel Costs ($000) | 8,719 | | 11,304 | 8,993 | 8,993 |
| Non-Personnel Costs ($000) | 2,862 | | 3,724 | 2,968 | 2,968 |
| Total Obligations ($000) | 11,581 | | 14,315 | 11,961 | 11,961 |
| Budget Authority ($000) | 11,581 | | 14,315 | 11,961 | 11,961 |
| (Trust Funds) ($000) | --- | | --- | --- | --- |
| Outlays ($000) | 11,349 | | 14,028 | 11,722 | 11,722 |
| | | | | | |
| **Workload Tables:** | | | | | |
| New claims | | | 115,000 | 125,000 | 125,000 |
| Claims processed | | | 120,000 | 125,000 | 125,000 |
| Backlog: begin year | | | 15,000 | 10,000 | 10,000 |
| end year | | | 10,000 | 10,000 | 10,000 |
| Avg. processing time | | | 24.2 days | 30.0 days | 30.0 days |

| Five-Year Estimates: | 1979 | 1980 | 1981 | 1982 | 1983 |
|---|---|---|---|---|---|
| Budget Authority | 11,961 | 13,157 | 14,472 | 15,919 | 17,510 |
| Outlays ($000) | 11,722 | 13,157 | 14,472 | 15,919 | 17,510 |

EXHIBIT 3-9A

EXAMPLE

CONSOLIDATED DECISION PACKAGE (CONT'D)

ESA                    OWCC                              Package 1 of 4

Short-term objectives:

Funding at this level is for only one objective--processing workers' compensation claims in 30 days, which is the maximum time allowed by statute.   This is six days longer than the present processing time.   FY 1978 functions which could not be carried on at this level are supervising rehabilitation services, monitoring medical care, and monitoring insurance carriers who write workers' compensation under the Act, and monitoring employers' insurance coverage.  Contract funds for the development of the ADP management  information system approved in FY 1978 would not be available at this level.

Impact on major objectives:

The accomplishments expected at this level would fulfill only one objective of the workers' compensation program, that of processing claims of employees with work-related illnesses or injuries to assure that they receive monetary compensation which is adequate to avoid undue disruption of their lives.

Other Information:

If this package is not approved and OWCC is disbanded, the workers covered by this Act will be forced to deal directly with their employers on compensation claims, without the benefit of assistance from the Federal Government, both in administrative and procedural matters and in enforcement of the employers' responsibilities.  The loss of this administrative remedy for problems would leave court action as the only mechanism for settling disputes, resulting in undue financial hardship for employees, as well as heavily burdening the court system.  Failure to maintain the program would also be a violation of the statutes, which require the Department to administer the program.  This level was developed using the assumptions that all activities not directly related to claims processing may be deleted.  Therefore, this level covers only salaries and expenses for program managers, claims examiners and clericals.

**EXHIBIT 3-9B**

EXAMPLE

| | |
|---|---|
| **CONSOLIDATED DECISION PACKAGE** | PAS CODE 990.00 |
| (Agency) <u>ESA</u> | Account I.D. No. <u>16-0105-01-505</u> |
| (Title) <u>Office of Workers'</u> <u>Compensation Claims</u> | Program Manager <u>(Signature)</u> |

Package <u>2</u> of <u>4</u>

Level: <u>Improvement (below current)</u>

Activity Description:

Process workers' compensation claims at the current rate, monitor medical care, supervise rehabilitation programs, and monitor insurance coverage.

| Resource Requirements: | 1977 | 1978 This Package | 1978 Cumulative Total | 1979 This Package | 1979 Cumulative Total |
|---|---|---|---|---|---|
| Budgeted Positions: FTP | 397 | | 447 | 60 | 420 |
| Other | 25 | | 25 | 20 | 20 |
| Staff Years | 411 | | 461 | 73 | 422 |
| | | | | | |
| Personnel Costs ($000) | 8,719 | | 11,304 | 1,882 | 10,875 |
| Non-Personnel Costs ($000) | 2,862 | | 3,724 | 619 | 3,587 |
| Total Obligations ($000) | 11,581 | | 14,315 | 2,501 | 14,462 |
| Budget Authority ($000) | 11,581 | | 14,315 | 2,501 | 14,462 |
| (Trust Funds) ($000) | --- | | --- | --- | --- |
| Outlays ($000) | 11,349 | | 14,028 | 2,450 | 14,172 |
| | | | | | |
| Workload Tables: | | | | | |
| New claims | | | 115,000 | | 125,000 |
| Claims processed | | | 120,000 | | 125,000 |
| Backlog: begins year | | | 15,000 | | 10,000 |
| end year | | | 10,000 | | 10,000 |
| Avg. processing time | | | 24.2 days | -5.8 days | 24.2 days |

| Five-Year Estimates: | 1979 | 1980 | 1981 | 1982 | 1983 |
|---|---|---|---|---|---|
| Budget Authority ($000) | 14,462 | 15,908 | 17,498 | 19,247 | 21,171 |
| Outlays ($000) | 14,172 | 15,908 | 17,498 | 19,247 | 21,171 |

**EXHIBIT 3-10A**

CONSOLIDATED DECISION PACKAGE (CONT'D)

ESA                OWCC                                    Package 2 of 4

Short-term objectives:

The goal at this level is to continue unabated the full range of services provided to victims of employment-related illness and injury. Included expected accomplishments are maintenance of the current 24.2-day average processing time for claims, full supervision of physical and vocational rehabilitation programs (estimated 1,200 cases), continued monitoring of insurance companies in the workers' compensation field, and monitoring employers' insurance coverage.

Impact on major objectives:

This level provides for the accomplishment of all major programmatic objectives, except for the solution of problems concerning insurance provision and coverage.

Other Information:

This package provides the same level of service to clients that is currently being provided. This is possible at a reduced resource level due to changes in the Act which go into effect at the beginning of FY 1979 and which will reduce the work required for processing claims. If the package is not approved, the efforts of the Department to assure the adequacy of the programs which prepare employees to return to a normal life--medical care and physical and vocational rehabilitation--will be discontinued. Also lost will be the Department's enforcement of insurance requirements. As in the minimum level package, the only remedy for employers' problems in these areas will be through the courts.

**EXHIBIT 3-10B**

CONSOLIDATED DECISION PACKAGE

Package 3 of 4
Level Current

(Agency) ESA  PAS CODE 990.00
(Title) Office of Workers' Compensation Claims  Account I.D. No. 16-0105-01-505
Program Manager (Signature)

Activity Description:

Process workers' compensation claims at an acculerated rate, certify insurers and insured employers.

| | 1977 | 1978 This Package | 1978 Cumulative Total | 1979 This Package | 1979 Cumulative Total |
|---|---|---|---|---|---|
| Resource Requirements: | | | | | |
| Budgeted Positions: FTP | 397 | | 447 | 27 | 447 |
| Other | 25 | | 25 | 5 | 25 |
| Staff Years | 411 | | 461 | 39 | 461 |
| | | | | | |
| Personnel Costs ($000) | 8,719 | | 11,304 | 642 | 11,517 |
| Non-Personnel Costs ($000) | 2,862 | | 3,724 | 213 | 3,800 |
| Total Obligations ($000) | 11,581 | | 14,315 | 855 | 15,317 |
| Budget Authority ($000) | 11,581 | | 14,315 | 855 | 15,317 |
| (Trust Funds) ($000) | --- | | --- | --- | --- |
| Outlays ($000) | 11,349 | | 14,028 | 838 | 15,011 |
| | | | | | |
| Workload Tables: | | | | | |
| New Claims | | | 115,000 | --- | 125,000 |
| Claims processed | | | 120,000 | --- | 125,000 |
| Backlog: begin year | | | 15,000 | --- | 10,000 |
| end year | | | 210,000 | --- | 210,000 |
| Avg. processing time | | | 24.2 days | - 1.2 days | 23.0 days |

Five-Year Estimates:

| | 1979 | 1980 | 1981 | 1982 | 1983 |
|---|---|---|---|---|---|
| Budget Authority ($000) | 15,317 | 16,848 | 18,532 | 20,385 | 22,423 |
| Outlays ($000) | 15,011 | 16,848 | 18,532 | 20,385 | 22,423 |

EXHIBIT 3-11A

CONSOLIDATED DECISION PACKAGE (CONT'D)

ESA                    OWCC                    Package 3 of 4

Short-term objectives:

Two major accomplishments are expected for this level, in addition to those in package 2. The first is reduction of the average claim processing time to 23.0 days, the shortest time possible due to legislative and procedural requirements. The second is the establishment of a program to investigate and certify insurance companies who wish to write insurance under the Act, and to certify the adequacy of employers' insurance coverage (or self-insurance program).

Impact on major objectives:

This package provides resources to acheive all major programmatic objectives.

Other Information:

Changes in the Act which take effect at the beginning of FY 1979 eliminate some of the present requirements for processing claims, thus reducing the amount of work which must be done on each claim. These changes allow reduction of processing time to the minimum possible, and will make resources available for use in the insurance certification program. Disapproval of this package would result in continued inadequate insurance coverage by employers, with the resulting hardships placed on injured employees.

**EXHIBIT 3-11B**

CONSOLIDATED DECISION PACKAGE

Package 4 of 4

Level Improvement

(Agency) ESA

(Title) Office of Worker's Compensation Claims

PAS CODE 990.000

Account I.D. No. 16-0105-01-505

Program Manager(Signature)

Activity Description:

Process worker's compensation claims at present rate, establish a task force to review the current program and identify improvements which can be made.

| Resource Requirements: | 1977 | 1978 This Package | 1978 Cumulative Total | 1979 This Package | 1979 Cumulative Total |
|---|---|---|---|---|---|
| Budgeted Positions: FTP | 397 | | 447 | 12 | 459 |
| Other | 25 | | 25 | -5 | 20 |
| Staff Years | 411 | | 461 | 10 | 471 |
| Personnel Costs ($000) | 8,719 | | 11,304 | 250 | 11,767 |
| Non-Personnel Costs ($000) | 2,862 | | 3,724 | 82 | 3,882 |
| Total Obligations ($000) | 11,581 | | 14,315 | 332 | 15,649 |
| Budget Authority ($000) | 11,581 | | 14,315 | 332 | 15,649 |
| (Trust Funds) ($000) | --- | | --- | --- | --- |
| Outlays ($000) | 11,349 | | 14,028 | 325 | 15,336 |
| Workload Tables: | | | | | |
| New claims | | | 115,000 | --- | 125,000 |
| Claims processed | | | 120,000 | --- | 125,000 |
| Backlog: begin year | | | 15,000 | --- | 10,000 |
| end year | | | 10,000 | --- | 10,000 |
| Average processing time | | | 24.2 days | 1.2 days | 24.2 days |

| Five-Year Estimates: | 1979 | 1980 | 1981 | 1982 | 1983 |
|---|---|---|---|---|---|
| Budget Authority($000) | 15,649 | 17,213 | 18,934 | 20,827 | 22,909 |
| Outlays($000) | 15,336 | 17,213 | 18,934 | 20,827 | 22,909 |

EXHIBIT 3-12A

CONSOLIDATED DECISION PACKAGE (CONT'D)

ESA                OWCC                Package 4 of 4

Short-term objectives:

This package will allow OWCC to conduct a study of the efficiency and effectiveness of the program. The study will concentrate on how well the current program is meeting the needs of workers and will look at both the adequacy of the Department's efforts under the Act, as well as the adequacy of the Act itself.

Impact on major objectives:

This package allows the Department to initiate a long-term effort to acheive the major objective of assessing the needs of employees in the workers compensation area, as well as the adequacy of the Department's program in meeting those needs. This is in addition to accomplishing all programmatic objectives.

Other Information:

Resources made available by the statutory changes in claims processing will be applied to the study. Failure to approve this package will adversely affect the ability of the Department's workers' compensation programs to make adjustments to better meet the needs of the workers.

**EXHIBIT 3-12B**

Agency ___ESA___

Title ___Office of Workers' Compensation Claims___

Object Classification (in thousands of dollars)

|  | Improvement (Cumulative)1/ | Current (Cumulative) | Improvement | |
|---|---|---|---|---|
|  |  |  | (This Package) | (Cumulative) |
| 11. Total personnel compensation..... | 9,932 | 10,518 | 228 | 10,746 |
| 12. Personnel benefits.............. | 943 | 999 | 22 | 1,021 |
| 21. Travel and transportation of persons................... | 327 | 340 | 20 | 360 |
| 22. Transportation of things.......... | 48 | 49 | 1 | 50 |
| 23.1 Standard level user charges...... | 582 | 601 | 18 | 619 |
| 23.2 Other rent, communications and utilities.................. | 272 | 276 | 4 | 280 |
| 24. Printing and reproduction........ | 50 | 50 | 4 | 54 |
| 25. Other services.............. | 2,195 | 2,365 | 31 | 2,396 |
| 26. Supplies and materials........... | 43 | 46 | 2 | 48 |
| 31. Equipment.................. | 20 | 23 | 2 | 25 |
| 41. Grants, subsidies and contributions.................. | 50 | 50 | --- | 50 |
| Other.................. |  |  |  |  |
| Total obligations............ | 14,462 | 15,317 | 332 | 15,649 |
| (Working Capital Fund included above).................. | (800) | (860) | (26) | (886) |

1/ This column is necessary only if an improvement package falls between the minimum and the current level.

**EXHIBIT 3-13**

20.  Ibid.

21.  Ibid.

22.  Executive Office of the President, Office of Management and Budget, *U.S. Budget of FY 1978*, Washington, D.C., January 1977

23.  U.S. Department of Health, Education, and Welfare, *ZBB for Public Health Service*, Washington, D.C., April 1977

24.  U.S. Department of Labor, ZBB Instructions for FY 1979, Washington, D.C., 1977

# CHAPTER 4
# STEP 3: REVIEW AND RANKING OF DECISION PACKAGES

# STEP 4: PREPARATION AND SUBMISSION OF THE BUDGET

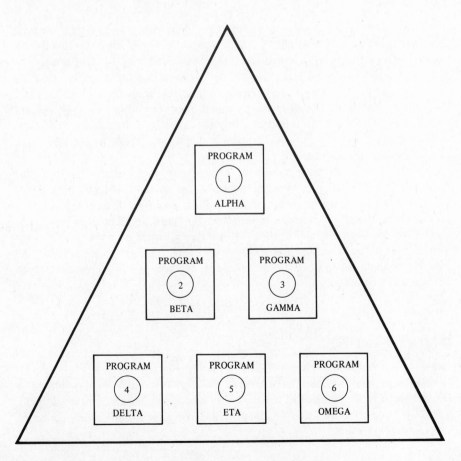

## STEP 3: REVIEW AND RANKING OF DECISION PACKAGES

Once the decision packages are developed, they are ranked in order of priority. The ranking process provides management with a technique for allocating resources by focusing on the questions: "What goals or objectives should the agency be attempting to achieve first?" and "How much resources should be allocated in attempting to achieve these objectives?" Thus, the prioritizing of the decision packages allows managers at each level of the organization to determine which specific goals and objectives are more important than others and to allocate limited resources to these important objectives. The completed decision packages are ranked initially by the decision unit manager who has developed the decision packages. They are then sent upward through the management hierarchy whereby the decision packages are once again reviewed and ranked along with the other decision unit packages at selected levels; the decision packages are consolidated again, bringing a broader perspective at this level of review and ranking.

### Type of Review

The review can be conducted more effectively at each management level if the type of review is determined beforehand. This is especially important in the middle and higher levels in the agency, where the review workload may be significant, even with consolidation of packages. As a means of increasing the effectiveness of its review, mid-level management may decide to limit its review of the higher-ranked packages to that necessary to provide a sound basis for ranking the packages and may choose to examine in more depth only the lower-ranked packages. The lower-ranked packages would be the first to be affected by an increase or decrease in the expected budgetary resources.

   The mid-level manager should review decision packages slightly above his "psychological line" drawn between high-and low-ranked packages. This avoids the unnecessary purging of potential high-ranking packages that could have been inadvertently placed by the decision unit manager below the "imaginary line." The higher-level manager may find it effective to review all packages given to him by his subordinates because the decision packages are being consolidated at each level. All packages recommending program improvement, deletion, and new programs should be thoroughly reviewed.

### Definition of Ranking

"Ranking is a process by which managers array program or activity levels (as shown in decision packages) in decreasing order of priority. This ranking process identifies the relative priority assigned to each decision package increment contained in the manager's budget request based on the benefits to be gained or the consequences of various spending levels."[1]

## RANKING SHEET

| | | | | | | A-11-24C |
|---|---|---|---|---|---|---|

The ranking sheet will show the priority assigned to all decision packages comprising the agency budget request.

If budget authority is not available for a decision package, an appropriate alternative measure will be used and identified.

If budget authority is not provided for all decision packages, this column will be omitted.

DEPARTMENT OF GOVERNMENT
Priority Ranking of Decision Packages, 19BY Budget
(In thousands of dollars)

| Rank | Decision Package Name and Number | BA | Outlays | Cumulative BA | Cumulative Outlays |
|---|---|---|---|---|---|
| 1 | Interest on borrowings (8932-1) | 809 | 809 | 809 | 809 |
| 2 | General administration (6931-1) | 582 | 582 | 1,391 | 1,391 |
| 3 | Budgetary and financial administration and service (1234-1) | 585 | 583 | 1,976 | 1,974 |
| 4 | Plant maintenance (5477-1) | 1,014 | 1,014 | 2,990 | 2,988 |
| 5 | Budgetary administration (4433-1) | 650 | 650 | 3,640 | 3,638 |
| 6 | Production of power (6625-1) | 7,250 | 7,250 | 10,890 | 10,888 |
| 80 | Construction grants (4777-2) | 23,000 | 21,200 | 762,126 | 668,221 |
| 81 | Sales program equipment (5517-1) | 600 | 600 | 762,726 | 668,821 |
| 82 | Budgetary and financial administration and service (1234-2) | 85 | 83 | 762,811 | 668,904 |
| 83 | Budgetary and financial administration and service (1234-3) | 80 | 78 | 762,891 | 668,982 |
| 84 | Plant maintenance (5477-2) | 234 | 234 | 763,125 | 669,216 |
| 85 | General administration (6931-2) | 45 | 45 | 763,170 | 669,261 |
| 86 | Power program equipment (5138-3) | 317 | 275 | 763,487 | 669,536 |
| 372 | Seaside Park Construction (1174-7) | 450 | 20 | 1,344,487 | 1,258,417 |
| 373 | Budgetary and financial administration and service (1234-4) | 18 | 16 | 1,344,505 | 1,258,433 |
| 374 | Service facilities grants (6326-4) | 5,000 | 4,500 | 1,349,505 | 1,262,933 |
| 375 | General management (2121-3) | 63 | 63 | 1,349,568 | 1,262,996 |
| | Total | | | 1,460,000 | 1,373,000 |

**EXHIBIT 4-1**

## Ranking Sheet

Each subordinate review level will prepare a ranking sheet to submit to the next higher review level. This ranking sheet should generally contain the information shown in Exhibit 4-1 for the budget year.

"In instances (e.g., revolving funds) where budget authority and net outlays *are not a factor in reflecting the appropriate or priority level of performance,* managers should use other measures (e.g., total obligations, employment)."

## INITIAL REVIEW AND RANKING OF DECISION PACKAGES

The developers of the decision packages, the decision unit managers, will rank the decision packages initially and then submit to higher level managers for review. Agencies may use whatever review and ranking techniques appropriate to their needs. However, ranking rule I should always be followed.

**Ranking Rule I**

*"The minimum level for a decision unit is always ranked higher than any increment for the same unit."*

The minimum level represents the level below which the programs or activities can not be conducted effectively.

*Example:*

Managers of decision units A, B, and C each rank packages for their units and send ranking sheet to managers of decision unit X. Decision Packages A1, B1, and C1 are minimum level packages for their respective decision unit. These packages are then sent to decision unit manager X for review and ranking.

|  | Package Number | Funding Increment | Funding Total |
|---|---|---|---|
|  | A1 | 100 | 100 |
| Decision | A2 | 15 | 115 |
| Unit A | A3 | 5 | 120 |
|  | A4 | 30 | 150 |
|  | B1 |  |  |
|  | B2 |  |  |
| Decision | B3 |  |  |
| Unit B | B4 |  |  |
|  | B5 |  |  |
|  | C1 |  |  |
|  | C2 |  |  |
| Decision | C3 |  |  |
| Unit C | C4 |  |  |
|  | C5 |  |  |
|  | C6 |  |  |

## HIGHER-LEVEL REVIEW AND RANKING

At higher management levels, the ranking sheet and related decision packages are reviewed. Before ranking is done by this management level, the reviewer may require the subordinate managers to revise, delete, or add to the decision packages and reorder the priority rankings.

*Examples:*

1. *Review by Higher-Level Manager X*

| | | | | Manager X Reviews | |
|---|---|---|---|---|---|
| | Package Number | Funding Increment | Funding Total | Revised Package Number | Funding Increment | Funding Total |
| | A1 | 100 | 100 | A1 | 100 | 100 |
| Decision | A2 | 15 | 115 | A2 | 5 | 105 |
| Unit A | A3 | 5 | 120 | A3 | 30 | 135 |
| | A4 | 30 | 150 | A4 | 15 | 150 |

"Higher-level manager reorders the proposed priorities of the subordinate decision unit managers. The packages may be revised by either the initial decision unit manager or the higher-level manager." (Initial packages, A2, revised down to A4.)

2.

| | Package Number | Accepted Package Number |
|---|---|---|
| | B1 | B1 |
| | B2 | B2 |
| Decision | B3 | B3 |
| Unit B | B4 | B4 |
| | B5 | B5 |

"Higher-level manager accepts proposed priorities of the subordinate manager."

3.

| | Package Number | Revised Package Number |
|---|---|---|
| | C1 | C1 |
| | C2 | C2 |
| Decision | C3 | C3 |
| Unit C | C4 | C4 |
| | C5 | C5 |
| | C6 | |

"Higher-level manager accepts proposed priorities of the subordiante manager, but chooses not to propose funding of lowest priority package, C6."

## CONSOLIDATION PROCESS

After the packages are reviewed, evaluated, and possibly revised, the higher level manager will *rank* all decision packages for all decision units under his control against each other and send a new ranking sheet to his superior.

*Example:*

Manager X will rank packages for decision units A, B, and C against each other and send the new ranking sheet to Manager R.

Ranking minimum level decision packages is accomplished by using Ranking Rule II.

## Ranking Rule II

*"A minimum level package for a given decision unit* does not *need to be ranked higher than any other decision package of other decision units."*

Once the subordinate packages are reviewed and ranked, the consolidation process is completed. The ranking identification number of the decision packages is changed.

*Example:*

Manager X evaluates and ranks decision packages received from subordinate managers A, B, and C.

Manager X renumbers the decision packages, A1 as X1, and C5 as X14.

| | Revised Package Number | Funding Increment | Funding Total[1] | Manager X | | |
|---|---|---|---|---|---|---|
| Manager A | A1 | 100 | 100 | X1 | A1 | |
| | A2 | 5 | 105 | X2 | B1 | |
| | A3 | 30 | 135 | X3 | A2 | |
| | A4 | 15 | 150 | X4 | C1 | |
| | | | | X5 | B2 | |
| | B1 [2] | | | X6 | A3 | To |
| | B2 | | | X7 | B3 | Manager R |
| Manager B | B3 | | | X8 | C2 | |
| | B4 | | | X9 | C3 | |
| | B5 | | | X10 | A4 | |
| | | | | X11 | B4 | |
| | C1 [3] | | | X12 | C4 | |
| | C2 | | | X13 | B5 | |
| Manager C | C3 | | | X14 | C5 | |
| | C4 | | | | | |
| | C5 | | | | | |

This process can be repeated as many times as necessary before a final consolidation of decision packages is prepared.

Cross indexing of decision packages for purposes of "tracking" would be advisable, especially if computerized.

*Example:*

"The consolidation process is explicitly designed to allow higher level managers the opportunity to bring their broader perspectives to bear on program priorities by allowing them to rank the decision packages and make program trade-offs. Higher level management's decision-making needs are better met by recasting all or some of the initial decision packages into a lesser number of consolidated decision packages. The consolidated packages would be based upon the more detailed information in the initial packages, but the information would be recast or reinterpreted in a broader frame of reference to focus on significant program alternatives or issues. The objectives are redefined to reflect the higher level manager's program perspective. This consolidation helps to reduce what would otherwise be an excessive paperwork and review burden at higher levels."

## Ranking Rule III

*"The agency head or his designee should determine at which review level(s) decision packages should be consolidated into a lesser number of packages before submission to the next higher review level."*

Example:

The Mental Health Administration decides that identified manager X will consolidate packages received from his subordinate manager A, B, and C for his decision unit. Numbering of decision packages would appear as follows:

| Subordinate Ranking | Manager X Consolidation |
|---------------------|-------------------------|
| A1                  | X1                      |
| B1                  |                         |
| A2                  | X2                      |
| C1                  |                         |
| B2                  | X3                      |
| A3                  |                         |
| B3                  |                         |

*Example:*

The Mental Health Administration decides that Manager X's supervisor will rank and consolidate decision packages. Here is how the process would flow:

| Manager X's Ranking | | Manager R's Ranking | | Manager R's Consolidation |
|---|---|---|---|---|
| X1 | A1 | | | |
| X2 | B1 | | | |
| X3 | A2 | | | |
| X4 | C1 | | | |
| X5 | B2 | 1 | X1 | |
| X6 | A3 | 2 | X2 | |
| X7 | B3 | 3 | Y1 | R2 |
| | | 4 | Y2 | |
| | | 5 | Y3 | |
| | | 6 | Y4 | |
| | | 7 | Y5 | R2 |
| | | 8 | Y6 | |
| | | 9 | Y7 | |
| | | 10 | X3 | |
| | | 11 | X4 | |
| | | 12 | X5 | R3 |
| | | 13 | X6 | |
| Y1 | A1 | 14 | X7 | |
| Y2 | B1 | | | |
| Y3 | B2 | | | |
| Y4 | B3 | | | |
| Y5 | A2 | | | |
| Y6 | A3 | | | |
| Y7 | A4 | | | |

### Ranking Rule IV

*"In all instances a minimum level consolidated decision package should be prepared.*

*This package may or may not include information from each of the minimum level packages from the decision package sets being consolidated."*

### Example:

A minimum level package R1 was developed by Manager R in the previous example. Decision unit package X1's information was not included in the consolidated package. Package X1 ensures access to mental health services to 45% of the population and package Y1 ensures access to mental health services to only military dependents.

This consolidation ranking process shows the relative priority that discrete increments of services or outputs of one decision unit have in relation to other increments of services or outputs of another decision unit.

Consolidated packages could differ greatly from the initial packages developed at the lower levels of management. This consolidated package reflect the "big picture" and different priorities, including the addition of new programs or the abolition of existing ones. "This consolidation should be based on natural groupings of subordinate decision units. Decision units in different budget subfunctions generally should not be consolidated." (See Exhibit 4-2 OMB's view of the ranking process.)

The key to effective ranking and consolidation is for top management to give subordinate managers the proper program and budget guidance before developing the initial decision packages. Once the decision packages are reviewed and ranked, the agency is then ready to prepare and submit their budget to the budget office.

## STEP 4: PREPARATION OF THE BUDGET

### OVERVIEW OF FORMULATION PHASE OF THE FEDERAL BUDGET PROCESS

Before explaining how detailed budget materials are developed and prepared using the ZBB process, it would be appropriate to regress and review the *executive formulation and transmittal phase* of the Federal budget process as described in "The Budget of the United States Government, FY 1978" which is written by Office of Management and Budget.

"The budget sets forth the President's financial plan of operation and thus indicates his priorities for the Federal Government during the coming year. The calendar year is the climax of many months of planning and analysis throughout the Executive Branch. Formulation of the 1978 budget began in the spring of 1976, although tentative goals for some programs were set earlier — when the 1977 budget was transmitted to the Congress in January of 1976.

"During the period when a budget is being formulated for the Executive Branch, there is a continuous exchange of information, proposals, evaluations, and policy decisions among the President, the Office of Management and Budget (OMB), and the various Government agencies.

In the spring, agency programs are evaluated, policy issues are identified, and budgetary projections are made, giving attention both to important modifications and innovations in programs and to alternative long-range program plans. These budgetary projections, including projections of estimated receipts prepared by the Treasury Department, are then presented to the President for his consideration, and the major issues are discussed. About the same time, the President receives projections of the economic outlook that are prepared jointly by the Council of Economic Advisers, the Treasury Department, and OMB.

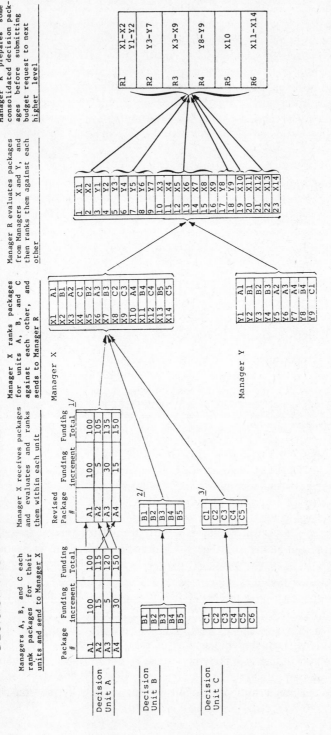

DECISION PACKAGE RANKING AND CONSOLIDATION PROCESS ILLUSTRATED

Managers A, B, and C each rank packages for their units and send to Manager X

Manager X receives packages and evaluates and ranks them within each unit

Manager X ranks packages for units A, B, and C against each other, and sends to Manager R

Manager R evaluates packages from Managers X and Y, and then ranks them against each other

BULLETIN NO. 77-9

Manager R prepares some consolidated decision packages before submitting budget request to next higher level

EXHIBIT 4-2

1/ Higher level manager reorders the proposed priorities of the subordinate decision unit managers. The packages may be revised by either the initial decision unit manager or the higher level manager.
2/ Higher level manager accepts proposed priorities of the subordinate manager.
3/ Higher level manager accepts proposed priorities of the subordinate manager, but chooses not to propose funding of lowest priority package.

"Following a review of these projections, the President establishes general budget and fiscal policy guidelines for the fiscal year that will begin about 15 months later. Tentative policy decisions and planning targets are then given to the agencies to govern the preparation of their budgets.

"Throughout the fall and early winter the Executive Branch is involved in two related budgetary processes. One is the preparation of the current services estimates, which are required by the Congressional Budget Act to be transmitted to the Congress by November 10 of each year. These estimates are projections of budget authority and outlays required to continue ongoing Federal programs and activities in the upcoming fiscal year without policy changes from the fiscal year in progress at the time the estimates are submitted.

"The second process is the preparation of the President's budget for transmittal to the Congress. This process involves a detailed review of agency budget requests by OMB. These requests and OMB's recommendations on them are presented to the President for decision. Overall fiscal policy issues — relating to total budget outlays and receipts — are again examined. The effects of budget decisions on outlays in the years that follow are also considered and are explicitly taken into account. Thus, the budget process involves the simultaneous consideration of the resource needs of individual programs, and the total outlays and receipts that are appropriate in relation to current and prospective economic conditions. The budget reflects the results of both of these considerations."[2]

## ZERO-BASE BUDGETING'S ROLE IN THE FEDERAL BUDGET PROCESS

Earlier in the budget process, decision packages are developed and reviewed to assist the agency in evaluating programs, identifying policy issues, and making budgetary projections in the spring. These projections based on the decision packages are then presented to the OMB for review and consideration. A question of importance to the reader would be, Why should the agency develop and rank decision packages before this planning stage? The answer is relatively simple. If an agency waits until the President establishes general budget and fiscal policy guidelines for the fiscal year, a major purpose of the ZBB process would be lost. The zero-base budgeting process has been adopted by the Federal Government to assist the President as well as the agencies to make the proper decisions on the cost and usefulness of Federal programs and activities.

Program and budget guidance prior to the development of decision packages is given by the higher level management within the agency. Earlier in Chapter 3, "Development of Decision Packages," it was explained that before a decision unit manager can be expected to develop decision packages competently, the manager has to receive program and budget guidance from higher level management. This program guidance could also be obtained through new legislation by Congress. The President would not establish budget and policy guidelines until *after* he received budgetary projections based on the decision packages from the agencies, projections of estimated receipts by the Treasury Department, and projections of the economic outlook by the Council of Economic Advisers.

# FORMULATION OF PRESIDENT'S BUDGET

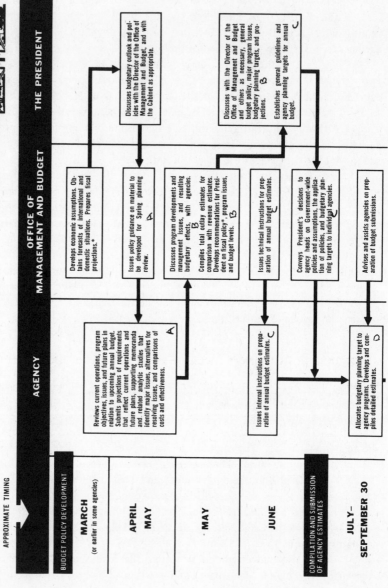

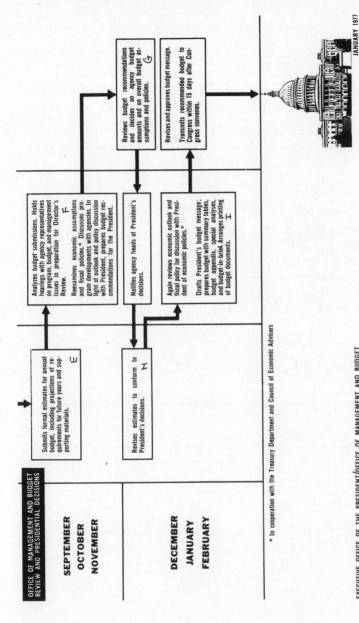

OFFICE OF MANAGEMENT AND BUDGET
REVIEW AND PRESIDENTIAL DECISIONS

SEPTEMBER
OCTOBER
NOVEMBER

Submits formal estimates for annual budget, including projections of requirements for future years and supporting materials.

Analyzes budget submissions. Holds hearings with agency representatives on program, budget, and management issues in preparation for Director's Review.

Reexamines economic assumptions and fiscal policies.* Discusses program developments with agencies. In light of outlook and policy discussion with President, prepares budget recommendations for the President.

Reviews budget recommendations and decides on agency budget amounts and on overall budget assumptions and policies.

Notifies agency heads of President's decisions.

DECEMBER
JANUARY
FEBRUARY

Revises estimates to conform to President's decisions.

Again reviews economic outlook and fiscal policy for discussion with President of economic policies.*

Drafts President's budget message; prepares budget with summary tables, budget appendix, special analyses, and budget-in-brief. Arranges printing of budget documents.

Revises and approves budget message.

Transmits recommended budget to Congress within 15 days after Congress convenes.

JANUARY 1977

* In cooperation with the Treasury Department and Council of Economic Advisers

EXECUTIVE OFFICE OF THE PRESIDENT/OFFICE OF MANAGEMENT AND BUDGET

EXHIBIT 4-3

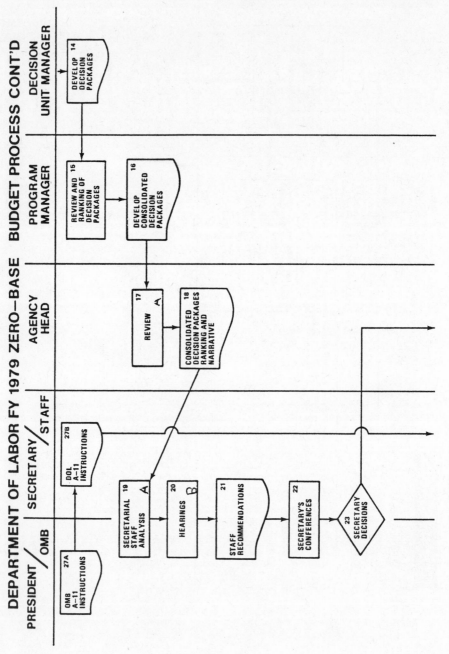

DEPARTMENT OF LABOR FY 1979 ZERO—BASE BUDGET PROCESS CONT'D

EXHIBIT 4-4A

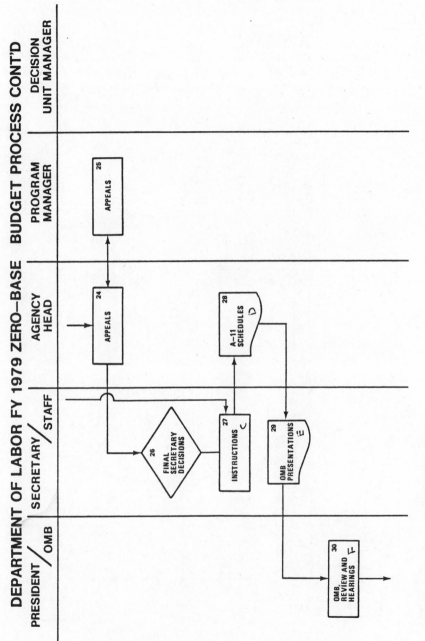

DEPARTMENT OF LABOR FY 1979 ZERO–BASE BUDGET PROCESS CONT'D

EXHIBIT 4-4B

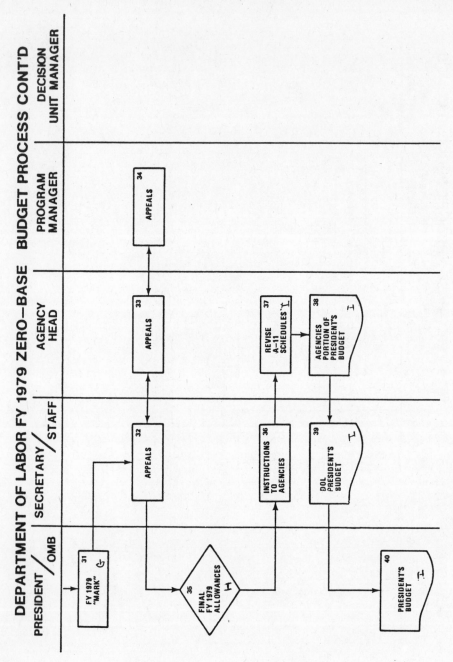

DEPARTMENT OF LABOR FY 1979 ZERO—BASE BUDGET PROCESS CONT'D

EXHIBIT 4-4C

**EXHIBIT 4-5**     Calendar of events — formulation of president's budget

---

March, April and May

A.   *Planning Stage:* Agency reviews and ranks ZBB Consolidated Decision Packages (CDP) and prepares narrative. Along with the Department's Office of the Secretary the agency reviews using the ranking and CDP, current operations, program objectives, issues, and future plans in relation to upcoming annual budget. It prepares projections of requirements that reflect current operations and future plans, supporting memoranda and related analytic studies that identify major issues, alternatives for resolving issues, and comparisons of costs and effectiveness.

May

B.   *Spring Planning Review:* Agency submits projections of requirements to OMB who discusses program development and management issues, and resulting budgetary effects, with agencies. OMB compiles total outlay estimates and develops recommendations for President on fiscal policy, program issues, and budget level.

June

C.   *Preparation of Budget Estimates:* The agency issues internal instructions on preparation of annual budget estimates based on OMB Bulletin A-11. The President establishes general guidelines and agency planning targets for annual budget. These guidelines are communicated to those preparing the budget estimates.

July through September 30

D.   Agency develops and compiles detailed estimates.

September through November

E.   The agency submits formal estimates for annual budget to OMB.

F.   *Director's Review:* OMB analyzes budget submissions and holds hearings with agency representatives on program, budget, and management issues for Director's Review. OMB submits budget recommendations to the President.

December through February

G.   *President's Mark:* The President reviews budget recommendations and decides on agency budget amounts (President's Mark) and on overall budget assumptions and policies.

H.   *Estimate Revision:* Agency receives President's decision on budget amounts and revises estimates to conform to it.

I.   *The President's Budget:* Agency submits budget revision to OMB who drafts the President's budget.

---

Source: Office of OMB — Formulation of President's Budget, January 1977.

## FORMULATION STAGES OF THE PRESIDENT'S BUDGET

It would be difficult to emphasize zero-base budgeting while explaining all the details of the Federal Budget Process. So, here is a condensed version that will enable you to visualize the impact that ZBB has on the Federal Budget Process. Printed in this book is the Department of Labor's Budget Process Flowchart (Exhibit 4-4) and OMB's Budget Formulation Chart for January 1977 (Exhibit 4-3). These charts are supported by a calendar of events narrative (Exhibit 4-5) which shows the interrelationship of the agency and the Executive Office of the President. The connated letters of the narrative steps are referenced on Exhibits 4-4 and 4-3 and throughout the chapter to assist the reader in following the calendar of events in the formulation of the President's budget.

### Planning Stage (A)

"Each spring attention is given to the planning of programs for the upcoming fiscal year and the development of preliminary plans and policies for the succeeding fiscal year. Attention is also given to projecting the effect of program decisions on subsequent budgets and to identifying major issues or problems affecting the budgets in the future. Discussions between OMB and the agencies often help to clarify specific problem areas.

"Upon request, agencies provide OMB with future work plans, program and financial plans, proposed new initiatives, special studies, program evaluations, and other data bearing on identified issues. Issue papers are developed on the basis of a systematic analysis and evaluation of the programs, plans, and work design implemented by the agency to accomplish its various objectives. These papers present alternative solutions to the problems and issues discussed, and include the agency head's recommended choice. These materials are critically examined in OMB. Proposed program expansions and new programs are viewed in terms of anticipated measurable benefits while efforts are also made to identify marginal and obsolete activities for which funding should be discontinued."[3]

In the planning stage, under ZBB process, the public manager has an important role. Done properly at this stage, the manager will determine alternative methods and program priorities in conjunction with the program analyst. If managers do not contribute their expertise through the ZBB process to this stage where agency programs are evaluated, policy issues are identified and budgetary projections are made, the manager remains a "puppet" or "paperpusher." He has not helped his agency one iota to prepare their plans. True zero-base budgeting then becomes nonexistent; a paper exercise takes its place. Preparing decision packages for budget estimates does not by itself provide the "spirit" for the successful implementation of ZBB.

### Spring Planning Review (B)

"In the late spring, OMB conducts the Spring Planning Review. Estimates are prepared indicating a probable range of outlays for each of the major programs and agencies for the forthcoming budget. These estimates are based on knowledge by

OMB staff of agency programs and are supplemented by discussions with agency budget and planning personnel. Information is also developed to relate résource requirements to program objectives, and papers are prepared discussing program, budgeting, and management issues.

"The Director reviews and evaluates the fiscal and economic situation, the spending outlook, and the individual program, budget, and management issues presented for the agencies. The results of the review are discussed with agency heads, covering both important program modifications and alternative long-range plans.

"Budgetary projections, including projections of estimated taxes and other receipts prepared by the Treasury Department, are then presented to the President for his consideration and the major issues are discussed. About the same time, the President receives projections of the economic outlook that are prepared jointly by the Council of Economic Advisers, the Treasury Department, and OMB, and are reviewed by the Economic Policy Board."[4]

### Establishment of Presidential Policy Guidelines (C)

"After review of these projections and alternative long-range program plans, the President will establish general budget and fiscal policy guidelines for the fiscal year. At this time the tentative policy decisions and planning targets are given to the agencies to govern the preparation of their budgets."[5]

At this point in our chapter, we will explain in more detail the agency's role in the budget preparation process.

## DEVELOPMENT OF BUDGET ESTIMATES
## AND THE NEW ZBB PROCESS (C & D)

The Office of Management and Budget issues technical instructions (OMB Circular No. A-11) for preparation of annual budget estimates as the next step in formulation of the President's budget. The agency then issues internal instructions on how to prepare the annual budget estimates. OMB conveys the President's decisions to agency heads on Government-wide policies and assumptions, the application of policies, and budgetary planning targets. The agency then allocates this budgetary planning target to agency programs. At this point the agency is ready to develop and prepare detailed estimates according to OMB Circular A-11, using the zero-base budgeting process.[6]

By reviewing the agency's final budget output, the reader can receive a clearer picture of the ZBB role in an agency's budget preparation stage. As an example, we will review the Food and Drug Administrations's budget as printed in the U.S. Budget for FY 1978 (Exhibit 4-6). This appropriation for general and special funds is represented by detailed salaries and expense information. The appropriation amount is supported by the program and financing schedule and the object classification schedule. In both schedules, direct obligations amount to $276,408. This is known as a *crosswalk*. In addition, the agency's printed budget includes the total budget authority, outlays, and personnel summary.

# DEPARTMENT OF HEALTH, EDUCATION, AND WELFARE

## FOOD AND DRUG ADMINISTRATION

### *Federal Funds*

General and special funds:

SALARIES AND EXPENSES

For necessary expenses[, not otherwise provided for,] of the Food and Drug Administration; for payment of salaries and expenses for services as authorized by 5 U.S.C. 3109, but at rates for individuals not to exceed the per diem rate equivalent to the rate for GS-18; for rental of special purpose space in the District of Columbia or elsewhere; for miscellaneous and emergency expenses of enforcement activities, authorized or approved by the Secretary and to be accounted for solely on his certificate, not to exceed $10,000; [$241,977,000] *$275,743,000. (Public Law No. 94-351, making appropriations for Agriculture and related agencies, 1977.)*

**Program and Financing** (in thousands of dollars)

| Identification code 75-0600-0-1-553 | 1976 act. | TQ act. | 1977 est. | 1978 est. |
|---|---|---|---|---|
| **Program by activities:** | | | | |
| Direct program: | | | | |
| 1. Foods | 70,031 | 18,742 | 79,006 | 81,724 |
| 2. Drugs and devices | 83,282 | 22,444 | 108,509 | 124,965 |
| 3. Radiological products | 18,088 | 4,664 | 19,001 | 19,216 |
| 4. National Center for Toxicological Research | 12,873 | 3,212 | 13,251 | 13,489 |
| 5. Program management | 29,376 | 9,539 | 30,252 | 37,249 |
| Total direct program | 213,650 | 58,601 | 250,019 | 275,743 |
| Reimbursable program | 1,268 | 465 | 4,000 | 665 |
| Total program costs, funded [1] | 214,918 | 59,066 | 254,019 | 276,408 |
| Change in selected resources (undelivered orders) | −8,386 | −2,858 | | |
| 10.00    Total obligations | 206,532 | 56,208 | 254,019 | 276,408 |
| **Financing:** | | | | |
| 11.00 Offsetting collections from: Federal funds | −1,268 | −465 | −4,000 | −665 |
| 21.00 Unobligated balance available, start of period | | −2,541 | | |
| 24.00 Unobligated balance available, end of period | 2,541 | | | |
| 25.00 Unobligated balance lapsing | | 24 | | |
| Budget authority | 207,805 | 53,226 | 250,019 | 275,743 |
| Budget authority: | | | | |
| 40.00 Appropriation | 207,805 | 53,226 | 241,977 | 275,743 |
| 44.10 Supplemental now requested for wage-board pay raises | | | 217 | |
| 44.20 Supplemental now requested for civilian pay raises | | | 7,254 | |
| 44.30 Supplemental now requested for military pay raises | | | 571 | |
| Relation of obligations to outlays: | | | | |
| 71.00 Obligations incurred, net | 205,264 | 55,743 | 250,019 | 275,743 |
| 72.00 Obligated balance, start of period | 63,788 | 53,211 | 54,301 | 67,570 |
| 74.00 Obligated balance, end of period | −53,211 | −54,301 | −67,570 | −70,137 |
| 90.00 Outlays, excluding pay raise supplemental | 215,841 | 54,653 | 231,593 | 270,291 |
| 91.10 Outlays from wage-board pay raise supplemental | | | 133 | 84 |
| 91.20 Outlays from civilian pay raise supplemental | | | 4,453 | 2,801 |
| 91.30 Outlays from military pay raise supplemental | | | 571 | |

[1] Includes capital outlay as follows: 1976, $5,314 thousand; TQ, $2,585 thousand; 1977, $6,631 thousand; 1978, $6,565 thousand.

**EXHIBIT 4-6**    Excerpt from the Budget of the U.S. — FY 1978

The Food and Drug Administration (FDA) administers and enforces consumer protection laws concerning dangerous, misbranded, and adulterated foods, drugs, human biologics, medical devices, cosmetics, and man-made sources of radiation.

1. *Foods.*—To insure the safety of the U.S. food and cosmetic supply, FDA reviews industry petitions and publishes tolerances for food additives, conducts research, develops improved methods to detect adulteration, sets standards for classes of food, and defines industry good manufacturing and sanitary practices. FDA inspects food and cosmetic processing plants and marketing establishments, analyzes samples to verify that these products are safe and properly labeled, and—when necessary—takes regulatory action to obtain compliance with the law.

2. *Drugs and devices.*—FDA insures that human and animal drugs, human biologics, and medical devices are safe, effective, and properly labeled. FDA reviews data to support the safety and efficacy of these products prior to marketing, evaluates reports of industry and the medical profession, and conducts research. FDA also inspects manufacturing firms, reviews labeling, analyzes samples, and—when necessary—takes regulatory action to enforce the legal requirements.

3. *Radiological products.*—FDA is responsible for eliminating unnecessary exposure to electronic product radiation through research, surveillance, and voluntary and mandatory performance standards.

4. *National Center for Toxicological Research.*—FDA conducts research programs to study the biological effects of potentially toxic chemical substances found in man's environment.

5. *Program management.*—This activity includes FDA's executive and administrative functions.

Object Classification (in thousands of dollars)

| Identification code 75–0600–0–1–553 | 1976 act. | TQ act. | 1977 est. | 1978 est. |
|---|---|---|---|---|
| Direct obligations: | | | | |
| Personnel compensation: | | | | |
| 11.1   Permanent positions | 110,041 | 29,364 | 133,782 | 145,937 |
| 11.3   Positions other than permanent | 4,854 | 1,308 | 7,350 | 8,089 |
| 11.5   Other personnel compensation | 1,535 | 405 | 2,070 | 2,237 |
| Total personnel compensation | 116,430 | 31,077 | 143,202 | 156,263 |
| 12.1   Personnel benefits: Civilian | 12,187 | 3,408 | 14,493 | 15,833 |
| 21.0   Travel and transportation of persons | 6,281 | 1,444 | 7,142 | 8,203 |
| 22.0   Transportation of things | 514 | 142 | 643 | 667 |
| Rent, communications, and utilities: | | | | |
| 23.1   Standard level user charges | 9,937 | 5,541 | 11,511 | 15,886 |
| 23.2   Other rent, communications, and utilities | 8,855 | 2,024 | 10,939 | 11,186 |
| 24.0   Printing and reproduction | 1,804 | 391 | 2,223 | 2,473 |
| 25.0   Other services | 33,716 | 6,443 | 41,856 | 46,873 |
| 26.0   Supplies and materials | 7,619 | 1,863 | 9,741 | 10,048 |
| 31.0   Equipment | 5,103 | 2,585 | 6,631 | 6,673 |
| 32.0   Lands and structures | 3 | 3 | | |
| 41.0   Grants, subsidies, and contributions | 2,721 | 781 | 1,521 | 1,521 |
| 42.0   Insurance claims and indemnities | 94 | 41 | 117 | 117 |
| Total direct obligations | 205,264 | 55,743 | 250,019 | 275,743 |

**EXHIBIT 4-6 (cont.)**

| | | | | | |
|---|---|---|---|---|---|
| | Reimbursable obligations: | | | | |
| 11.1 | Personnel compensation: Permanent positions | 193 | 74 | 618 | 172 |
| 12.1 | Personnel benefits: Civilian | 16 | 6 | 52 | 14 |
| 21.0 | Travel and transportation of persons | 14 | 5 | 79 | 5 |
| 22.0 | Transportation of things | 3 | 1 | 8 | |
| 23.2 | Rent, communications, and utilities: Other rent, communications, and utilities | 2 | 1 | 8 | |
| 24.0 | Printing and reproduction | 1 | 1 | 3 | 1 |
| 25.0 | Other services | 667 | 244 | 2,092 | 346 |
| 26.0 | Supplies and materials | 164 | 60 | 523 | 127 |
| 31.0 | Equipment | 193 | 70 | 617 | |
| 32.0 | Lands and structures | 15 | 3 | | |
| | Total reimbursable obligations | 1,268 | 465 | 4,000 | 665 |
| 99.0 | Total obligations | 206,532 | 56,208 | 254,019 | 276,408 |

**Personnel Summary**

| | | | | |
|---|---|---|---|---|
| Total number of permanent positions | 6,362 | | 7,339 | 7,491 |
| Full-time equivalent of other positions | 316 | | 542 | 542 |
| Average paid employment | 6,675 | | 7,475 | 8,033 |
| Average GS grade | 9.39 | | 9.31 | 9.31 |
| Average GS salary | $14,829 | | $15,570 | $16,349 |

**EXHIBIT 4-6 (cont.)**

This appropriation passed through a very intricate and complex process; however, the preparation of an agency's budget using the ZBB concept is quite simple. Imagine the printed page without the new budget year amounts as shown in Exhibit 4-7. I will explain how the zero-base budgeting process will be used to formulate the budget for the FY 1978. *However, notice that the ZBB process complements the normal budget preparation process, and no major changes have to be made.* The reader has seen the end result; now the ZBB process leading to this output will be discussed.

### Preparation of Budget Estimates Using the ZBB Process

The agency submits budget data and estimates to OMB, prepared in a manner similar to this process. After the consolidated decision packages and rankings are completed, the packages provide the budget information to be posted to different types of work-sheets including "crosswalk" work-sheets. These "crosswalk" work-sheets are (1) the object classification and program worksheet and (2) the budget account structure and decision unit worksheet. The worksheets assist in the final preparation of various budget schedules and estimates to be submitted to the OMB.

The process of preparing an agency's budget estimates will not be explained in more detail. Although OMB Circular A-11 requires various schedules to be submitted, here is an explanation of some of the important ones. Information for the budget estimates and justifications to be submitted to OMB are *initially provided by the consolidated decision packages* developed by the agency. The first step is to post information from these decision packages to a number of worksheets.

# DEPARTMENT OF HEALTH, EDUCATION, AND WELFARE

## FOOD AND DRUG ADMINISTRATION

### *Federal Funds*

General and special funds:

SALARIES AND EXPENSES

For necessary expenses[, not otherwise provided for,] of the Food and Drug Administration; for payment of salaries and expenses for services as authorized by 5 U.S.C. 3109, but at rates for individuals not to exceed the per diem rate equivalent to the rate for GS–18; for rental of special purpose space in the District of Columbia or elsewhere; for miscellaneous and emergency expenses of enforcement activities, authorized or approved by the Secretary and to be accounted for solely on his certificate, not to exceed $10,000; [$241,977,000] *$275,743,000. (Public Law No. 94–351, making appropriations for Agriculture and related agencies, 1977.)*

**Program and Financing** (in thousands of dollars)

| Identification code 75–0600–0–1–553 | 1976 act. | TQ act. | 1977 est. |
|---|---|---|---|
| **Program by activities:** | | | |
| Direct program: | | | |
| 1. Foods | 70,031 | 18,742 | 79,006 |
| 2. Drugs and devices | 83,282 | 22,444 | 108,509 |
| 3. Radiological products | 18,088 | 4,664 | 19,001 |
| 4. National Center for Toxicological Research | 12,873 | 3,212 | 13,251 |
| 5. Program management | 29,376 | 9,539 | 30,252 |
| Total direct program | 213,650 | 58,601 | 250,019 |
| Reimbursable program | 1,268 | 465 | 4,000 |
| Total program costs, funded [1] | 214,918 | 59,066 | 254,019 |
| Change in selected resources (undelivered orders) | −8,386 | −2,858 | --------- |
| 10.00   Total obligations | 206,532 | 56,208 | 254,019 |
| **Financing:** | | | |
| 11.00 Offsetting collections from: Federal funds | −1,268 | −465 | −4,000 |
| 21.00 Unobligated balance available, start of period | --------- | −2,541 | --------- |
| 24.00 Unobligated balance available, end of period | 2,541 | --------- | --------- |
| 25.00 Unobligated balance lapsing | --------- | 24 | --------- |
| Budget authority | 207,805 | 53,226 | 250,019 |
| Budget authority: | | | |
| 40.00 Appropriation | 207,805 | 53,226 | 241,977 |
| 44.10 Supplemental now requested for wage-board pay raises | --------- | --------- | 217 |
| 44.20 Supplemental now requested for civilian pay raises | --------- | --------- | 7,254 |
| 44.30 Supplemental now requested for military pay raises | --------- | --------- | 571 |
| Relation of obligations to outlays: | | | |
| 71.00 Obligations incurred, net | 205,264 | 55,743 | 250,019 |
| 72.00 Obligated balance, start of period | 63,788 | 53,211 | 54,301 |
| 74.00 Obligated balance, end of period | −53,211 | −54,301 | −67,570 |
| 90.00 Outlays, excluding pay raise supplemental | 215,841 | 54,653 | 231,593 |
| 91.10 Outlays from wage-board pay raise supplemental | --------- | ------- | 133 |
| 91.20 Outlays from civilian pay raise supplemental | --------- | --------- | 4,453 |
| 91.30 Outlays from military pay raise supplemental | --------- | --------- | 571 |

[1] Includes capital outlay as follows: 1976, $5,314 thousand; TQ, $2,585 thousand; 1977, $6,631 thousand; 1978, $6,565 thousand.

EXHIBIT 4-7

**Object Classification** (in thousands of dollars)

| Identification code 75–0600–0–1–553 | 1976 act. | TQ act. | 1977 est. |
|---|---|---|---|
| Direct obligations: | | | |
| Personnel compensation: | | | |
| 11.1  Permanent positions_____ | 110, 041 | 29, 364 | 133, 782 |
| 11.3  Positions other than permanent_____ | 4, 854 | 1, 308 | 7, 350 |
| 11.5  Other personnel compensation_____ | 1, 535 | 405 | 2, 070 |
| | | | |
| Total personnel compensation_____ | 116, 430 | 31, 077 | 143, 202 |
| 12.1  Personnel benefits: Civilian_____ | 12, 187 | 3, 408 | 14, 493 |
| 21.0  Travel and transportation of persons_____ | 6, 281 | 1, 444 | 7, 142 |
| 22.0  Transportation of things_____ | 514 | 142 | 643 |
| Rent, communications, and utilities: | | | |
| 23.1  Standard level user charges_____ | 9, 937 | 5, 541 | 11, 511 |
| 23.2  Other rent, communications, and utilities_ | 8, 855 | 2, 024 | 10, 939 |
| 24.0  Printing and reproduction_____ | 1, 804 | 391 | 2, 223 |
| 25.0  Other services_____ | 33, 716 | 6, 443 | 41, 856 |
| 26.0  Supplies and materials_____ | 7, 619 | 1, 863 | 9, 741 |
| 31.0  Equipment_____ | 5, 103 | 2, 585 | 6, 631 |
| 32.0  Lands and structures_____ | 3 | 3 | _____ |
| 41.0  Grants, subsidies, and contributions_____ | 2, 721 | 781 | 1, 521 |
| 42.0  Insurance claims and indemnities_____ | 94 | 41 | 117 |
| | | | |
| Total direct obligations_____ | 205, 264 | 55, 743 | 250, 019 |
| Reimbursable obligations: | | | |
| 11.1  Personnel compensation: Permanent positions_____ | 193 | 74 | 618 |
| 12.1  Personnel benefits: Civilian_____ | 16 | 6 | 52 |
| 21.0  Travel and transportation of persons_____ | 14 | 5 | 79 |
| 22.0  Transportation of things_____ | 3 | 1 | 8 |
| 23.2  Rent, communications, and utilities: Other rent, communications, and utilities_____ | 2 | 1 | 8 |
| 24.0  Printing and reproduction_____ | 1 | 1 | 3 |
| 25.0  Other services_____ | 667 | 244 | 2, 092 |
| 26.0  Supplies and materials_____ | 164 | 60 | 523 |
| 31.0  Equipment_____ | 193 | 70 | 617 |
| 32.0  Lands and structures_____ | 15 | 3 | _____ |
| | | | |
| Total reimbursable obligations_____ | 1, 268 | 465 | 4, 000 |
| | | | |
| 99.0  Total obligations_____ | 206, 532 | 56, 208 | 254, 019 |

**Personnel Summary**

| | 1976 act. | TQ act. | 1977 est. |
|---|---|---|---|
| Total number of permanent positions_____ | 6, 362 | _____ | 7, 339 |
| Full-time equivalent of other positions_____ | 316 | _____ | 542 |
| Average paid employment_____ | 6, 675 | _____ | 7, 475 |
| Average GS grade_____ | 9. 39 | _____ | 9. 31 |
| Average GS salary_____ | $14, 829 | _____ | $15, 570 |

**EXHIBIT 4-7 (cont.)**

Although agencies use their own formats two important "crosswalk" worksheets will be explained in this book. Other budget preparation information can be obtained by reading OMB Circular A-11. A common worksheet used currently is the "crosswalk" which assists the agencies in the preparation of the schedules Object Classification and Program and Financing (Exhibit 4-7) printed in the President's Budget Package. Verification is made if total costs ($275,743) on the worksheet (Exhibit 4-8) agree with totals of the ranking summary (Exhibit 4-9). If these amounts coincide, then Standard Form 300 (Exhibit 4-10) is used to complete the program and financing schedule and Standard Form 304 (Exhibit 4-11) is used for completion of the object classification schedule.

FOOD AND DRUG ADMINISTRATION

"Crosswalk" Worksheet

Accumulation of Projected Costs for 19BY
by Object Class and Activity

| Object | Foods | Radiological Products | National Center for TR | Program Management | Drugs & Devices | Total Costs by Object |
|---|---|---|---|---|---|---|
| Personnel Compensation: | | | | | | |
| 11.1 Permanent positions | 43933 | 10215 | 7010 | 19502 | 65277 | 145937 |
| 11.3 Positions other than permanent | 2345 | 566 | 404 | 1051 | 3723 | 8089 |
| 11.5 Other personal compensation | 648 | 156 | 111 | 290 | 1032 | 2237 |
| 11.8 Special personal service payments | - | - | - | - | - | - |
| Personnel Benefits: | | | | | | |
| 12.1 Civilian | 4591 | 1008 | 791 | 2058 | 7285 | 15883 |
| 21.0 Travel | 2378 | 575 | 410 | 1060 | 3780 | 8203 |
| 22.0 Transportation of Things | 193 | 47 | 33 | 86 | 308 | 667 |
| 23. Standard Level User Charges | 4595 | 1110 | 794 | 2069 | 7318 | 15886 |
| 23.2 Other Rent, Comm. & Util. | 3243 | 782 | 559 | 1454 | 5148 | 11186 |
| 24.0 Printing and Reproduction | 717 | 173 | 123 | 321 | 113 | 2473 |
| 25.0 Other Services (Contracts) | 13593 | 3208 | 2343 | 6088 | 21641 | 46873 |
| 26.0 Supplies and Materials | 2913 | 703 | 502 | 1306 | 4624 | 10098 |
| 31.0 Equipment | 2002 | 467 | 333 | 867 | 3004 | 6673 |
| 41.0 Grants, Subsidies and Contributions | 456 | 106 | 76 | 197 | 686 | 1521 |
| 42.0 Insurance Claims | 117 | - | - | - | - | 117 |
| Total Costs by Activity | 81724 | 19216 | 13489 | 36349 | 124965 | 275743 |

EXHIBIT 4-8

PUBLIC HEALTH SERVICE

PRIORITY RANKING SUMMARY

FOOD & DRUG ADMINISTRATION

Exhibit 4-9

| RANK | DECISION PACKAGE NAME | BUDGET AUTHORITY | OUTLAYS | CUMULATIVE BUDGET AUTHORITY | CUMULATIVE OUTLAYS | (BY)/(CY) % |
|---|---|---|---|---|---|---|
| 1 | Program Management (1 of 2) | 36,349 | 36,349 | 36,349 | 36,349 | 15 |
| * 2 | Drugs & Devices (1 of 4) | 50,000 | 50,000 | 86,349 | 86,349 | 35 |
| 3 | Foods (1 of 1) | 81,724 | 81,724 | 168,073 | 168,073 | 67 |
| * 4 | Drugs & Devices (2 of 4) | 58,509 | 58,509 | 226,582 | 226,582 | 90 |
| * 5 | Drugs & Devices (3 of 4) | 16,456 | 16,456 | 243,038 | 243,038 | 97 |
| 6 | Nat'l Cntr for TR (1 of 1) | 13,489 | 13,489 | 256,520 | 256,520 | 103 |
| 7 | Radiological Prod. (1 of 1) | 19,216 | 19,216 | 275,743 | 275,743 | 110 FL |
| * 8 | Drugs & Devices (4 of 4) | 10,000 | 10,000 | 285,743 | 285,743 | 114 |
| 9 | Program Management | 20,000 | 20,000 | 305,743 | 305,743 | 122 |

(FL—Funding Levels)

**EXHIBIT 4-9**   Ranking summary

STANDARD FORM 300-T
June 1975, Office of Management and Budget
Circular No. A-11, Revised.

| Identification code<br>75-0600-0-1-553 | 19 76<br>actual | 19 | 19 77<br>estimate | 19 78<br>estimate |
|---|---|---|---|---|
| Program by activities: | | | | |
| Direct program: | | | | |
| 1. Foods . . . . . . . . . . . | 70,031 | | 79,006 | 81,724 |
| 2. Drugs and devices . . . . | 83,282 | | 108,509 | 124,965 |
| 3. Radiological products. . . | 18,088 | | 19,001 | 19,216 |
| 4. National Center for | | | | |
| Toxicological Research. | 12,873 | | 13,251 | 13,489 |
| 5. Program management . . | 29,376 | | 30,252 | 36,349 |
| | | | | |
| Total direct program | 213,650 | | 250,019 | 275,743 |
| | | | | |
| (Mono cast: 22.13) | (Mono cast: 5.9) | (Mono cast: 5.9) | (Mono cast: 5.9) | (Mono cast: 5) |

EXHIBIT 4-10

Another "crosswalk," a tabulation showing the relationship of decision units to account structure (Exhibit 4-12), is to be included with the agency budget submission because of a new OMB requirement as stated in Section 22.2 of the revised Circular A-11 in June 1977. Here is an excerpt:

*Relationship of decision units to account structure.*

A tabulation will be prepared in the format of Exhibit 5-8 to show the relationship between the budget account structure and the decision units identified in the agency justification materials. This "crosswalk" should list, by bureau, each account and the related decision units as well as the total budget year budget authority and outlay amounts associated with each. When decision units are financed by more than one appropriation or fund account, the portion of the decision unit funded under each account will be shown. Accounts should be listed in budget sequence.[7] (Refer to Chapter 3 — Account Identification Codes.)

It should be noted that the decision unit, Bureau of Hospital Care, has two appropriation numbers, 2361 and 2345. This is the reason why amounts are kept separate. Exhibit 4-12 can be prepared using *one* of three methods:

1. By posting from the cumulative columns of the last *decision package* of a set as illustrated below (note that this package represents the decision unit #1234):

STANDARD FORM **304**
May 1969, Bureau of the Budget
Circular No. A-11, Revised.
304-103

### OBJECT CLASSIFICATION (in thousands of dollars)

| Identification code<br>75-0600-01-553 | 19 76<br>actual | 19 77<br>estimate | 19 78<br>estimate |
|---|---|---|---|
| **Personnel compensation:** | | | |
| 11.1  Permanent positions | 110,041 | 133,782 | 145,937 |
| 11.3  Positions other than permanent | 4,854 | 7,350 | 8,089 |
| 11.5  Other personnel compensation | 1,535 | 2,070 | 2,237 |
| 11.8  Special personal services payments | | | |
| Total personnel compensation | 116,430 | 143,202 | 156,263 |
| **Personnel benefits:** | | | |
| 12.1   Civilian | 12,187 | 14,493 | 15,833 |
| 13.0  Benefits for former personnel | | | |
| 21.0  Travel and transportation of persons | 6,281 | 7,142 | 8,203 |
| 22.0  Transportation of things | 514 | 643 | 667 |
| 23.0  Rent, communications, and utilities | 9,937 | 11,511 | 15,886 |
| 23.1   Standard level user charges | 8,855 | 10,939 | 11,186 |
| 23.2   Other rent, communications & util. | | | |
| 24.0  Printing and reproduction | 1,804 | 2,223 | 2,473 |
| 25.0  Other services | 33,716 | 41,856 | 46,873 |
| 26.0  Supplies and materials | 7,619 | 9,741 | 10,048 |
| 31.0  Equipment | 5,103 | 6,631 | 6,673 |
| 32.0  Lands and structures | 3 | ------- | ------- |
| 33.0  Investments and loans | | | |
| 41.0  Grants, subsidies, and contributions | 2,721 | 1,521 | 1,521 |
| 42.0  Insurance claims and indemnities | 94 | 117 | 117 |
| 43.0  Interest and dividends | | | |
| 44.0  Refunds | | | |
| 99.0   Total obligations | 205,264 | 250,019 | 275,743 |

(Mono cast: 20.11)        (Mono cast: 5.9)        (Mono cast: 5.9)        (Mono cast: 5)

## EXHIBIT 4-11

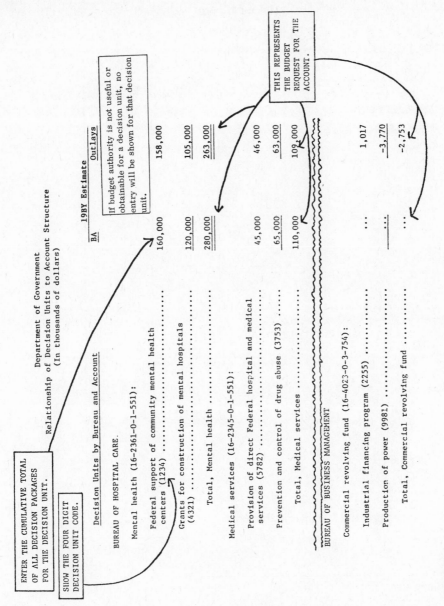

Department of Government
Relationship of Decision Units to Account Structure
(In thousands of dollars)

ENTER THE CUMULATIVE TOTAL OF ALL DECISION PACKAGES FOR THE DECISION UNIT.

SHOW THE FOUR DIGIT DECISION UNIT CODE.

If budget authority is not useful or obtainable for a decision unit, no entry will be shown for that decision unit.

THIS REPRESENTS THE BUDGET REQUEST FOR THE ACCOUNT.

| Decision Units by Bureau and Account | 19BY Estimate BA | Outlays |
|---|---|---|
| BUREAU OF HOSPITAL CARE. | | |
| Mental health (16-2361-0-1-551): | | |
| Federal support of community mental health centers (1234) .............. | 160,000 | 158,000 |
| Grants for construction of mental hospitals (4321) .............. | 120,000 | 105,000 |
| Total, Mental health .............. | 280,000 | 263,000 |
| Medical services (16-2345-0-1-551): | | |
| Provision of direct Federal hospital and medical services (5782) .............. | 45,000 | 46,000 |
| Prevention and control of drug abuse (3753) ...... | 65,000 | 63,000 |
| Total, Medical services .............. | 110,000 | 109,000 |
| BUREAU OF BUSINESS MANAGEMENT | | |
| Commercial revolving fund (16-4023-0-3-754): | | |
| Industrial financing program (2255) .............. | ... | 1,017 |
| Production of power (9981) .............. | ... | -3,770 |
| Total, Commercial revolving fund | ... | -2,753 |

EXHIBIT 4-12

Package 4 of 4

*DECISION PACKAGE (1234-4)*
Department of Government
Bureau of Hospital Care
Federal Support of Community Health Services
Mental Health: 16-2361-0-1-551

*Activity Description:* For every CHMC whose eight-year eligibility periods ends, fund two newly qualifying CMHC's.

STANDARD FORM
Office of Management and Budget
Circular No. A-11, Revised.

Mental Health
Bureau of Hospital Care, Department of Government

| Identification code 16-2361-0-1-551 | 19BY BA | 19BY Outlays | | |
|---|---|---|---|---|
| Decision Packages | | | | |
| Federal support of Community Mental Health Centers | | | | |
| (1234-1) | 120,000 | 119,000 | | |
| (1234-2) | 20,000 | 19,000 | | |
| (1234-3) | 10,000 | 10,000 | | |
| (1234-4) | 10,000 | 10,000 | | |
| Total (1234) | 160,000 | 158,000 | | |
| Grants for construction of mental hospitals | | | | |
| (4321-1) | 100,000 | 85,000 | | |
| (4321-2) | 20,000 | 20,000 | | |
| Total (4321) | 120,000 | 105,000 | | |
| Total Mental Health | 280,000 | 263,000 | | |

**EXHIBIT 4-13**

*Resource Requirements:* Dollars in thousands

| | | | 1979 | |
|---|---|---|---|---|
| | 1977 | 1978 | This Package | Cumulative Total |
| Planning grants (S) | 1,000 | 1,000 | 0 | 0 |
| Operating grants ($) | 97,000 | 147,000 | 10,000 | 160,000 |
| Total obligations | 98,000 | 148,000 | 10,000 | 160,000 |
| Budget authority | 98,000 | 148,000 | 10,000 | 160,000 |
| Outlays | 97,000 | 145,000 | 10,000 | 158,000 |

2. By listing decision packages on a worksheet as illustrated (Exhibit 4-13), then completing the schedule.

3. By running off a data processing listing using the same format as that used in the second method.

Bureau of Hospital Care
Department of Government
ADP Listing of Decision Packages

|  | BA | Outlays |
|---|---|---|
| 1234-1 | 120,000 | 119,000 |
| 1234-2 | 20,000 | 19,000 |
| 1234-3 | 10,000 | 10,000 |
| 1234-4 | 10,000 | 10,000 |
| 1234 | 160,000 | 158,000 |
| 4321-1 | 100,000 | 85,000 |
| 4321-2 | 20,000 | 20,000 |
| 4321 | 120,000 | 105,000 |
| *16-236-0-1-551 | 280,000 | 263,000 |

OMB Circular A-11 lists other supporting documents and data such as the Detail of Permanent Position Schedule. This document is relatively unchanged by the new zero-base budgeting process; thus, we have not explained them in this text. The next step after preparation of the budget estimates and supporting data for the budget year is to submit these documents to OMB in the required format.

## SUBMISSION OF THE BUDGET ESTIMATES TO OMB (E)

Annually Federal departments and agencies submit budget estimates to the Office of Management and Budget (OMB). Agencies must provide budget justification and information regarding their financial and personnel requirements. These budget requirements are transmitted to OMB in the format prescribed by OMB Circular A-11.

In June 1977, OMB Circular A-11 was revised to include zero-base budgeting. "These are as follows:

Section 11.4    Advance consultation with OMB is required in developing the decision units that will form the basis for the agency's zero-base budget submission.

Section 13.1    Agency budget proposals should result from a comprehensive zero-base budgeting system.

Section 21.1    The concepts of zero-base budgeting

Section 22.1    Key agency objectives will no longer be listed in summary and highlight memoranda. Objectives will be identified in decision unit overviews and decision packages.

Section 24.1    Instructions have been added prescribing the zero-base budget justification material required in support of agency estimates.

Section 24.4    Supplemental requests will be supported by zero-base justifications.

Section 36.1    Narrative statements for the appendix should now reflect certain information contained in the zero-base justification materials.

Section 39.4    Instructions on the preparation of ZBB documents to accompany supplementals and budget amendments."[8]

Revisions of Sections 13.1, 21.1 and 22.2 of OMB Circular A-11 have been included in appropriate chapters throughout the book. Other sections are explained in the next paragraphs.

### Section 24.1 – Justification of Programs and Financing

"All estimates reflected in agency budget submissions will be supported by zero-base budget justifications.

1.  *Material Required.* A decision unit overview and set of decision packages or consolidated decision packages (see Exhibits 3-4 and 3-5) will be prepared and submitted to OMB for each decision unit identified by the agency in consultation with OMB. Agencies will also submit a ranking sheet that lists, in priority order, the decision packages that comprise the agency's budget request (Exhibit 4-1).

2.  *Derivation of Amounts Requested.* Agencies should base justification on or be prepared to submit additional information covering the following:

    a.  Detailed analyses of workload, employment requirements, productivity trends, the impact of capital investment proposals on productivity, and changes in quality of output.

    b.  Basis for distribution of funds (i.e., formulas or principles for allocation, matching, the awarding of loans, grants, or contracts, etc.) and data on resulting geographic distribution (e.g., by state, etc.) with identification of any issues. (OMB will issue separate instructions requiring agencies to report state-by-state obligations for all formula grant programs.")[9]

### Section 24.4 – Explanations Relating to Supplemental Estimates

Another important revision of OMB Circular A-11 is explained in Section 24.4, as follows: "When the need for a program supplemental appropriation is forecast, a decision package set should be prepared. In addition, the Other Information section on the decision package should set forth the reasons for the omission of the request from the regular estimates of the period concerned, and the reasons why it is considered essential that the additional appropriation be granted during the period instead of obtaining the money in a regular appropriation the following year.

"Whenever possible, requests for supplementals, whether under existing or proposed legislation, should be accompanied by recommendations as to where corresponding offsets can be made elsewhere in the agency. If the estimate is approved for later transmittal (rather than in the budget), further justification of the supplemental estimate will be required when it is formally submitted. In every case, the effect of requested supplementals will also be shown in decision packages covering the budget year.

"For anticipated supplementals in the current year to meet the cost of pay increases, decision packages need not be prepared. However, in any case, information should be provided identifying, for each appropriation or fund, the total cost of the pay increases and the amount that is being absorbed in accordance with related policy guidance. Any difference from information submitted with the apportionment request for the current year should be explained."[10]

### Section 36.1 – Purpose and Content of Narrative Statements

"The activities listed in the program and financing schedule must be described in a narrative statement.

"The primary purpose of the narrative statement is to present briefly in a form suitable for printing in the budget, the objectives, the work program financed from the account, a measure of expected performance (compared with past and present), and the relation of expected performance to the financial estimates. Narrative statements should focus on work to be accomplished under each account *during the budget year,* including significant work performed on a reimbursable basis. Significant increases and decreases from the current year to the budget year will be explained.

"These statements should be mission-oriented and set forth the significant long-range and short-range objectives of the activities financed by the account. Information should be provided on the impact of proposed budget year funding on the accomplishment of objectives. Such information should be derived from the zero-base justification materials. Whenever possible, objectives should be stated and performance measured in quantitative terms."[11]

### Section 39.3 – Budget Amendments and Supplemental Estimates

"During the congressional budget process agencies may determine the need for revising the original estimates upward or downward, due to developments since the estimates were originally transmitted to the Congress. For example, additional funds for the current or budget year may be necessary to meet unforeseen requirements or emergencies that have arisen since the budget was prepared. The specific amounts subsequently recommended to the Congress are the result of detailed analysis and review, based on the conditions at the time the recommendation is transmitted. These revisions can take one of two forms: 'budget amendments' or 'supplementals.'

'Budget amendments' are estimates transmitted to the Congress that 'amend' (revise) budget estimates transmitted previously on which the Congress has not completed action. 'Supplementals' are normally transmitted to Congress as requests to provide funds in addition to amounts already appropriated. It should be noted that it is not in order for Congress to consider a supplemental that would cause total outlays or budget authority to exceed the limits of the most recently approved concurrent resolution on the budget. To the extent that previously unforeseen requirements for the current year can be identified before January, supplemental appropriation requests are included in the budget document. Additional requests to carry out new legislation enacted since the budget was formulated may be prepared and transmitted to the Congress as budget amendments or supplementals, as appropriate."[1,2]

Those estimates representing additional requests to regular annual appropriations (supplementals) or modification of estimates previously submitted (budget amendments) should be presented in the following manner:

- Justify the need for the appropriation in a decision package format

- Prepare at least two decision packages representing one at a minimum level and the other at a requested level[13]

### Review of Agency Estimates in the Office of Management and Budget (F)

"When the estimates are received in OMB, they are referred to the examiners responsible for the programs involved. All the knowledge that the examiners possess about the agency — based on long-term analysis, field investigations, special studies, and conferences held with agency officials — is brought to bear at this time. The examiners must be thoroughly familiar with the President's budget policy and previous congressional action, as well as with the programs of the agency and their relationship to activities of other agencies. Considerable attention is given to the basis for the individual estimates, the current and projected volume of work, the methods by which the agency proposes to accomplish its objectives, the costs of accomplishment, and the estimates of requirements in terms of supplies, equipment, facilities, and numbers of people. Examiners review past performance, check the accuracy of factual information presented, and consider the future implications of the program. *They identify significant program, budget, and management issues to be raised for discussion with agency representatives at hearings conducted in OMB during September and October.*

"After the hearings are completed, the examiners prepare summaries of the issues and their recommendations for the Director's Review. This Review concentrates attention on the major issues involving Presidential policy, but also provides a check on other aspects of the recommendations.

"The Director's Review provides an opportunity for the principal officials of OMB to obtain from the examiners an understanding of agency program aspirations and budget requests, and analysis of the significant issues involved, and the relationship of the agency requests to the planning targets recommended for the agency as a result of the Spring Planning Review. *The Review process is directed toward applying the President's policies to each agency's budget requests, identifying the aspects of the agency's budget that require specific Presidential attention, and developing OMB recommendations that the Director will make to the President regarding such items.*

"The process of review occupies OMB from the early part of September through December. During this period, the economic outlook is again assessed by the staffs of the Treasury Department, the Council of Economic Advisers, and OMB, and revenue estimates are prepared for presentation to the President."[14]

### Decision by the President – President's Mark (G)

"Going through another priority review, the President is faced with the task of recommending a budget that meets the most urgent needs of the country within the constraints imposed by the availability of resources. This task is complicated by the fact that a large segment of the budget is mandatory under existing law. Spending that is relatively uncontrollable in this sense, including interest on the public debt, social security, veterans benefits, general revenue sharing, and similar programs, accounts for over three-quarters of total budget outlays. Outlays for such programs depend upon provisions of the laws that authorize the programs and on other factors not readily subject to annual budgetary control. They can be affected by the annual budget process only to the extent that they are accompanied by proposed changes in law. Because of the size and complexity of the budget, the Director's recommendations together with those of the agency are placed before the President as portions of the review are completed. As soon as the President makes decisions on portions of the budget, agency heads are notified of the amounts that will be recommended to Congress for each agency's programs for the ensuing fiscal year."[15]

### Preparation of the Budget Document (H & I)

"When the agency receives its budget allowance, the initial budget estimates are revised – in conformity with the President's decisions – for inclusion in the printed budget documents. The Budget Appendix sets forth the exact wording of the appropriation language last enacted by the Congress, with changes proposed by the President for the upcoming fiscal year, followed by detailed schedules supporting each estimate. In line with the policies set forth in Public Law 84-863, cost-based budget presentations are used for most accounts. This type of presentation, based on data in agency accounting systems, provides information on inventories and other resources available to finance the agency's program and on the costs for the resources consumed within each fiscal year.

"As soon as revisions of the individual budget schedules for each agency are completed, the figures from the revised schedules are summarized by agency. The figures are also consolidated to make up overall summary tables that present agency, as well as functional and various other tabulations. These summary tables

Table 3. BUDGET OUTLAYS BY FUNCTION AND SUBFUNCTION: 1970-79 (in billions of dollars)—Continued

| Function and subfunction | Actual | | | | | | | | Estimate | | |
|---|---|---|---|---|---|---|---|---|---|---|---|
| | 1970 | 1971 | 1972 | 1973 | 1974 | 1975 | 1976 | TQ | 1977 | 1978 | 1979 |
| **Community and regional development:** | | | | | | | | | | | |
| Community development | 2.3 | 2.6 | 3.1 | 3.1 | 3.0 | 3.1 | 3.5 | 1.1 | 4.9 | 5.1 | 4.9 |
| Area and regional development | .6 | .7 | .8 | .9 | 1.1 | .9 | 1.3 | .3 | 2.2 | 2.3 | 1.8 |
| Disaster relief and insurance | .3 | .4 | .4 | 1.6 | .8 | .4 | .5 | .1 | .6 | .5 | .5 |
| Deductions for offsetting receipts | -* | -* | -* | -* | -* | -* | -* | -* | -* | -* | -* |
| **Total community and regional development** | 3.2 | 3.6 | 4.3 | 5.5 | 4.9 | 4.4 | 5.3 | 1.5 | 7.7 | 7.9 | 7.1 |
| **Education, training, employment, and social services:** | | | | | | | | | | | |
| Elementary, secondary, and vocational education | 3.1 | 3.5 | 4.0 | 3.7 | 3.8 | 4.7 | 4.7 | 1.2 | 5.2 | 5.5 | 5.4 |
| Higher education | 1.4 | 1.4 | 1.4 | 1.5 | 1.3 | 2.1 | 2.7 | .7 | 3.4 | 2.9 | 2.9 |
| Research and general education aids | .5 | .5 | .5 | .7 | .9 | .9 | .8 | .2 | 1.1 | 1.2 | 1.2 |
| Training and employment | 1.6 | 2.0 | 2.9 | 3.3 | 2.9 | 4.1 | 6.3 | 1.9 | 6.8 | 5.3 | 4.3 |
| Other labor services | .1 | .2 | .2 | .2 | .2 | .3 | .3 | .1 | .4 | .4 | .4 |
| Social services | 1.1 | 1.4 | 2.7 | 2.5 | 2.5 | 3.3 | 3.5 | .9 | 4.1 | 4.0 | 4.0 |
| Deductions for offsetting receipts | -* | -* | -* | -* | -* | -* | -* | -* | -* | -* | -* |
| **Total education, training, employment, and social services** | 7.9 | 9.0 | 11.7 | 11.9 | 11.6 | 15.2 | 18.2 | 5.0 | 21.1 | 19.4 | 18.1 |
| **Health:** | | | | | | | | | | | |
| Health care services | 10.6 | 12.1 | 14.5 | 15.5 | 18.5 | 23.4 | 28.7 | 7.6 | 34.5 | 26.0 | 28.2 |
| Health research and education | 1.6 | 1.7 | 2.0 | 2.3 | 2.3 | 2.7 | 3.1 | .9 | 2.8 | 2.6 | 2.5 |
| Prevention and control of health problems | .4 | .5 | .5 | .6 | .8 | .9 | 1.0 | .3 | 1.1 | .9 | .9 |
| Health planning and construction | .5 | .5 | .4 | .4 | .5 | .7 | .8 | -* | .9 | 1.3 | 1.3 |
| General health financial assistance | ... | ... | ... | ... | ... | ... | ... | ... | ... | 12.3 | 13.8 |
| Deductions for offsetting receipts | -* | -* | -* | -* | -* | -* | -* | -* | -* | -* | -* |
| **Total health** | 13.1 | 14.7 | 17.5 | 18.8 | 22.1 | 27.6 | 33.4 | 8.7 | 39.3 | 43.2 | 46.7 |

Source: Budget of U.S. FY 1978.

EXHIBIT 4-14

together with final revenue estimates prepared by the Treasury Department set forth the Government-wide budget totals. (These summary tables will be discussed in detail in the next paragraphs.) The President then transmits his recommended budget to the Congress."[16]

## The Federal Program by Function (Exhibit 4-14)

The Office of Management and Budget drafts the President's budget message; prepares budget with summary tables, budget appendix, special analyses, and budget-in-brief. The President then revises and approves the budget message and transmits recommended budget to Congress within 15 days after Congress convenes.

This section is intended only to give the reader background information on parts of format and content of the budget draft by OMB. The budget is discussed in terms of major functions or purposes being served. "The functional structure groups the budget authority and outlays of budget accounts and off-budget Federal entities as well as tax expenditures into *relatively* homogeneous categories to facilitate understanding and analysis of the budget. To the extent feasible, these groupings are made without regard to agency or organizational lines. They are the categories used by the Congress in developing concurrent resolutions on the budget.

"Federal activities are classified in one, and only one, function. Because many activities serve more than one purpose, it is often necessary to make judgments as to their single most important purpose. Consequently, the total in a function is not a complete measure of all Federal activity serving that purpose.

*Example:*

Outlays for medical care of military personnel are included in the national defense function as part of the cost of maintaining a national military establishment, even though such outlays clearly contribute to health and, therefore, could legitimately be included in a broadly defined health function.

"Some important ways of classifying Federal activities are not explicitly identified in the functional classification structure. For example, there is no separate function for housing programs. While all housing programs may be seen as having the common purpose of promoting good housing, this purpose is subordinated in the present functional classification to such other purposes as community and regional development, income support, aid to business, national defense, and veterans benefits and services.

"Despite its limitations and the need for periodic reviews and changes where appropriate, the functional classification has proven to be a useful structure for the presentation of the Federal program for three decades. Functional data appear in several places in budget documents."[17] There are tables for (1) Budget Authority by Function and Agency (Exhibit 4-15) and Budget Account Listing (Exhibit 4-16), and (2) Budget Outlays by Function and Agency (Exhibit 4-17), which "presents budget authority and outlays by agency and appropriation account and includes an identification number indicating the functional classification of each budget account.

THE BUDGET FOR FISCAL YEAR 1978

Table 14. BUDGET AUTHORITY BY FUNCTION AND AGENCY—Continued

(In millions of dollars)

| Function and department or other unit | 1976 act. | TQ act. | 1977 est. | 1978 est. | 1979 est. |
|---|---|---|---|---|---|
| **500 EDUCATION, TRAINING, EMPLOY- MENT, AND SOCIAL SERVICES— Continued** | | | | | |
| **506 Social services:** | | | | | |
| Department of Health, Education, and Welfare | 4,095 | 935 | 4,197 | 3,940 | 4,008 |
| Department of Housing and Urban Development | | | 3 | 5 | · 5 |
| Total 506 | 4,095 | 935 | 4,200 | 3,945 | 4,013 |
| Deductions for offsetting receipts [2] | −5 | −1 | −5 | −6 | −5 |
| Total education, training, employment, and social services | 21,217 | 5,321 | 21,762 | 17,967 | 18,471 |
| **550 HEALTH** | | | | | |
| **551 Health care services:** | | | | | |
| Department of Health, Education, and Welfare [1] | 32,463 | 8,448 | 41,257 | 36,303 | 40,688 |
| Other independent agencies: Civil Service Commission [1] | 348 | 99 | 452 | 506 | 596 |
| Deductions for offsetting receipts | −3,598 | −878 | −5,997 | −7,077 | −7,500 |
| Total 551 | 29,214 | 7,669 | 35,712 | 29,733 | 33,784 |
| **552 Health research and education:** | | | | | |
| Department of Health, Education, and Welfare | 2,981 | 555 | 3,188 | 2,439 | 2,400 |
| **553 Prevention and control of health problems:** | | | | | |
| Department of Agriculture | 228 | 65 | 241 | 242 | 242 |
| Department of Health, Education, and Welfare | 612 | 103 | 553 | 341 | 341 |
| Department of the Interior | 84 | 21 | 98 | 106 | 111 |
| Department of Labor | 117 | 29 | 130 | 135 | 135 |
| Other independent agencies: | | | | | |
| Consumer Product Safety Commission | 40 | 10 | 40 | 40 | 40 |
| Occupational Safety and Health Review Commission | 6 | 1 | 6 | 7 | 7 |
| Total 553 | 1,087 | 231 | 1,069 | 871 | 876 |
| **554 Health planning and construction:** | | | | | |
| Department of Health, Education, and Welfare [1] | 378 | 53 | 394 | 1,210 | 1,236 |
| Deductions for offsetting receipts | −2 | −1 | −1 | −1 | −1 |
| Total 554 | 376 | 52 | 393 | 1,208 | 1,235 |
| **555 General health financing assistance:** | | | | | |
| Department of Health, Education, and Welfare | | | | 13,172 | 13,830 |
| Deductions for offsetting receipts [2] | −8 | −1 | −8 | −8 | −8 |
| Total health | 33,649 | 8,505 | 40,354 | 47,416 | 52,118 |

See footnotes at end of table.

Source: Budget of U.S. FY 1978.

EXHIBIT 4-15

THE FEDERAL PROGRAM BY AGENCY AND ACCOUNT

## BUDGET ACCOUNTS LISTING (in thousands of dollars)—Continued

| Account and functional code | | 1976 actual | TQ actual | 1977 estimate | 1978 estimate |
|---|---|---|---|---|---|

### DEPARTMENT OF DEFENSE—CIVIL—Continued

**SUMMARY—Continued**
**Trust funds:—Continued**

| | | | | | |
|---|---|---|---|---|---|
| 705 | BA} O } | −163 | −23 | −1,345 | −1,795 |
| Total trust funds | BA | 15,502 | 3,862 | 14,759 | 14,566 |
| | O | 17,888 | 4,422 | 9,011 | 14,550 |
| Total Department of Defense—Civil. | BA | 2,196,097 | 659,075 | 2,494,692 | 2,644,839 |
| | O | 2,124,252 | 582,546 | 2,468,553 | 2,627,512 |

## DEPARTMENT OF HEALTH, EDUCATION, AND WELFARE

**PUBLIC HEALTH SERVICE**
*Food and Drug Administration*
*Federal Funds*

**General and special funds:**

| | | | | | |
|---|---|---|---|---|---|
| Salaries and expenses ............553 | BA | 207,805 | 53,226 | 241,977 $^{C}$217 $^{D}$7,254 $^{E}$571 | 275,743 |
| | O | 215,841 | 54,653 | 236,750 | 273,176 |
| Buildings and facilities.............554 | BA | 1,000 | 750 | 3,125 | 3,515 |
| | O | 1,858 | 496 | 3,413 | 3,606 |

**Public enterprise funds:**

| | | | | | |
|---|---|---|---|---|---|
| Revolving fund for certification and other services.........................553 | O | 762 | −352 | ............. | ............. |
| Total Federal funds Food and Drug Administration. | BA | 208,805 | 53,976 | 253,144 | 279,258 |
| | O | 218,461 | 54,797 | 240,163 | 276,782 |

*Health Services Administration*
*Federal Funds*

**General and special funds:**

| | | | | | |
|---|---|---|---|---|---|
| Health services .........................(..551) | BA | 994,706 | 243,088 | 1,077,175 $^{C}$807 $^{D}$3,471 $^{E}$122 | $^{K}$902,041 $^{J}$−844,012 |
| | O | 1,119,744 | 191,391 | 1,117,863 | 847,118 $^{J}$−407,000 |
| ndian health services...................551 | BA | 283,310 | 75,528 | 349,788 $^{C}$1,155 $^{D}$3,442 | 362,424 |
| | O | 273,190 | 74,916 | 341,470 | 358,732 |
| Indian health facilities.................554 | BA | 55,616 | 11,084 | 88,163 | 74,425 |
| | O | 59,303 | 16,260 | 59,389 | 77,731 |
| Emergency health.........................054 | O | 94 | ............. | ............. | ............. |

**Public enterprise funds:**

| | | | | | |
|---|---|---|---|---|---|
| Health maintenance organization loan and loan guarantee fund.551 | O | 9,074 | 7,270 | 15,575 | 14 |
| Total Federal funds Health Services Administration. | BA | 1,333,632 | 329,700 | 1,524,123 | 494,878 |
| | O | 1,461,405 | 289,837 | 1,534,297 | 876,595 |

See footnotes at end of table.

Source: Budget of U.S. FY 1978.

**EXHIBIT 4-16**

THE BUDGET FOR FISCAL YEAR 1978

Table 15. OUTLAYS BY FUNCTION AND AGENCY (in millions of dollars)—Con.

| Function and department or other unit | 1976 act. | TQ act. | 1977 est. | 1978 est. | 1979 est. |
|---|---|---|---|---|---|
| **550  HEALTH** | | | | | |
| **551   Health care services:** | | | | | |
| Department of Health, Education, and Welfare [1] | 31,933 | 8,344 | 40,010 | 32,615 | 35,152 |
| Other independent agencies: Civil Service Commission [1] | 320 | 91 | 441 | 482 | 573 |
| Deductions for offsetting receipts | −3,598 | −878 | −5,997 | −7,077 | −7,500 |
| Total 551 | 28,655 | 7,556 | 34,454 | 26,020 | 28,225 |
| **552   Health research and education:** | | | | | |
| Department of Health, Education, and Welfare | 3,086 | 934 | 2,762 | 2,623 | 2,454 |
| Department of Housing and Urban Development | —* | —* | —* | —* | —* |
| Total 552 | 3,086 | 934 | 2,762 | 2,623 | 2,454 |
| **550   HEALTH—Continued** | | | | | |
| **553   Prevention and control of health problems:** | | | | | |
| Executive Office of the President | 13 | 1 | 6 | | |
| Department of Agriculture | 217 | 50 | 239 | 241 | 241 |
| Department of Health, Education, and Welfare | 496 | 138 | 567 | 421 | 412 |
| Department of the Interior | 84 | 21 | 102 | 105 | 108 |
| Department of Labor | 109 | 31 | 129 | 132 | 132 |
| Other independent agencies: | | | | | |
| Consumer Product Safety Commission | 38 | 10 | 46 | 39 | 46 |
| Federal Metal and Nonmetallic Mine Safety Board of Review | * | | | | |
| Occupational Safety and Health Review Commission | 6 | 1 | 7 | 7 | 7 |
| Total 553 | 963 | 251 | 1,096 | 945 | 947 |
| **554   Health planning and construction:** | | | | | |
| Department of Health, Education, and Welfare [1] | 754 | −19 | 949 | 1,323 | 1,305 |
| Department of the Interior | —* | * | | | |
| Deductions for offsetting receipts | −2 | −1 | −1 | −1 | −1 |
| Total 554 | 752 | −20 | 947 | 1,322 | 1,304 |
| **555   General health financing assistance:** | | | | | |
| Department of Health, Education, and Welfare | | | | 12,302 | 13,774 |
| Deductions for offsetting receipts [2] | −8 | −1 | −8 | −8 | −8 |
| Total health | 33,448 | 8,720 | 39,251 | 43,205 | 46,696 |

**EXHIBIT 4-17**

"While budget outlays have been presented on a functional basis since 1948, this classification has taken on new importance with enactment of the Congressional Budget Act of 1974 (Public Law 93-344). Under terms of this act, the Congress is now required to adopt at least two concurrent resolutions on the budget each year. The first resolution is to provide targets, by major function, for the authorization and appropriation actions that take place in the Congress after the first resolution. The Second Concurrent Resolution, which is intended to take place after completion of the authorization and appropriation process, adjusts the overall budget authority and outlay targets of the first resolution and converts them into firm ceilings, and includes any directions to congressional committees necessary to meet these ceilings. As a result, the functional structure is now being used as a basis for congressional budget control as well as a means of displaying budget information."[18]

## Functional Classification

"The functional classification arrays budgetary data according to the major purpose served by the unit being classified (usually, a budget account). In accordance with the Congressional Budget Act, the Congress must pass resolutions establishing budget targets and ceilings by functional categories.

"The following criteria are used in establishing and in assigning activities to functional categories:

- "A function must have a common end or ultimate purpose addressed to an important national need. (The emphasis is on what the Federal Government seeks to accomplish rather than the means of accomplishment, what is purchased, or the clientele or geographic area served.)

- "A function must be of continuing national importance and be significant in size, i.e., normally account for at least 2% of total budget outlays over a number of years.

- "The basic unit of classification generally is the appropriation or fund account. Occasionally, an appropriation account serves more than one major purpose. Accordingly, an account may be divided into two or more subfunctions. Any such division requires a compelling reason, and must involve relatively large amounts for each subfunction.

- "Each unit is classified into the single best or predominant purpose served. Thus, a unit is assigned to only one function.

- "Activities and programs are normally classified by common purpose (or function) regardless of which agencies conduct the activities."[19]

## The Congressional Budget Process (Exhibit 4-18)

"The Congressional budget process has undergone significant changes due to the enactment of the Congressional Budget and Impoundment Control Act of 1974

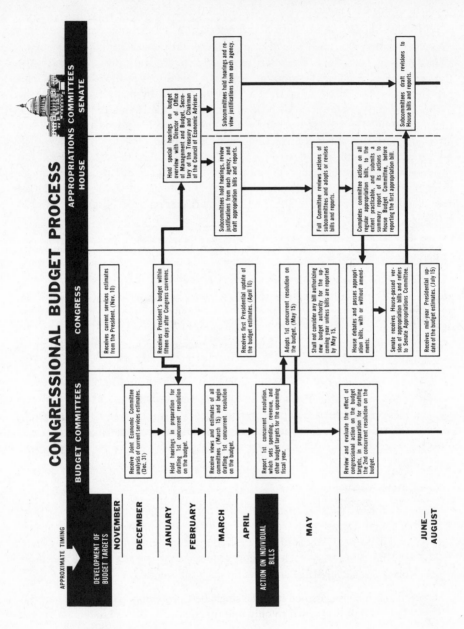

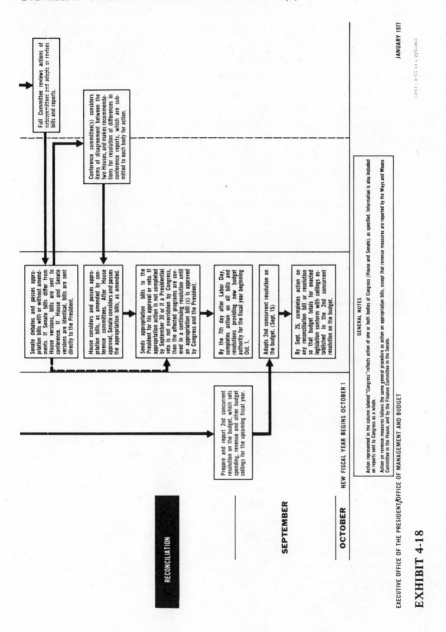

Full Committee reviews actions of subcommittee and adopts or revises bills and reports.

Conference committee(s) considers items of disagreement between the two Houses, and makes recommendations for resolution of differences in conference reports, which are submitted to each body for action.

Senate debates and passes appropriation bills with or without amendments. If Senate bills differ from House versions, bills are sent to conference. If House and Senate versions are identical, bills are sent directly to the President.

House considers and passes appropriation bills, as amended by conference committees. After House approval, Senate considers and passes the appropriation bills, as amended.

Sends appropriation bills to the President for his approval or veto. If appropriation action is not completed by September 30 or if a Presidential veto is not overridden by Congress, then the affected programs are covered in a continuing resolution until an appropriation bill (s) is approved by Congress and the President.

By the 7th day after Labor Day, completes action on all bills and resolutions providing new budget authority for the fiscal year beginning Oct. 1.

Adopts 2nd concurrent resolution on the budget. (Sept. 15)

By Sept. 25, completes action on any reconciliation bill or resolution so that budget totals for enacted legislation conform with ceilings established in the 2nd concurrent resolution on the budget.

Prepare and report 2nd concurrent resolution on the budget, which sets spending, revenue and other budget ceilings for the upcoming fiscal year.

**RECONCILIATION**

**SEPTEMBER**

**OCTOBER**   NEW FISCAL YEAR BEGINS OCTOBER 1

JANUARY 1977

GENERAL NOTES

Action represented in the column labeled "Congress:" reflects action of one or both bodies of Congress (House and Senate), as specified. Information is also included on reports sent to Congress as a whole.

Action on revenue measures follows the same general procedure as action on appropriation bills, except that revenue measures are reported by the Ways and Means Committee in the House, and by the Finance Committee in the Senate.

EXECUTIVE OFFICE OF THE PRESIDENT/OFFICE OF MANAGEMENT AND BUDGET

**EXHIBIT 4-18**

(P.L. 93-344). Under this Act, the Congress focuses on over-all budget totals and relates individual appropriation actions to one another within a general set of spending priorities. To aid in this process, the Act established a new committee on the Budget in each House and a new, professionally staffed Congressional Budget Office (CBO). The Act also provides a tight timetable for the new budget process and shifts the fiscal year from July 1 through June 30 to October 1 through September 30, in order to give the Congress three additional months to complete action on the Federal budget.

"Congressional action on the budget commences with the receipt of the current services estimates, due approximately 2 months before the President's budget is transmitted in January. These estimates are submitted by the President and represent the amount of budget authority and outlays that would be necessary to continue existing programs at their current operating levels (without policy changes) during the budget year. While the current services estimates are neither recommended amounts nor estimates as to what will be in the President's budget, the Congress may use them as a base upon which to review the President's proposed budget.

"The President's budget is required to be transmitted to the Congress within 15 days after the start of each new session in January. Shortly after the receipt of the budget, the Director of OMB and the Secretary of the Treasury are usually invited to appear before the House and Senate Budget Committees and Appropriations Committees to explain the general basis for the budget proposals. These Committees then hold additional hearings and receive testimony from Members of Congress and such representatives of Federal departments and agencies, the general public, and organizations, as the Committees deem appropriate.

"Under the procedures established by the Congressional Budget Act, the Congress considers budget totals prior to completing action on individual appropriations. Thus, the Act requires that by March 15, the House and Senate Budget Committees will receive reports from all other Congressional committees on their respective views and estimates of the appropriate level of total budget outlays, total new budget authority, the public debt, the surplus or deficit, and Federal revenues. These reports, along with an April 1 fiscal policy report from the CBO, form the basis of the first concurrent resolution on the budget, which by law must be adopted no later than May 15. The first concurrent resolution fixes new budget authority and outlay targets for the budget as a whole and for each major functional category. Targets for the public debt, Federal revenues, and the surplus or deficit are also established.

"Once Congress has completed action on the first concurrent resolution, it may begin to consider individual spending and revenue bills. Accompanying the conference report on the concurrent resolution is a joint explanatory statement which includes an estimated allocation of the budget total to each committee having jurisdiction over spending or revenue measures. Thereafter, the Appropriations Committees and the other committees that have received allocations, subdivide the allocations among their subcommittees."[20]

## Congressional Action on Appropriations (and Revenue Measures)

"About 13 regular appropriations bills are prepared for adoption each year. Once the first concurrent resolution has been agreed to by both Houses, Congressional consideration of requests for appropriations and changes in revenue law follow an established pattern. These requests are considered first in the House of Representatives. Agencies prepare and submit justifications, providing detailed information to support the President's budget requests, for consideration by the Appropriations Committee. Agency witnesses appear before Appropriations Subcommittees to explain the estimates and answer questions. The justification material presented to the subcommittee generally is the same type of material given to OMB earlier, revised to reflect the President's decisions on the budget. However, if the subcommittee wishes, additional information or a different format of justification, is provided.

"The subcommittee reviews performance in the past year and the latest available information on the status of current year programs, as well as the estimates proposed for the budget year. Agencies also present information on balances of prior year appropriations. In the case of major procurement programs (as in Defense) that require a long period of time between placing the orders and the delivery of material, the justification usually includes information on delivery schedules.

"In many cases, the Appropriations Committee regularly receives agencies' financial and work reports and information from the General Accounting Office on the results of its audits. The Committee also has available as a resource its own staff, as well as investigative staff on detail to the Committee from the GAO and from executive branch agencies. Once the Appropriations Committee has completed review of an appropriation bill, it reports the bill with any recommended changes to the full House of Representatives for action. Following passage by the House, the bill is referred to the Senate for action, where the process of Appropriations Committee review and full Senate action is again completed.

"Requests to change revenue laws, which are referred to the Ways and Means Committee in the House and to the Finance Committee in the Senate, follow the same pattern of Congressional action as do appropriations bills. In the case of disagreement between the two Houses on an individual appropriation or revenue bill, a conference committee (consisting of members of both Houses) meets to resolve the issues. The report of the conference committee is returned to each House for approval, and, when agreed to by both, the measure is presented to the President in the form of an enrolled bill, for approval or veto in its entirety."[21]

## The Congressional Reconciliation Process

"The Budget Act requires that the Congress complete action on all bills providing new budget authority by the 7th day after Labor Day. By September 15, the Congress must complete action on a concurrent resolution on the budget that sets ceilings for budget authority and floors for revenue. This second concurrent resolution reaffirms or revises the targets set earlier in the year under the first concurrent resolution. It also, to the extent necessary, directs the Appropriations Committees and other committees having jurisdiction over spending and revenue measures to recommend changes in existing or pending legislation so as to conform with the ceilings and floors established therein.

"Changes recommended by the various committees, pursuant to the second concurrent resolution, are reported in a reconciliation bill (if adjustments affect enacted legislation) or a reconciliation resolution (where changes affect legislation not yet enacted into law), or both Congressional action on such measures is to be completed by September 25. Nonetheless, Congress cannot adjourn until the second required concurrent resolution on the budget has been adopted; and, if required, the reconciliation process has been completed."[22]

## NOTES

1.  Executive Office of the President, Office of Management and Budget, Zero-Base Budgeting, OMB Bulletin 77-9, April 19, 1977. All remaining parts of Reviewing and Ranking were predominately taken from OMB Bulletin 77-9

2.  Executive Office of the President, Office of Management and Budget, "Executive Formulation and Transmittal Phase," The Budget of the United States Government, FY 1978, 1977

3.  Ibid.

4.  Ibid.

5.  Ibid.

6.  Ibid.

7.  Executive Office of the President, Office of Management and Budget, "Preparation and Submission of Budget Estimates," OMB Circular A-11, July 1977

8.  Ibid.

9.  Ibid.

10.  Ibid.

11.  Ibid.

12.  Ibid.

13.  Ibid.

14.  Executive Office of the President, Office of Management and Budget, "Preparation and Execution of the Federal Budget," 1977

15.  Ibid.

16.  Ibid.

17.  Executive Office of the President, the Budget of the U.S. Government, FY 1977

18.  Ibid.

19.  Ibid.

20.   Ibid.

21.   Executive Office of the President, "Preparation and Execution of the Federal Budget,"

22.   Ibid.

# CHAPTER 5
# IMPLEMENTATION OF
# THE ZBB PROCESS

Peter Pyhrr states that there are several factors to consider before installing ZBB, such as top management policy, organizational size and location, management capabilities, adequate time, and ZBB formats.[1] There are other factors to be considered also before designing and implementing zero-base budgeting:

- Principal users of the generated information
- Objectives and expectations of ZBB
- Linkage to existing agency systems

Once the principal users of the information produced by the zero-base budgeting process have been determined, designing and implementing the ZBB system can be accomplished effectively. Setting objectives of what an agency hopes to achieve by the use of the zero-base technology would save valuable implementation time. The average manager is comfortable with existing management systems; every effort should be made to link the new zero-base procedures with the current planning and information systems. The success of any new system is dependent upon the acceptance of the ZBB process by the manager. Therefore, strategy for implementing ZBB would be to supplement the existing process, not replace it. The ZBB system becomes even more popular if it is flexible and satisfies other agency needs than just using ZBB for budget justification.

To what am I alluding? A Government agency should be aware that the OMB is, in accordance with the President's direction, only providing guidance on the use of zero-base budgeting techniques for the preparation and justifications of budget requests within each agency. It is true that the Office of Management and Budgeting is asking each agency to develop a zero-base budgeting system to be used in the preparation of the 1979 Budget. However, OMB Bulletin No. 77-9 also states, "These (ZBB) concepts and guidelines are a framework within which *each agency should develop necessary procedures to meet its individual requirements.*"[2]

## INSTRUCTIONS TO IMPLEMENT ZBB

Before proceeding any further, of interest are the instructions that have been issued to departments and agencies on implementing zero-base budgeting in the Federal Government.

On February 14, 1977, President Carter sent a Memorandum to the Heads of Executive Departments and Agencies directing them ". . . .to develop a zero-base system within the agency in accordance with instructions to be issued by the Office of Management and Budget. The Fiscal Year 1979 budget will be prepared using this system." Subsequently, on April 19, 1977, the Office of Management and Budget issued *Bulletin 77-9.* This instruction provided specific guidance to the agencies on the use of zero-base budgeting techniques for the preparation and justification of fiscal year 1979 budget requests. In June 1977, OMB advised agencies of revision in OMB Circular No. A-11, "Preparation and Submission of Budget Estimates." This OMB Circular No. A-11 contained guidance to the agencies of ZBB materials to be submitted in their FY 1979 agency budget submissions.

## COMMITMENT IN IMPLEMENTING ZBB

Analyzing your own commitment to implementing ZBB is important before making an assessment of expectations from others. The implementation plan would be affected if higher-level managers or subordinates have a degree of commitment substantially higher or lower. There are a number of options toward an agency's approach to implementing ZBB. Common sense should dictate the proper approach to be used. Continuous visible commitment by key managers must be made, not just fanfare at the initial "throwing out of the ball." The best played game is that which the President stays to watch.

After the initial novelty has worn off, the agencies must guard against possible disenchantment. Some managers will feel that the results of implementing this system will figure in their individual performance evaluations. The manager begins to resent that a significant portion of their operating time has been taken away. Confusion sets in when management direction shifts too many times. Poorly worded memos begin to weigh on the manager's mind. "You must turn in your decision packages within 20 days." Managers, who want to look instantly successful, "bite off more than they can chew." A manager of a large agency inadvertently selects a decision unit at the "zero" line. After developing 30,000 decision packages he becomes discouraged by his mistake.

Some managers cannot get "turned on" by possible advantages of implementing an effective zero-base budgeting system such as expanding lower-level management participation in planning, evaluation, and budgeting. Then, how about appealing to their pride of accomplishment — attempting to install a ZBB system might give the citizens of the United States a feeling that Federal employees are trying to give them more for their tax dollar.

## STEPS IN THE IMPLEMENTATION OF ZBB

Guidelines or steps that could be used by an agency in the implementation of ZBB are:
1. Selection of advisory team
2. Training
3. Preparing calendar of events
4. Development of implementation manual

### Selection of an Advisory Implementation Team

ZBB links planning, budgeting, and review stages of an agency. Members of the ZBB implementation team should initially have employees from various functional units on the committee, such as program analysts, budget analysts, accountants, ADP specialists, and representatives from the top and bottom levels of management. Representatives from regional offices should be on the team. Otherwise, "catch-up ball" will have to be played in the regions.

This type of selection will assist in the proper communication and training needed to successfully implement ZBB. Here is a negative example. If one of my classes, program analysts and accountants were asked if a copy of OMB Bulletin 77-9 issued to their agencies 3 weeks ago had been communicated to them. An employee of the Office of the Secretary of one agency stated that the budget office had received it but had not shared it with other departments.

In Georgia, ZBB was administered with 10 analysts connected with the Budget Bureau and very little representation from other disciplines. In the Federal Government, ZBB will be administered and coordinated by a small staff also. Most of the implementation of ZBB will be accomplished by agency managers supported by a team of administrative, financial, and operating managers. Each team will vary depending on the size of its agency. The number of representatives from the different disciplines will determine whether ZBB will be just a budget technique or whether it will also be a management tool to implement more efficiency and effectiveness in the public sector.

Agency teams could be aligned as illustrated above. They could have a steering committee composed of coordinators. Each coordinator would assist a number of decision units in the implementation of ZBB.

### Duties of the ZBB Advisory Staff

Duties of the implementation team should involve keeping all management levels informed of new developments, problems, and progress. This enables managers to avoid wasting time and effort. The team also provides assistance and conducts meetings to explain the various ZBB procedures. The team would be the liaison

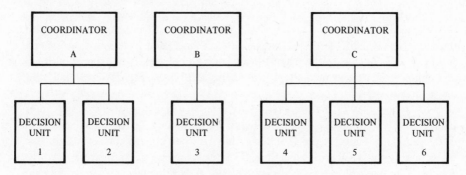

Steering committee

between OMB and the agency's manager. The Georgia Budget Bureau administered the ZBB process and assisted each agency in developing its own ZBB team. In the Federal Government, OMB has directed the budget examiners to assist the agencies in implementing ZBB.

Duties of the advisory staff would be to:

1.  Coordinate the ZBB process

2.  Determine decision units (organizational level) where decision packages would be developed

3.  Develop program, planning, or budgetary guidelines or assumptions for the agency and communicate down to the decision units

4.  Establish time requirements and draft calendar of events for the ZBB process

5.  Communicate ZBB concepts and draft instructions to other members of the agency

6.  Develop zero-base budgeting manual

## Training

On a record by comedian Bill Cosby, it was stated, "and the Lord asked Noah to build an ark. Noah replied, 'Lord, what's an ark?' " The message is quite clear. Before agencies can begin to implement ZBB, managers need sufficient training in ZBB concepts especially at the executive level. A manager should receive rigid training in the use of ZBB principles and techniques before introducing ZBB to his organization. At a certain point of time these managers will then become the trainers and coach their subordinates. If top-level managers do not receive quality training initially, then by the time training filters down to a lower level, it could leave much to be desired.

Managers should take recommended training programs such as those given by the Management Sciences Training Center at the U.S. Civil Service Commission, the U.S. Department of Agriculture Graduate School, and by known professional groups. These courses can be attended by State employees. Other suggested forms of training would be to read a text such as this, *ZBB in the Public Sector* and other periodicals on ZBB.

In January 1977, before President Carter issued his executive memo to establish zero-base budgeting in the Federal Government, 38 top executives from different agencies met at the first accredited 10 week college course in Zero-Base Budgeting at the Office of Education (U.S. Department of Agriculture Graduate School). The basic objectives included learning ZBB principles and techniques and applying them to their agency. Teams were set up in the classroom and the final outputs of the teams efforts were (1) development of ZBB manuals and (2) preparation of decision packages. (The adjunct professor of this class was the author, Peter Sarant.)

Developed as a project for the zero-base budgeting course was a realistic zero-base budgeting manual conceptualized for the Office of the Deputy Assistant Secretary, Finance, HEW. The team which represented all necessary functional areas had produced by March 17, 1977, a HEW manual which was "on the money." It developed instructions to their subordinates and designed decision packages which were appropriate using the States' experience. It should be noted that the class did not have any OMB guidance because OMB's Bulletin 77-9 was not issued until a month later. In short, the Department of Health, Education, and Welfare exexutives had a 3-month training start in learning all the principles and techniques in ZBB. It was this class which achieved the conquest of ZBB "real world" situations prematurely, which encouraged me to write this book. This text is based on principles and concepts that were taught in this classroom, and, of course, it has been updated with OMB instructions and the experiences of other State and Federal agencies.

**Prepare Calendar of Events**

The calendar of events (Exhibit 5-1) should be developed by the team and submitted with the ZBB manual. "How much time do we need for the ZBB process?" is a question always asked by managers developing the calendar of events. Before preparing the calendar consider the following:

1.  Additional time should be allowed for analysis and review of current activities.

2.  Allowance should be made for training and communication.

3.  Development, review, ranking, and revision of decision packages will add to the time necessary to prepare budgets, especially the review and analysis phase of ZBB. (The State of Georgia took 4 weeks to do this.)

CALENDAR OF EVENTS

| Date | Event |
|------|-------|
| 28 Mar 77 | Initiate a series of three day instructional periods for all action personnel involved in formulating ZBB activities. Attendance will be mandatory. |
| 4 Apr 77 | Initiate a series of instructional seminars for mid level managers involved in evaluating and ranking decision packages. Seminars will consist of two four-hour sessions. Attendance will be mandatory. |
| 11 Apr 77 | Initiate a series of instructional seminars for top management. Seminars will consist of two three-hour sessions and more if desired. |
| 15 Apr 77 | Issue manual of instructions. |
| 13 May 77 | Meet with all action personnel to answer questions on manual. |
| 3 Jun 77 | Outline of decision packages submitted to managers for approval of decision package organization. |
| 17 Jun 77 | Marked up outlines returned to action personnel for revising. |
| 22 Jul 77 | Action personnel develop complete decision packages and first line managers rank packages. |
| 29 Jul 77 | Submit packages and rankings to the first consolidation level for review, ranking, and revision, as required. |
| 12 Aug 77 | Make intermediate level rankings and revise, as required. |
| 26 Aug 77 | Review and rank packages at the final consolidation level. |
| 2 Sep 77 | Packages and rankings reviewed by top management; preliminary funding decisions made. |
| 8 Sep 77 | Revise planning assumptions if necessary; make changes, as required. Apply latest fiscal data to all packages, changing levels where required. |
| 22 Sep 77 | Managers at the final consolidation level review changes and rerankings to be submitted for the final top management review. |
| 30 Sep 77 | Final review of packages and rankings by top management. |
| 3 Oct 77 - 31 Jan 78 | Preparation of congressional justification material. |

Source: ZBB project by U.S.D.A. Graduate School – ZBB Budgeting Conceptualized for the U.S. Department of Health, Education, and Welfare.

**EXHIBIT 5-1**    Calendar of events

In subsequent years the ZBB process will take less time because of the "learning curve" changing its direction as a result of the additional experience by managers and subordinates alike. In Georgia, agencies were given 3 months additional time to implement ZBB; however, it took less time to complete the entire process.

Time requirements can initially be reduced if:

1.  More training at lower levels is given

2.  Revisions of decision packages are kept to a minimum through proper communication

3.  Managers are allowed sufficient time to analyze and develop decision packages. This saves time at the consolidation phase because top-level managers can save time because of budget justifications

4.  The level at which well-written decision packages are developed is raised. This reduces the number of rankings, reviews, and revisions of these decision packages.

5.  ZBB is realistically implemented as a complementary system and not implemented as a replacement for the entire system. Paperwork would decrease because current forms now used in planning and budgeting are still used.

### Development of ZBB Manual

We began the implementation phase by developing ZBB teams, training managers, and scheduling events. The next important step in implementing ZBB effectively is proper communication. The agencies can communicate instructions through verbal briefings as well as through the issuance of a manual of instructions (see Appendix, Conceptualized ZBB Budgeting Manual for the Office of the Deputy Assistant Secretary of Finance, HEW). A manual's contents could include at a minimum:

1.  Letter of introduction

2.  Planning assumptions and expenditure guidelines

3.  Calendar of events required

4.  Purposes, philosophy, procedures, and concepts of ZBB

5.  Explanation of all steps in ZBB process

6.  Examples and instructions for completing ZBB forms and schedules

### ZERO-BASE BUDGETING AUTOMATION

Pete Pyhrr states, "The computer can become a tool that makes the difference between failure or success of zero-base budgeting in that it provides management . . . with a viable analysis and decision making tool."[3]

Mr. Ken Burroughs from the State of Georgia has established a "Special Interest Group on Zero-Base Budgeting and Automated Data Processing" in Washington, D.C., to gather, develop, and exchange information and guidelines for supporting ZBB with computer resources and applying ZBB techniques to ADP budgeting. He states, "ZBB and Data Processing can, if used properly, reinforce each other and provide the organization with much greater effectiveness in the overall use of its resources. These two powerful techniques working in close cooperation give mangement at all levels the tools to make significant short run impact on the allocation of resources within the organization. However, in order to achieve a high level of effectiveness through use of these techniques at least a broad understanding must be obtained by all concerned managers of the workings of both disciplines."

To write the finish to this book I discovered two people who were knee deep in the "nuts and bolts" of ZBB computer applications, Mr. Fred Porter and Ms. Rita Henry from the State of Arkansas. Mr. Porter is the State Budget Manager and Ms. Henry is the Applications Development Manager for the State of Arkansas. The next section of the book "Automating the Zero-Base Concept" is coauthored by them. They "baby-sat" with the initial Arkansas Automated System. It is my intent to have the reader benefit by another "real world" experience; in this case, the State of Arkansas's experiences with zero-base automation.


## AUTOMATING THE ZERO-BASE BUDGET CONCEPT
### by Fred Porter and Rita Henry

---

## I.    INTRODUCTION

The zero-base budget concept does not readily lend itself to the standardization that many may feel is inherent to an automated process of budget formulation. Indeed, the major value of zero-base budgeting lies in giving program managers flexibility and making them responsible for assessing their operations to determine which programs or alternatives should be given their highest priorities. However, it is in this very area of making assessments and priority determinations that many program managers have had the least experience. A well-developed and responsive automated budget system can become an invaluable tool to managers in assisting them to make program decisions throughout both the preparation and implementation processes of the budget cycle.

To have an automated zero-base budget system that is well developed and responsive to program managers' needs you must first attain agreement among the various interests involved — be they legislative, executive, administrative, or combinations of these interest groups — as to which areas of the zero-base budget system will receive the greatest benefits through automation. Areas to consider are the ranking process, the legislative summary, intermediate summaries for analysis and recommendation, detail budget preparation, budget implementation, or combinations of any or all these areas. Reaching a consensus as to the priorities of these various areas can be, and generally is, the most difficult portion of automating a budget concept. Once a consensus has been reached, automation of the various areas in accordance with set priorities must allow for the greatest amounts of simplicity and flexibility for the program managers as can be made possible.

If the zero-base budget system can be made to function as a planning tool for program managers it will receive their full support, and this may ultimately determine the success of the budget system. A legitimate budget system from which rational, sound recommendations can be made must offer something back to the program managers. By offering them a much-simplified and useful system that will present their needs and assist them in their planning functions, the executive and legislative leaders will receive the information they need to make informed recommendations and the decisions necessary for utilizing the resources of the governmental organization to their maximum.

## II.    FACTORS OF A GOVERNMENTAL ENVIRONMENT

The governmental environment surrounding the budget system in each instance will dictate to a large degree whether or not automating the zero-base budget concept will prove successful or even feasible.

Several factors should be considered. Legislative acceptance of the zero-base concept is necessary. Also their familiarity and attitude toward the automation of governmental functions in general should be of a strong, positive nature. Strong support within the executive branch, from the top down, will assist the central budget office and the computer services personnel in obtaining the information they need to develop an automated system that will be useful to the persons involved at each of the various stages of the budget cycle.

Frequency of budget preparation — annual or biennial — will play an important role in determining formats for budget preparation and presentation. However, this should receive minor consideration as a determining factor for automating the budget process. In the final analysis, basically the same amount of information must be generated whether it is in larger amounts every other year or smaller amounts every year.

The organization of computer facilities within a governmental organization can easily play a paramount role in implementing an automated zero-base budget system. A centralized computer services facility through which all information can be processed and all budgets produced is highly conducive to a successful automated budget system. This is not to say that attempting to automate the zero-base budget process around a decentralized or geographically disbursed computer services facility would be futile or unrealistic. However, it would be much more difficult for the central budget office to provide adequate coordination or assistance during the preparation phase of the budget process. Decentralization would also require the development of a duplicate or similar system for each facility in order to maintain budget continuity. This in turn would make the implementation and maintenance of the automated budget system more expensive and difficult.

The ability to interface with other automated systems is highly desirable and useful when considering the automation of the budget process. Automated accounting, payroll/personnel, and acquisition systems can all be used as primary data sources either through data base extractions or file duplication for use in generation of budgetary information. Use of these types of systems for primary data sources not only eliminates the man hours and expense involved with manually producing and establishing the data in the budget system, but also assures that a much higher level of data accuracy is attained.

The format of legislative authorization for expenditures and the formats used for recording cost data within the accounting system have large impact on the way budgetary information can be collected and displayed. Commonly, legislative authorization is either by line item or by program. If authorization is by line item there must be some mechanism either within a centralized accounting system or within the individual agency's accounting system to allow for the allocation of line item authorization to specific programs. Without this program allocation, development of discrete decision packages by the program managers would be impossible. Of course, legislative authorization by program naturally lends itself to the zero-base budget concept and can make the automation of the concept much easier and more flexible.

## III.   INFORMATION FOR LEGISLATIVE PRESENTATION OF THE BUDGET

Different governmental organizations require that different budgetary information be made available to the legislative branch for review and authorization purposes. This can be the submission of the chief executive's budget derived from his recommendations on departmental or agency budgets. It can also be the actual departmental or agency budget submissions with chief executive recommendations attached, or perhaps other information with little or no chief executive input. What all methods of presentation generally have in common is that the information provided tends to be summarized at a very broad level. This summarization is, of course, necessary to allow the legislative branch time to act upon all budgetary measures during the brief time spans commonly allowed for legislative sessions.

In the zero-base budget concept the program ranking document is the ideal document from which the legislative recommendations and subsequent appropriations should be made. To manually compile the ranking document, which may well include all decision packages from all programs of an agency or department, is a very painstaking and tedious task, and a later revision of the rankings can easily mean repeating the entire process again. Automating the zero-base budget concept and having the cost data for each decision package included in the system and readily identifiable makes the development of the ranking document for the department or agency very easy. Merely assigning a ranking number to each decision package identification code and requesting that all decision packages be summarized and printed in order by ranking number automatically generates the ranking document. A revision in decision package rankings requires only reassigning the rankings to the affected decision packages and requesting the generation of a new ranking document with the old one to be discarded.

Although program information is being highly demanded and used more and more in the recommendation processes of the budget cycle, many legislative bodies are reluctant to deviate from the line item approach for the appropriation of revenues. Reconciling the differing concepts presented when using a zero-base budget approach to program recommendations and a line item approach to legislative appropriation can be made much easier with the assistance of an automated budget system.

Illustrations III A, B, C, and D depict how, through automation of the budget preparation process, program recommendations made from the ranking document can be translated into line item appropriations and then further translated into program operating budgets after authorization by utilizing in various formats the accumulation of selective detail data.

Also, within many governmental organizations the legislative branch retains the authority for creation of personnel positions. Although position authorization may be very specific as to number, classifications, and compensation rates, in most cases it is summarized at the major division or agency level. Herein lies the problem of identifying those positions which coincide with the program decision package requests previously addressed. The ability to identify, compile into legislative authorization format, and then reallocate these position authorizations back to individual programs for utilization can be greatly enhanced through a well designed automated budget system.

Illustrations III E, F, G, and H depict how through automating the budget preparation process, specific position authorization can be maintained throughout the stages of decision package development, program/decision package ranking, executive and legislative recommendation, legislative authorization, and program allocation for operations.

It would be irrational to assume that all appropriation or position recommendations would precisely follow the ranking format, or that in the final analysis all appropriation measures and personnel authorizations would balance back exactly to the decision package requests as the previous illustrations have depicted. However, what is important is that in many cases they may do so or that changes in personnel authorizations and appropriations may have been specific and noted so that adjustments can be easily made when final translation of appropriations and personnel authorizations into program operating budgets does occur. Having this automated capability to manipulate the budgetary data with minimal effort allows much more time to be devoted to analyzing those changes for which only vague or insufficient information is available for determining program allocations.

By utilizing computer capabilities to accumulate and display selective detail information in a number of different formats, it indeed becomes possible to apply the zero-base approach to line item budgeting.

In many governmental organizations the success or failure of the zero-base budget approach may well hinge around the ability to provide the executive and legislative branches with the program information they desire yet retain the line item controls they demand. However, an overzealous attempt to satisfy both these ends without careful planning and communication between the Executive Branch,

|                      | AGENCY   PROGRAM   A |                    |                    |
| LINE ITEMS           | DECISION PKG.  A 1    | DECISION PKG A 2   | DECISION PKG  A 3  |
|----------------------|-----------------------|--------------------|--------------------|
| SALARIES             | $    300              | $  400             | $   150            |
| NUMBER POSITIONS     | 4                     | 12                 | 4                  |
| EMPLOYER MATCHING    | 100                   | 130                | 50                 |
| GENERAL MAINTENANCE  | 200                   | 250                | 100                |
| GRANTS               | 500                   | 0                  | 0                  |
| OTHER                | 50                    | 320                | 0                  |
| TOTAL                | $ 1,150               | $ 1,100            | $   300            |

|                      | AGENCY   PROGRAM   B |                     |                    |
| LINE ITEMS           | DECISION PKG.  B 1    | DECISION PKG.  B 2  | DECISION PKG  B 3  |
|----------------------|-----------------------|---------------------|--------------------|
| SALARIES             | $    350              | $   500             | $   700            |
| NUMBER POSITIONS     | 4                     | 16                  | 19                 |
| EMPLOYER MATCHING    | 200                   | 350                 | 400                |
| GENERAL MAINTENANCE  | 700                   | 900                 | 300                |
| DATA PROCESSING      | 800                   | 200                 | 100                |
| TOTAL                | $ 2,050               | $ 1,950             | $1,500             |

**ILLUSTRATION III A**    Individual decision package summaries

| RANK | TITLE/DESCRIPTION | AMOUNT/# POSITION. | CUMMULATIVE AMT/# POSITION |
|------|-------------------|--------------------|----------------------------|
| 1    | B 1               | $  2,050 /  4      | $  2,050  /  4             |
| 2    | A 1               | $  1,150 /  7      | $  3,200  /  11           |
| 3    | A 2               | $  1,100 / 12      | $  4,300  /  23           |
| 4    | B 3               | $  1,500 / 19      | $  5,800  /  42           |
| 5    | B 2               | $  1,950 / 16      | $  7,750  /  58           |
| 6    | A 3               | $    300 /  4      | $  8,050  /  62           |

**ILLUSTRATION III B**    Agency ranking document
(Assume revenue ceiling of $5,800)

|                       | AGENCY AMOUNT |
|-----------------------|---------------|
| SALARIES              | $   1,750     |
| EMPLOYER MATCHING     | 830           |
| GENERAL MAINTENANCE   | 1,450         |
| GRANTS                | 500           |
| DATA PROCESSING       | 900           |
| OTHER                 | 370           |
| TOTAL APPROPRIATION   | $   5,800     |

**ILLUSTRATION III C**   Line item
appropriation measure

the Legislative Branch, and the Central Budget Office can result in inundating the Chief Executive and the Legislature with reams of documentation which they may neither understand nor have the time to wade through. This can be crippling at least, and perhaps fatal, to implementing an automated zero-base budget. By communicating with the Chief Executive and the Legislative Branch, and through orientation and joint planning, the "paper mill" can be controlled and the Central Budget Office can gain executive and legislative support for automating the zero-base budget concept.

|                       | PROGRAM A | PROGRAM   B | TOTAL     |
|-----------------------|-----------|-------------|-----------|
| SALARIES              | $   700   | $   1,050   | $   1,750 |
| EMPLOYER MATCHING     | 230       | 600         | 830       |
| GENERAL MAINTENANCE   | 450       | 1,000       | 1,450     |
| GRANTS                | 500       | 0           | 500       |
| DATA PROCESSING       | 0         | 900         | 900       |
| OTHER                 | 370       | 0           | 370       |
| TOTAL                 | $   2,250 | $   3,550   | $   5,800 |

**ILLUSTRATION III D**   Program operations allocations

AGENCY    PROGRAM   A

| DECISION PKG.  A1 | | | DECISION PKG. A2 | | | DECISION    PKG.  A 3 | | |
|---|---|---|---|---|---|---|---|---|
| Classification | Grade | # Req. | Classification | Grade | # Req. | Classification | Grade | # Req. |
| DIRECTOR | 23 | 1 | SUPERVISOR | 16 | 2 | SUPERVISOR | 16 | 1 |
| ASST. DIRECTOR | 18 | 1 | ACCOUNTANT | 14 | 2 | INVESTIGATOR | 13 | 1 |
| RESEARCH ASSOC. | 14 | 2 | BOOKKEEPER | 12 | 4 | SECRETARY | 9 | 1 |
| SECRETARY | 9 | 3 | CLERK TYPIST | 7 | 4 | CLERK | 6 | 1 |
| TOTAL | $300 | 7 | TOTAL | $400 | 12 | TOTAL | $150 | 4 |

AGENCY    PROGRAM   B

| DECISION PKG.   B1 | | | DECISION PKG.   B2 | | | DECISION   PKG.   B3 | | |
|---|---|---|---|---|---|---|---|---|
| Classification | Grade | # Req. | Classification | Grade | # Req. | Classificiation | Grade | #Req. |
| DIRECTOR | 23 | 1 | SUPERVISOR | 16 | 3 | ADMINISTRATOR | 20 | 1 |
| ATTORNEY | 22 | 1 | TRAINING COORD. | 14 | 3 | ACCOUNTANT | 14 | 3 |
| LEGAL ASST. | 19 | 1 | TRAINING ASST. | 12 | 6 | BOOKKEEPER | 12 | 6 |
| LEGAL SECRETARY | 12 | 1 | CLERK TYPIST | 7 | 4 | CLERK TYPIST | 7 | 9 |
| TOTAL | $350 | 4 | TOTAL | $500 | 16 | TOTAL | $700 | 19 |

**ILLUSTRATION III E**     Individual decision package position listings

|  |  | AGENCY REQUEST |  |
| --- | --- | --- | --- |
| CLASSIFICATION | GRADE | NO. REQUESTED | NO. RECOMMENDED 1/ |
| DIRECTOR | 23 | 2 | 2 |
| ATTORNEY | 22 | 1 | 1 |
| ADMINISTRATOR | 20 | 1 | 1 |
| LEGAL ASSISTANT | 19 | 1 | 1 |
| ASST. DIRECTOR | 18 | 1 | 1 |
| SUPERVISOR | 16 | 6 | 2 |
| ACCOUNTANT | 14 | 5 | 5 |
| RESEARCH ASSOC. | 14 | 2 | 2 |
| TRAINING COORD. | 14 | 3 | 0 |
| INVESTIGATOR | 13 | 1 | 0 |
| BOOKKEEPER | 12 | 10 | 10 |
| LEGAL SECRETARY | 12 | 1 | 1 |
| TRAINING ASSIT. | 12 | 6 | 0 |
| SECRETARY | 9 | 4 | 3 |
| CLERK TYPIST | 7 | 17 | 13 |
| CLERK | 6 | 1 | 0 |
| TOTAL | $2,400 | 62 | 42 |

1/  Refer to Illustration III  B

**ILLUSTRATION III F**    Summary position request/recommendation

## AGENCY POSITION AUTHORIZATION

| CLASSIFICATION | GRADE | NUMBER AUTHORIZED |
|---|---|---|
| DIRECTOR | 23 | 2 |
| ATTORNEY | 22 | 1 |
| ADMINISTRATOR | 20 | 1 |
| LEGAL ASSISTANT | 19 | 1 |
| ASSISTANT DIRECTOR | 18 | 1 |
| SUPERVISOR | 16 | 2 |
| ACCOUNTANT | 14 | 5 |
| RESEARCH ASSOCIATE | 14 | 2 |
| BOOKKEEPER | 12 | 10 |
| LEGAL SECRETARY | 12 | 1 |
| SECRETARY | 9 | 3 |
| CLERK TYPIST | 7 | 13 |
| TOTAL POSITIONS AUTHORIZED | | 42 |

**ILLUSTRATION III G**    Summary, position recommendation legislative authorization

| CLASSIFICATION | GRADE | PROGRAM A | PROGRAM B | TOTAL |
|---|---|---|---|---|
| DIRECTOR | 23 | 1 | 1 | 2 |
| ATTORNEY | 22 | 0 | 1 | 1 |
| ADMINISTRATOR | 20 | 0 | 1 | 1 |
| LEGAL ASSISTANT | 19 | 0 | 1 | 1 |
| ASSISTANT DIRECTOR | 18 | 1 | 0 | 1 |
| SUPERVISOR | 16 | 2 | 0 | 2 |
| ACCOUNTANT | 14 | 2 | 3 | 5 |
| RESEARCH ASSOCIATE | 14 | 2 | 0 | 2 |
| BOOKKEEPER | 12 | 4 | 6 | 10 |
| LEGAL SECRETARY | 12 | 0 | 1 | 1 |
| SECRETARY | 9 | 3 | 0 | 3 |
| CLERK TYPIST | 7 | 4 | 9 | 13 |
| TOTAL POSITIONS ALLOCATED | | 19 | 23 | 42 |

**ILLUSTRATION III H**    Program position allocations

## IV.   INFORMATION FOR BUDGET ANALYSIS AND RECOMMENDATION

One of the major values of implementing a zero-base budget is that program managers are required to become more involved in the budget process. Only they can provide the in-depth program information that is necessary for decision package justifications. However, if the program manager has heretofore been either uninvolved or only casually involved with the development of the budget requests, problems can soon arise. He may soon find himself totally confused and engulfed in a barrage of budget forms, adding machine tapes, and program narratives with a clear idea neither of what he is requesting nor of which justification coincides with which decision package request. When this situation develops, program managers become avid opponents of zero-base budgeting.

A well-designed, automated system of budget formulation can relieve the program manager of virtually all manual calculations, simplify forms completion, and control the flow of budget development in an orderly fashion. When such an environment exists, the program manager can then clearly determine what his needs are and formulate his justification for those needs. Also, when the automated budget system relieves the program manager from many of the technical duties, it likewise reduces the technical assistance he requires from the budget analyst. Both are free then to spend much more of their time developing or analyzing program information.

By combining program narrative and decision package justifications with the decision package fiscal data, which is shown in Illustrations III A, B, and E, the budget analyst can get a very clear insight into what each decision package can be expected to accomplish and its relative value to the agency.

Although the budget analyst may use the individual decision package information to formulate his budget recommendations, it is generally desirable to use some higher level of summarization for presentation of these recommendations. Within an automated budget environment the budget analyst has a number of options he may utilize to present his recommendations. These options can include alternate ranking documents indicating his recommended arrangements of priorities for receipts of funding, or consolidation of related decision packages through automated cost center combinations with accompanying consolidated decision package recommendations. A third method could be accumulation of individual decision package recommendation data for reflection on the agency ranking document, thereby providing a budget recommendation for each ranking without physically changing the decision package's relative position on the ranking document.

Illustrations IV A, B, and C depict these three examples of recommendation formats. With a flexible, automated system of budget development, cost and recommendation data can be arranged and rearranged into any number of formats to best reflect the information desired at any particular stage of the budget process.

## V.   INFORMATION FOR DETAIL BUDGET PREPARATION

Normally budgets must be prepared at various levels due to varying agency structures. If an automated zero-base budget system is to be effective, it must support

RECOMMENDED RANKING DOCUMENT - ASSUME REVENUE CEILING OF $5,800.

| RANK | TITLE/DISCRIPT. | AMT./#POS. | CUMM. AMT./POS. |
|------|-----------------|------------|-----------------|
| 1 | B 1 | $2,050/4 | $2,050/4 |
| 2 | B 2 | 1,950/16 | 4,000/20 |
| 3 | B 3 | 1,500/19 | 5,500/39 |
| 4 | A 3 | 300/4 | 5,800/43 |
| 5 | A 1 | 1,150/7 | 6,950/50 |
| 6 | A 2 | $1,100/12 | $8,050/62 |

**ILLUSTRATION IV A**　　Budget analyst's recommended decision package ranking document.
(Refer to Illustration III B for comparison)

| | PROGRAM A | | | |
|-----------------|------------|------------|------------|------------|
| LINE ITEM | AGENCY | REQUEST | BUDGET | RECOMMENDATION |
| SALARIES | $ | 850 | $ | 150 |
| NO. POSITIONS | | 23 | | 4 |
| EMPLOYER MATCHING | $ | 280 | $ | 50 |
| GENERAL MAINTENANCE | $ | 550 | $ | 100 |
| GRANTS | $ | 500 | $ | 0 |
| OTHER | $ | 370 | $ | 0 |
| TOTAL | $ | 2,550 | $ | 300 |

| | PROGRAM B | | | |
|-----------------|------------|------------|------------|------------|
| LINE ITEM | AGENCY | REQUEST | BUDGET | RECOMMENDATION |
| SALARIES | $ | 1,550 | $ | 1,550 |
| NO. POSITIONS | | 39 | | 39 |
| EMPLOYER MATCHING | $ | 950 | $ | 950 |
| GENERAL MAINTENANCE | $ | 1,900 | $ | 1,900 |
| DATA PROCESSING | $ | 1,100 | $ | 1,100 |
| TOTAL | $ | 5,500 | $ | 5,500 |

**ILLUSTRATION IV B**　　Combination of related decision package requests with accompanying decision package recommendations

| RANK NO. | TITLE/ DISC. | AGENCY REQUEST | | BUDGET RECOMMENDATION | |
|---|---|---|---|---|---|
| | | AMT./POSITION | CUM. AMT. POSITION | AMT/POSITION | CUM. AMT. POSITION |
| 1 | B1 | $ 2,050 / 4 | $ 2,050 / 4 | $ 2,050 / 4 | $ 2,050 / 4 |
| 2 | A1 | 1,150 / 7 | 3,200 / 11 | 0 / 0 | 2,050 / 4 |
| 3 | A2 | 1,100 / 12 | 4,300 / 23 | 0 / 0 | 2,050 / 4 |
| 4 | B3 | 1,500 / 19 | 5,800 / 42 | 1,500 / 19 | 3,550 / 23 |
| 5 | B2 | 1,950 / 16 | 7,750 / 58 | 1,950 / 16 | 5,500 / 39 |
| 6 | A3 | $ 300 / 4 | $ 8,050 / 62 | 300 / 4 | 5,800 / 43 |

**ILLUSTRATION IV C**     Agency ranking document with budget recommendations included

these varying levels of organization. An example of the various levels of an agency is shown in Illustration V A. The agency has five activities. One of the activities has three sections, and one of the sections has three units. This agency may need to budget at unit level while another agency may only need activity level.

If a line item approach is used the budget at the cost center level should reflect budgeted expenditures for personnel positions, maintenance object categories, and grants/special line items. This detailed level of budgeting is generally an easy way for agency personnel to estimate costs. Most people tend to think at a detail level; for example, it's easier to say, "I will need $12,000 for position #1, $15,000 for #2," etc. than to say, "I will need $250,000 for salaries." Also, by developing detail budget requests, the likelihood of overlooking an expenditure item is much less than when budgeting at a high summary level.

If position authorization is required, budget reports for personnel positions should be produced at cost center level so that program managers can develop their

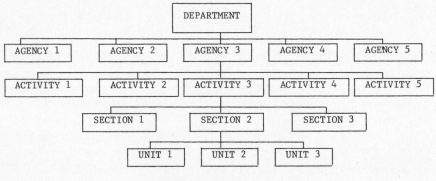

**ILLUSTRATION V A**

respective budgets. The designation of the position as a minimum, current, or priority item must be shown.

A special consideration for personnel positions is extra help or part-time positions. This information may or may not fit into the same reporting format as that for full-time personnel positions. Also, designation of upgrade/downgrade requests must be shown.

The budget reports for maintenance objects can provide the following data: object code and title, actual expenditures, budgeted expenditures, inflation amounts, adjustment amounts, percentage of increase/decrease, and amounts by minimum, current, and priority level.

Information on grants and special line items must also be provided. Space may be necessary on the form for the agency to describe the program and the reason for any increase or decrease.

There are numerous technical and analytical aids which can be generated to facilitate the budget process. The more important ones include the decision package percentage listings. These can show at the cost center, appropriation, and fund levels the various percentages necessary for analysis of the budget requests. Percentages such as minimum level to budgeted, current level to budgeted, etc. can be calculated at each of these expenditure levels. The report can be generated for all cost centers, appropriations, and funds or it can be created on an exception basis, such as for any budget for which the minimum level is greater than 80 percent of the budgeted amount. Such exception listing can enable the budget analysts to quickly locate possible "problem" areas.

Identification of positions in multiple cost centers is important. When budgets are prepared at the detailed level, it is necessary to know the various cost centers in which an individual position may appear. This situation is created when more than one cost center had expenditures for that particular position. This listing aids the budget analyst and agency personnel in ensuring that the data is uniform for each position regardless of where it appears. Also, various update error reports designate those budget modifications which were not performed due to incorrect or incomplete data. The generation of this type of aid is typical in any automated system.

Identification of errors in personnel position data is an aid when data for a personnel position does not coincide with that in other cost centers for the same position. These inconsistencies are noted so that they may be corrected.

There should be a code and description data listing. The various codes and their corresponding descriptions are listed for reference. These codes and descriptions may designate cost centers, agencies, departments, appropriations, characters, funds, maintenance objects, and employee classifications. Other data such as inflation factors, special classification, salaries, grades, and cross references to funds and departments (for appropriation) may also be included.

Identification of invalid decision package rankings is vital. In the event that two or more packages receive the same rank or if a package receives no ranking, notification of these facts must be made. This information assures agencies of having valid ranking documents produced. For large agencies this information can be of tremendous benefit when many priority programs must be ranked.

## VI.  ADDITIONAL BENEFITS MADE POSSIBLE THROUGH AUTOMATION

In an automated zero-base budget system the data which have been entered into the computer can be manipulated to provide information for a number of additional uses. When the budget system has been expanded in this manner the data which have been entered are being utilized to their fullest extent.

In budget systems which project personnel costs by position, classification conversion becomes a relatively straightforward function. It is necessary for the Personnel Office to determine how each classifications is to translate and to supply this information to the budget system, as shown in Illustration VI A. Through this approach all employees can be converted from one classification plan to another. There are always exceptions, so there must be a mechanism for translating special positions to their appropriate classification codes.

A sample document which can be used to designate positions that are exceptions to the conversion plan is shown in Illustration VI B.

A further application of the classification conversion process is for the converted data to be reentered into the payroll/personnel system after the budget cycle is complete. This reduces tremendously the amount of duplication of effort.

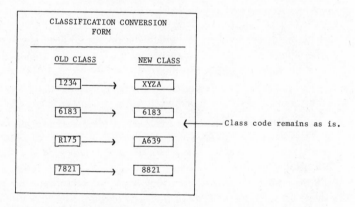

**ILLUSTRATION VI A**

**ILLUSTRATION VI B**

An additional benefit of an automated zero-base budget system can be that of pay plan conversion. This function is particularly beneficial if any necessary classification conversions have been performed. The various proposed pay plans can be entered into the budget system and calculations made to determine the different costs of implementing the various plans. The system should be capable of accepting any pay plan within a reasonable format (varying the number of grades or steps) and with reasonable variations on the time-in-step requirements.

The automated generation of personnel sections is a great aid if the appropriation bills are to reflect position authorizations. The positions budgeted for each classification within the agency or appropriation along with the associated grades can be produced and inserted directly into the appropriation bill. This feature of the budget system virtually eliminates errors resulting from manually typing the information onto the bills. It also greatly reduces the amount of time and effort required to prepare the appropriation bills for the legislative session. Also, online capability can allow immediate update and generation of personnel sections, which is important during the legislative session when time is of the essence.

## VII.   UTILIZING THE PREPARATION PROCESS FOR BUDGET IMPLEMENTATION

Where many budget systems fall short is in the area of budget implementation. After the preparation, recommendation, and legislative authorization processes have been completed, agency fiscal and program personnel then set about to determine their plans for expenditure of appropriated funds. Unfortunately the outcome of this process can sometimes bear little or no resemblance to the information contained in the budget request that had been previously submitted and appropriated. A zero-base budget can and should be used as an implied contract between the agencies and the Legislature. Agencies should be held accountable for the programs for which they requested and subsequently received funding. By completing the budget cycle with an automated phase of budget implementation, much can be gained toward ensuring that accountability can be attained. The question arises as to what level of detail should the budget data within the automated budget system be utilized for budget implementation. To reconcile the budget request information with the final budget authorization is the logical first step in the process. This should be done at either of two levels. Reconciliation can be at the detail unit or object of expenditure level with input going directly into the budget request so that in the final analysis the budget request data in the computer is identical to the budget authorization. This method is perhaps easier from a computer system development point of view since it is merely changing budget request data into budget authorization data. However, this method is at a level of detail that is not rationally necessary to determine the program allocations. Also, this method of reconciliation tends to be less flexible and more time consuming than is desirable. An alternate and easier method of reconciliation from the budget analyst's and program manager's point of view is to duplicate the budget request data at that program summary level from which the budget recommendations were formulated. Data inserted at this summary level (refer to Illustration III A) to only the duplicate records can simplify the reconciliation, and maintain the original request data for comparison and future reference as well. At this level it is also easier for the budget analyst and program manager to come to grips with those areas of change for which exists only the vague or insufficient information referred to previously. When reconciliation with the budget authorization is achieved, it is then only a simple matter of data combinations to provide the program managers with their program operating allocations (reference Illustrations III D and III H).

Utilizing an automated process of budget development and implementation such as just described can be one of the most valuable planning tools available to program managers. Eliminating the tedious and menial steps in the budget develop- ment stages enables program managers to devote serious time and effort to budget planning. If they then utilize an automated system to carry those plans forward through the recommendation and authorization stages to the implementation stage, program managers need no longer duplicate their planning processes.

## VIII.  TECHNICAL CONSIDERATIONS OF AN AUTOMATED SYSTEM

The development effort of an automated zero-base budget system must be well organized and properly planned. As with the development of any other data processing application, effective project management is a must. There are many of these methodologies which are successful, and most data processing organizations have a method which works for them. These guidelines serve several functions, such as:

1.  Delineating the various tasks necessary to be performed in the system's development (a checklist)

2.  Designating the organization's policies on project management

3.  Providing examples of various ways to accomplish those tasks

Another part of successful system development centers around having the "right" people involved from the very beginning of the project. Some of these "right" people would include the chief executive, key legislators, legislative staff personnel, personnel from other administrative offices (accounting, personnel), the budget staff, and agency personnel. Certainly, the highest-level personnel must be consulted for policy decisions, such as the implementation of an automated zero- base budget system. They should also be continually consulted and informed (at least at a high level) throughout the system's development in relation to its status, its features, and their decision needs.

Other personnel directly utilizing or interfacing with the budget system should be questioned for their ideas, and the impact of the system/procedures inter- face required. Strong backing by these individuals is absolutely necessary if the sys- tem is to be a success, since their attitude and enthusiasm will be transmitted to other program managers.

The involvement of the budget analysts is also essential. Their continued participation throughout the project will have many positive results by providing the analysts with such things as:

1.  A sense of ownership in the system

2.  A chance for them to express their ideas and think creatively

3.  An in-depth knowledge of the way in which the budgeting cycle works

4.  Training on a gradual basis, rather than a "crash" course once the system is up

Of course, the degree to which all analysts participate will depend upon the size of the budget staff. However, at a minimum they should all participate at major review points with further involvement desirable.

Agency personnel should be kept abreast of the work being done on the budget system, but primarily at the conceptual level, with detailed orientation occurring immediately preceding the actual utilization of the system. Their support of the system becomes very important as they are the people who will actually be preparing budget information.

Support from each of these groups is particularly important in light of the tremendous amount of time necessary for an effective system development. The decisions about how the system is to operate should be made a year or two prior to implementation.

An effective, automated, zero-base budget system cannot be developed overnight — a great deal of analysis and design time is required, particularly in today's sophisticated, integrated data base environment.

Many may immediately consider utilizing private consultant services to perform the design and development functions in automating the zero-base budget concept. This practice should be given very careful consideration in this particular instances for many reasons.

1.  Consultants cannot know more about the operations of the organization than those people who are employed there.

2.  Consultants may not be able to develop the most effective system (again because they are not as familiar with operations).

3.  Consulting services may be far more expensive then "in-house" services.

4.  Consultants may tend to develop standard systems which are designed to work in most organizations with easy transferability. In the case of automated zero-base budget systems they must be developed around the organization's environment (as described in the first part of this chapter) rather than attempting to alter the environment to fit the system.

5.  Also, when consulting agencies develop a system and leave actual operations and maintenance of the system to the data processing section of the govern-

mental organization, loose ends may be left and documentation may be poor, and if the budget office is unhappy, there is little which can be done.

Another matter which must be addressed in developing an automated zero-base budget system is the preparation of useful documentation. There are four types:

1. *Data Processing* — There are standards in most data processing organizations for strict documentation of programs and systems. This allows for reduced effort in maintaining the systems, especially in light of high employee-turnover rates in this profession.

2. *Budget Office* — In many cases the data entry/collection function lies in the budget office. The budget analysts must have thorough documentation on how to use the system in order to aid them in working with the computer and for assisting the agencies in developing their budgets.

3. *Zero-Base Budget Users* — The agency personnel must receive written procedures on how their budgets are to be developed. The better this documentation is, the less time the budget analyst will need to spend aiding them on the technical aspects of the system. This documentation should contain actual samples as they will appear when automatically generated — this will lessen confusion.

4. *Executive level* — A general overview of the zero-base budget system's functions and information generated might be supplied to executive-level personnel who will be reviewing or making recommendations on budgets (such as legislators). This can serve as a reference guide.

Along with documentation, an effective orientation program is needed. People at all levels of the organization will make much better use of the system if they feel comfortable with it. They also will tend to lend more support to the automated system.

Once the system has been developed, it must be thoroughly tested. A systems test is really a trial run through all parts of the system involving all the people who will be running the system and providing input. The test creation of the budget data base will ensure that capability when actual creation is performed. The update cycle and report generation cycles must also be tested. Thorough testing will ensure the system's accuracy before the agencies get involved. This also provides a chance for the budget analysts to actually use the procedures involved and to modify those which do not function properly. This will enable them to work knowledgeably with the agencies when the system becomes operational.

System tests, effectively done, generally take longer than anticipated, so ample time for this task should be allowed.

Developing an automated zero-base budget system can be very costly in both time and dollars; therefore, it must be flexible. That is, changes in the environment should not result in major redesign or reprogramming. This is an extremely difficult situation to avoid as many times it is not possible to anticipate all areas in which flexibility may be needed. It is easy to develop a standardized system, but it is most difficult to develop a system when many variable, and even unknown, conditions must be provided for. The analysis and design time increases manyfold and development costs also increase. However, when flexibility is a part of the design, the system will continue to be effective for many years after a system that is developed for meeting only today's needs has become obsolete. Nevertheless, this idea of flexibility must be approached with moderation. To gain total flexibility (which is probably impossible), the cost and time for development would be prohibitive and the system would encompass so many parameters that it would require a magician to operate it. Other factors which the computer analyst should keep in mind when attempting to maintain flexibility during system development include program design, file structure flexibility, the interface with other systems, and the flexibility to allow for changing computer hardware/software.

As well as being flexible, the system must also be simple to use. If the development is not carefully done, these two factors can easily become mutually exclusive. There are several aspects of simplicity to discuss. One of these is the "paper mill." In a zero-base budget system where there are numerous decision packages at numerous levels, it is very easy for the automated system to become a "paper mill," generating more reports, in more sequences, at more expenditure levels, for more decision levels than can ever possibly be looked at, and much less used. This situation is one that can be minimized if the system developers are cognizant of this fact. In a zero-base budget system, of course, the other side of the coin must also be considered. Information at many varying levels is needed to provide decision makers with data so that legitimate budgets can be prepared and recommendations made, but the information should be generated only as needed.

Another area in which simplification is needed is that of redundant data. Use of the budget system can become extremely cumbersome if data must be entered in more than one data base. The accounting and budget systems could share the same code data base and payroll/personnel and budget systems could share the same pay table and classification data bases, resulting in a code being in the computer system in only one place. This also prevents the data from becoming different in separate data bases due to human error.

Some other aspects of simplicity involve usage of meaningful codes, limitation of the number of forms, and having only a minimum amount of input data necessary.

The process of developing various report formats requires special attention. The appropriate amount of information must be provided and this necessitates thorough analysis of the needs for each report. If a particular report omits information, then it may not be used at all. On the other hand, if there are too much data on one page, it is cluttered and hard to read, and again will probably not be used. Also, each report should have a specific use. If this approach is used, the development of useless reports will be avoided and the determination of the data to appear on each report is much easier.

Reporting is the basis of an automated zero-base budget system and the importance of developing usable reports is a key step.

Another consideration of major importance is whether the automated zero-base budget system should have online functions and, if so, to what extent. Factors which should be evaluated include how responsive the system must be. If there is no significant time problem, then a batch system will probably be adequate. However, if many last minute budget changes are being made, an online system might be justifiable. What is the turnaround for batch processing? To be considered here is the location of the data entry and computer sites. If access is immediate and updates can be keyed and processed within an adequate time frame, then batch processing may again be sufficient. However, if turn around is slow or the computer facility cannot be reached on a daily basis, then an online system might be necessary. If online capability is needed the terminal must be compatible with the computer system hardware and software. If a terminal is already being utilized for accessing other data bases, it may or may not be possible to use it for access of the budget data. What is the cost of a terminal printer (if needed)? What is the cost of communication lines? These are provided by the telephone company and cost is computed by number of miles. What number of terminals are to be used? This could range from one in the budget office to a number of them remotely located in many of the agencies. What number and type of online transactions are to be done each day? Data base transactions can be expensive, and updating generally costs more per transaction than inquiring. Also, transactions which print out reports at the terminal are generally expensive.

An analysis of these cost estimates will aid in performing any costs/benefit analysis which might be needed. Is the lead time available for obtaining the online equipment? The decision should be made at the beginning of the system development so that ample time is provided for the equipment to be ordered, shipped, and installed. In fact, if there is not enough time then there is probably not enough time to get the system developed either. Can the computer support an online system? Most large computers will already have the hardware and software for support of online systems and will have several already running. If a zero-base budget system is to be the first online system for the organization, ample time must be allowed for getting the problems ironed out of the online systems software. Another consideration in this area is that the computer system may be at capacity and unable to handle a new online application. The benefits of having the system online should be documented in the case that justification is requested.

Whether the system is to be online or not must be determined in the very early stages of the system development. This is necessary as the design is dependent upon this capability, and the time required to develop the system will be longer if online functions are to be included.

There are a number of specific detail points which should be considered by the computer analyst during development of an automated zero-base budget system. Budgets may not be prepared at the level at which expenditures are recorded. To ensure that the cost data is extracted at the correct level, a budget level table is needed. It should be developed at the most convenient level. With these data supplied at the beginning of each budget cycle, the expenditure data will be collected (and accumulated, if necessary) at the proper level for budget preparation. Of course, care must be taken that an agency is not designated to budget at a level lower than that at which expenditures were recorded.

The way in which data are stored in the accounting and payroll/personnel systems determines the method in which the budget data base is created. At the correct point in time data bases from both of those systems can have the pertinent data extracted to create the budget data base.

There are calculations which can be performed to relieve agency personnel of repetitive functions. One of these is the calculation of step increases. This calculation assumes step increases as they are available, making no provision for promotions. To accurately perform this, several data items are utilized, such as the employee's grade, step, annual rate, increased eligibility date, and months budgeted (for positions in multiple cost centers).

Calculation of inflation on maintenance object expenditures is less complicated than that for step increases. For a biennial budget, it would be calculated for all object factors obtained from a code data base which has an inflationary percentage given for each year. These inflation factors can be initialized at zero and updated to reflect the projected rate of inflation. A third major calculation in an automated zero-base budget system is the computation of employee matching costs. The maximums and percentages should be maintained in a table for easy modification each budget cycle.

Because there can be zero to N priority programs, the manner in which these data are stored on the computer system requires careful thought so that great amounts of storage space are not wasted. This is especially true if the system is online. A variable length record or hierarchical file structure can easily support this.

The capability to combine and accumulate data to higher levels for reporting purposes should be present for a useful system. A cost center combination document can be submitted designating the cost centers to be combined for that particular generation of reports. Then, as the budget data base is being read, the appropriate records can have their corresponding amounts combined and the reports will be produced as requested.

The combination capability should be available for appropriations also. The method of processing would be similar to that for cost center combinations. A special consideration in processing combinations is whether there are any limits on which cost centers or appropriations can be combined. If appropriations are authorized within agencies, should appropriation combination be allowed to cross agency lines?

The use of combinations to report data in special groupings can be a tremendous time-saving capability. The types of combinations provided should be dependent upon the needs of the governmental entity.

The automated zero-base budget system should have the capability to rank programs at various levels. The programs which are actually ranked at a cost level may also be ranked at activity level, then agency level, and then at departmental level, through the use of priority identification. This requires that each program be ranked several different ways and that these data be maintained on the computer system with the capability to update the rankings as needed. Since various agencies may be at different points in the development of their budgets at any given time, all levels of reports may be needed in one night's generation of budget reports. The method of determining which reports to produce for which agencies can be complicated, and it is easy for the situation to develop in which several computer jobs must be run each night to produce all the various reports needed. One sophisticated method of streamlining report requests would be for the budget analysts to utilize the terminal and select reports for each agency on grids, as shown in Illustrations VIII A and B. In these examples the agencies needing reports and those specific reports requested can be entered into a table so the computer can then produce exactly the reports needed at one time. A request document containing the same information could also be used for batch input rather than terminal input.

|  |  | REPORTS |  |  |  |  |
|---|---|---|---|---|---|---|
| AGENCY | PERSONNEL |  | OBJECT |  | SPECIAL LINE ITEM |  |
|  | DETAIL | SUMMARY | DETAIL | SUMMARY | DETAIL | SUMMARY |
| 1 | Yes | Yes | Yes | Yes | Yes | Yes |
| 8 | Yes |  | Yes |  | Yes |  |
| 23 | Yes | Yes |  |  |  |  |
| 61 |  | Yes |  | Yes |  | Yes |
| 84 | Yes | Yes | Yes | Yes |  |  |

**ILLUSTRATION VIII A**

|  | OTHER SUMMARY REPORTS |  |  |
|---|---|---|---|
| AGENCY | APPROPRIATION | RANKING | COST CENTER |
| 1 | Yes |  | Yes |
| 8 |  | Yes |  |
| 23 |  | Yes |  |
| 61 | Yes |  | Yes |
| 84 |  | Yes |  |

**ILLUSTRATION VIII B**

```
┌─────────────────────────────────────────────────────────────────────┐
│                         REPORT DISTRIBUTION                           │
│  ┌──────────────────────┐                  ┌──────────────┐           │
│  │   RANKING            │                  │  AGENCY      │           │
│  └──────────────────────┘                  │    1         │           │
│  ┌──────────────────────┐                  └──────────────┘           │
│  │APPROPRIATION         │                  ┌──────────────┐           │
│  └──────────────────────┘                  │  AGENCY      │           │
│  ┌──────────────────────┐                  │    8         │           │
│  │COST CENTER           │                  └──────────────┘           │
│  └──────────────────────┘                  ┌──────────────┐           │
│  ┌──────────────────────┐                  │  AGENCY      │           │
│  │SPECIAL LINE ITEM     │                  │    23        │           │
│  │    SUMMARY           │                  └──────────────┘           │
│  └──────────────────────┘                  ┌──────────────┐           │
│  ┌──────────────────────┐                  │  AGENCY      │           │
│  │SPECIAL LINE ITEM     │                  │    61        │           │
│  │    DETAIL            │                  └──────────────┘           │
│  └──────────────────────┘                  ┌──────────────┐           │
│  ┌──────────────────────┐                  │  AGENCY      │           │
│  │   OBJECT             │                  │    84        │           │
│  │   SUMMARY            │                  └──────────────┘           │
│  └──────────────────────┘                                             │
│  ┌──────────────────────┐                                             │
│  │   OBJECT             │              PRINTOUT BY AGENCY              │
│  │   DETAIL             │                                             │
│  └──────────────────────┘                                             │
│  ┌──────────────────────┐                                             │
│  │PERSONNEL             │                                             │
│  │SUMMARY               │                                             │
│  └──────────────────────┘                                             │
│  ┌──────────────────────┐                                             │
│  │PERSONNEL             │                                             │
│  │DETAIL                │                                             │
│  └──────────────────────┘                                             │
│                                                                       │
│     PRINTOUT BY REPORT TYPE                                           │
│                                                                       │
└─────────────────────────────────────────────────────────────────────┘
```

## ILLUSTRATION VIII C

The process of report distribution to agencies is extremely time consuming for the budget office if they receive the reports such as shown on the left side of Illustration VIII C. If they are printed in agency sequence, rather than report type sequence, the result would be that shown on the right side of Illustration VIII C. There are several technical ways to accomplish the best printing sequence for reports, and by logically reviewing the requirements, an approach can be developed.

There are no data base designs shown in this chapter, but rather summarization of several of the higher-level application development considerations. There is truly a great amount of work required in automating a zero-base budget system, but it is far from impossible. With the proper support and the commitments and strategies suggested in this chapter, logical analysis and design of a custom tailored system is all that remains to be done for an effective automated zero base budget system.

## IN SUMMARY

Those who have read this book will arrive at their own conclusions about implementing zero-base budgeting successfully. There will be the realization that ZBB *is not* a system like Program Planning and Budgeting (PBB), but a complementary management technique influencing managers at all levels to evaluate in detail the cost effectiveness of their operations and specific activities, and permit the Executive Branch and Congress to better establish their priorities and allocate scarce resources. The four-step approach of the ZBB process is relatively easy to implement if the top and operational agency managers use it discretely in linking the planning, budgeting and reviewing stages into a single process.

Zero-base budgeting can coexist with all past management techniques such as Management-by-Objectives, Cost-benefit Analysis, and Economic Investment Analysis. In order for this management to be used successfully, commitment to ZBB must be made at the higher levels of management. Management should use every available technique to prevent the erosion of public confidence in the Government.

Although this book emphasizes ZBB implementation in the Federal Government, it should serve as a model for the implementation of ZBB in state, city, and local governments, also. In brief, ZBB is a technique which complements and links the existing planning, budgeting, and review processes. It identifies alternative and efficient methods of utilizing limited resources in the effective attainment of selected benefits. It is a flexible management approach which provides a credible rationale for reallocating resources by focusing on the systematic review and justification of the funding and performance levels of current programs or activities.

## NOTES

1. Pyhrr, Peter A., *Zero-Base Budgeting, A Practical Management Tool for Evaluating Expenses,* 1973 (John Wiley and Sons, Inc.)

2. Executive Office of the President, Office of Management and Budget, *Zero-Base Budgeting,* OMB Bulletin 77-9, April 19, 1977

3. Ibid.

# APPENDIX

**EXECUTIVE OFFICE OF THE PRESIDENT**
OFFICE OF MANAGEMENT AND BUDGET
WASHINGTON, D.C. 20503

Bulletin No. 77-9                                                April 19, 1977

TO THE HEADS OF EXECUTIVE DEPARTMENTS AND ESTABLISHMENTS

SUBJECT:  Zero-Base Budgeting

1.  <u>Purpose</u>.  The President, in a memorandum of February 14,
1977 (Attachment), asked each agency head to develop a zero-
base budgeting system to be used in the preparation  of  the
1979  Budget.  In accordance with the President's direction,
these instructions provide guidance on the use of  zero-base
budgeting  techniques  for the preparation and justification
of 1979 budget  requests  within  each  agency.  <u>Separate</u>
<u>instructions  will  be  issued  in  OMB  Circular No. A-11 to</u>
<u>advise agencies of budget materials to be submitted to  OMB</u>.
The  instructions  in  this  Bulletin lay the foundation for
agency budget submissions in September  in  accordance  with
Circular No. A-11.

2.  <u>Coverage</u>.  These instructions apply to all  agencies  in
the   executive   branch   whose   budgets  are  subject  to
Presidential review (see OMB  Circular  No.  A-11,  section
11.1).  These concepts and guidelines are a framework within
which  each  agency  should  develop necessary procedures to

meet its individual requirements. Agencies should insure
that the fundamental characteristics of zero-base budgeting
are retained. Agencies excluded from the coverage of this
bulletin are encouraged to develop zero-base budgeting
procedures.

3. <u>Definition</u> <u>of</u> <u>terms</u>.

    a. <u>Decision unit</u>. The program or organizational entity
for which budgets are prepared and for which a manager makes
significant decisions on the amount of spending and the
scope or quality of work to be performed.

    b. <u>Decision package</u>. A brief justification document
that includes the information necessary for managers to make
judgments on program or activity levels and resource
requirements. A series of decision packages (a decision
package set) is prepared for each decision unit and
cumulatively represents the total budget request for that
unit.

    c. <u>Consolidated decision packages</u>. Packages prepared
at higher management levels that summarize and supplement
information contained in decision packages received from
lower level units. Consolidated packages may reflect
different priorities, including the addition of new programs
or the abolition of existing ones.

    d. <u>Ranking</u>. The process by which managers array
program or activity levels (as shown in decision packages)
in decreasing order of priority. This ranking process
identifies the relative priority assigned to each decision
package increment contained in the manager's budget request
based on the benefits to be gained at and the consequences
of various spending levels.

    e. <u>Minimum level</u>. The program, activity, or funding
level below which it is not feasible to continue the
program, activity, or entity because no constructive
contribution can be made toward fulfilling its objective.
The minimum level:

    -- may not be a fully acceptable level from the program
manager's perspective; and

    -- may not completely achieve the desired objectives of
the decision unit.

    f. <u>Current level</u>. The level that would be reflected in
the budget if fiscal year 1978 activities were carried on at
1978 service or other output levels without major policy
changes. A concept, not unlike current services, that
nevertheless permits internal realignments of activities
within existing statutory authorization. Estimates of
personnel compensation and other objects of expenditure will
be made in accordance with OMB Circular No. A-11.

4. <u>The zero-base budgeting concept</u>. Zero-base budgeting is
a management process that provides for systematic
consideration of all programs and activities in conjunction

with the formulation of budget requests and program planning.

The principal objectives of zero-base budgeting are to:

  -- involve managers at all levels in the budget process;

  -- justify the resource requirements for existing activities as well as for new activities;

  -- focus the justification on the evaluation of discrete programs or activities of each decision unit;

  -- establish, for all managerial levels in an agency, objectives against which accomplishments can be identified and measured;

  -- assess alternative methods of accomplishing objectives;

  -- analyze the probable effects of different budget amounts or performance levels on the achievement of objectives; and

  -- provide a credible rationale for reallocating resources, especially from old activitites to new activites.

To accomplish these objectives zero-base budgeting requires these decision-makers to:

  -- use "decision packages" as the major tool for budgetary review, analysis, and decisionmaking; and

  -- rank program or activity levels in order of priority.

5. Benefits anticipated in the Federal Government. This new system can provide significant benefits at all levels throughout the Federal Government. These benefits include:

  -- focusing the budget process on a comprehensive analysis of objectives, and the development of plans to accomplish those objectives;

  -- providing better coordination of program and activity planning, evaluation, and budgeting;

  -- expanding lower level management participation in progam and activity planning, evaluation, and budgeting;

  -- causing managers at all levels to evaluate in detail the cost effectiveness of their operations and specific activities--both new and old-- all of which are clearly identified;

  -- requiring tnat alternative ways to meet objectives are identified;

  -- identifying trade-offs between and within programs; and

-- providing managers at all levels with better information on the relative priority associated with budget requests and decisions.

Many agency management processes are aimed at providing some if not all of these same benefits. In many instances, however, such processes do not operate agencywide and the information relevant to the processes is not gathered, analyzed and reviewed in a systematic manner for all programs and activities. The value of zero-base budgeting is that it provides a process requiring systematic evaluation of the total budget request and all program objectives.

6. The zero-base budgeting process. Agencies should develop their internal zero-base budgeting procedures within the following framework.

a. Identification of objectives. An important early step in zero-base budgeting is the identification of objectives for all managers preparing and reviewing decision packages.

Top level agency management should be involved in setting objectives for lower level agency managers to:

(1) help ensure that appropriate guidance is furnished to managers throughout the agency;

(2) aid managers preparing decision packages in defining, explaining, and justifying their work to be performed and the associated resources; and

(3) aid top and intermediate level managers in understanding and evaluating the budget requests.

Program and organization objectives should be explicit statements of intended output, clearly related to the basic need for which the program or organization exists. The task of identifying objectives requires the participation by managers at all levels to determine the ultimate realistic outputs or accomplishments expected from a program or organization (major objectives) and the services or products to be provided for a given level of funding during the budget year (short-term objectives).

However, lack of precise identification and quantification of such objectives does not preclude the development and implementation of zero-base budgeting procedures.

As objectives are identified, managers should simultaneously determine the key indicators by which performance and results are to be measured. Agencies should specify measures of effectiveness, efficiency, and workload for each decision unit. These measures can often be obtained from existing evaluation and workload measurement systems. If such systems do not exist, or if data are not readily available, desirable performance indicators should not be rejected because of apparent difficulties in measurement.

Indirect or proxy indicators should be considered initially, while evaluation and workload systems are developed to provide the necessary data for subsequent budget cycles.

    b. <u>Identification of decision units</u>. Another of the first steps in zero-base budgeting is the identification of the entities in the program or organization structure whose managers will prepare the initial decision packages. In all instances, the identification of the decision units should be determined by the information needs of higher level management. <u>Agencies should ensure that the basic decision units selected are not so low in the structure as to result in excessive paperwork and review. On the other hand, the units selected should not be so high as to mask important considerations and prevent meaningful review of the work being performed.</u> In general, the decision unit should be at an organizational or program level at which the manager makes major decisions on the amount of spending and the scope, direction, or quality of work to be performed. A decision unit normally should be included within a single account, be classified in only one budget subfunction, and to the extent possible, reflect existing program and organizational structures that have accounting support.

    c. <u>Preparation of decision packages</u>. The decision unit manager performs two types of analyses based on the program and budget guidance received from higher level management. First, the manager examines alternative ways of accomplishing the major objectives. Such alternatives may require legislation and may have been identified and developed as a result of a major reexamination of the program or activity. In other instances the alternatives identified may not be fully developed, but will serve as a basis for reexamining the program at a later date. In still other instances, the alternatives identified may be the first steps toward more significant changes that will take longer than one year to accomplish. Normally, the best alternative is then selected and used as the basis for the second type of analysis--the identification of different levels of funding, activity, or performance. The purpose of identifying these different levels is to provide information on: (1) where reductions from the total request may be made, (2) the increased benefits that can be achieved through additional or alternative spending plans, and (3) the effect of such additions and reductions. Again, legislation may be required to put into effect some level of funding or performance.

However, nothing in this process should inhibit or prohibit any decisionmaker from submitting, requesting, or reviewing any information needed for analyses and decisionmaking. For example, separate decision package sets may be prepared to examine the impact of different alternatives. Also, packages reflecting increased performance or funding levels may introduce alternative methods of accomplishment that were not feasible at a lower level.

The guidance received from higher level management may determine the specific service, performance, output, or funding levels and the objectives to be discussed. This helps to insure that information provided in the decision package is broken down and arrayed in a manner conducive to higher level review of issues concerning the decision unit and also covering more than one decision unit. However, in all instances the decision package set should include:

(1) A minimum level. In all instances, the minimum level should be below the current level (unless it is clearly not feasible to operate below the current level); and

(2) A current level (unless the total requested for the decision unit is below the current level).

The decision package set may also include, when appropriate:

(1) A level or levels between the minimum and current levels; and

(2) Any additional increments desired above the current level.

Proposed changes (supplementals, amendments, rescissions) in current year amounts should be shown in packages separate from the packages described above. However, the above packages should include any budget year effect of current year changes. New programs or activities (e.g., those resulting from new legislative authority or a new major objective) will be proposed in a separate decision package set. Proposals for abolition of current programs or activities normally will not be reflected in a decision package set. However, such proposals should be highlighted, as appropriate, in another part of the agency justification.

The decision unit manager prepares a decision package set that includes decision packages reflecting incremental levels of funding and performance, so the cumulative amount of all packages represents the total potential budget request of the decision unit. Each package shows the effect of that funding and performance level on meeting the assigned objectives. The decision packages serve as the primary tool for budgetary review, analysis, and decisionmaking, although additional material may also be made available or requested for review.

Generally, a series of packages should be prepared for all programs and activities where, through legislative or administrative means, there is discretion as to the amount of funds to be spent or the appropriate method or level of activity. This does not mean that where a spending level is mandatory under existing substantive law, only one level will be identified. There are many instances in which the decision on whether to propose legislative changes is made during the preparation of the budget. There are also instances in which changes in regulations or program administration can affect the amount of resources needed to carry out a mandatory program. In these instances, packages should be prepared that analyze the effects of different

funding or performance levels or alternative methods of
accomplishing the objectives. In any instance where there
is clearly no discretion in the amounts of funds to be spent
or the appropriate method or level of activity, at least one
decision package should be prepared that summarizes the
analysis and decisionmaking that resulted in that request.
That decision package should support the conclusion that
only one funding or activity level can be considered during
the budget process.

    d. Ranking of decision packages. Completed decision
packages should be ranked initially by the decision unit
manager. At higher management levels, the rankings of each
subordinate manager are reviewed and formed into a
consolidated ranking. This consolidation process is
illustrated in Exhibit 1. The ranking shows the relative
priority that discrete increments of services or other
outputs have in relation to other increments of services or
other outputs. The process is explicitly designed to allow
higher level managers the opportunity to bring their broader
perspectives to bear on program priorities by allowing them
to rank the decision packages and make program trade-offs.

Agencies may use whatever review and ranking techniques
appropriate to their needs. However, the minimum level for
a decision unit is always ranked higher than any increment
for the same unit, since it represents the level below which
the activities can no longer be conducted effectively.
However, the minimum level package for a given decision unit
need not be ranked higher than an incremental level of some
other decision unit. A minimum level for a decision unit
may be ranked so low in comparison to incremental levels of
other decision units that the funding level for the agency
may exclude that minimum level package. This would signify
the loss of funding for that decision unit.

Decision packages or decision package sets may be prepared
to examine the effect of alternative ways to meet an
objective (see Section 6.c.). In these instances, only
those decision packages that are part of the unit's request
should be ranked. The other decision packages should
accompany the submission, however, so higher review levels
may examine the alternatives and have an opportunity to
replace the requested packages with those representing an
alternative thus far not recommended.

    e. Higher level review. In all instances, the use of
decision packages and priority rankings are the major tools
for analysis, review, and decisionmaking. At each higher
management level:

    -- decision packages may be revised, deleted, or added;
and

    -- rankings submitted by subordinate managers may be
revised.

    (1) Consolidation of decision packages. In some
small agencies, it may be desirable for each higher

management level to review every decision package prepared by each decision unit. In other instances, however, higher level management's decisionmaking needs may better be met by recasting all or some of the initial decision packages into a lesser number of consolidated decision packages. The consolidated packages would be based upon the more detailed information in the initial packages, but the information would be recast or reinterpreted in a broader frame of reference to focus on significant program alternatives or issues. The objectives may be redefined to reflect the higher level manager's program perspective.

This consolidation process may also be used to reduce what would otherwise be an excessive paperwork and review burden at higher levels. The agency head or his designee should determine at which review level(s) all or some of the packages will be consolidated into a lesser number of packages before submission to the next higher review level (see Exhibit 1). This consolidation should be based on natural groupings of subordinate decision units. Decision units in different budget subfunctions generally should not be consolidated. The consolidated package will summarize the more detailed information contained in the individual packages and identify the subordinate decision units covered.

In all instances a minimum level consolidated decision package will be prepared. This package may or may not include each of the minimum level packages from the decision package sets being consolidated. There will be instances when the preparation of a current level consolidated package is not feasible (e.g., when a decision package for a new program or activity is ranked higher than a current level package). When appropriate, there should also be a level or levels identified between the minimum and current levels.

(2) Type of review. The review can be conducted more effectively at each management level if the type of review is determined beforehand. This is especially important in the mid and higher levels in the agency, where the review workload may be significant, even with consolidation of packages. As a means of increasing the effectiveness of its review, higher level management may decide to limit its review of the higher-ranked packages to that necessary to provide a sound basis for ranking the packages and may choose to examine in more depth only the lower-ranked packages. The lower-ranked packages would be the first to be affected by an increase or decrease in the expected budgetary resources.

7. Preparation of materials. The following materials should be prepared for each decision unit.

a. Decision unit overview. The overview provides information necessary to evaluate and make decisions on each of the decision packages, without the need to repeat that information in each package. It should be at most two pages long, prepared in the format of Exhibit 2, and contain the following information:

(1) <u>Identifying information</u>.  Include sufficient
information to identify the decision unit, and the
organizational and budgetary structure within which that
decision unit is located.  Each package should include the
title of the appropriation or fund account that finances the
decision unit, the account identification code (see OMB
Circular No. A-11, section 21.3), and any internal agency
code necessary.

(2) <u>Long-range goal</u>.  When appropriate, identify
the long-range goal of the decision unit.  Goals should be
directed toward general needs, to serve as the basis for
determining the major objective(s) undertaken to work
towards that goal.

(3) <u>Major objective(s)</u>.  Describe the major
objectives of the decision unit, the requirements these
objectives are intended to satisfy and the basic authorizing
legislation.  Major objectives normally are of a continuing
nature or take relatively long periods to accomplish.
Objectives should be measurable and should be those that
program managers employ; they should form the basis for
first determining and subsequently evaluating the
accomplishments of programs or activities.

(4) <u>Alternatives</u>.  Describe the feasible
alternative ways to accomplish the major objectives.
Identify which of the alternatives represents the method
proposed for the budget year.  Briefly explain how the
approach selected contributes to satisfying the major
objectives and the rationale for not pursuing other
alternatives.  This may include a discussion of
organizational structure and delivery systems; longer-range
cost factors; and when applicable, the unique aspects and
need for the program that cannot be filled by State or local
governments or the private sector (particularly for any
enlarged or new proposed action).

(5) <u>Accomplishments</u>.  Describe the progress of the
decision unit toward meeting the major objectives.  This
section should include both quantitative and qualitative
measures of results.

b. <u>Decision packages</u>.  Each (consolidated) decision
package should be no more than two pages long, be prepared
in a format similar to Exhibit 3, and contain at least the
following information:

(1) <u>Identifying information</u>.  This information
should include organizational identification (agency,
bureau), appropriation or fund account title and
identification number, specific identification of the
decision unit, the package number, and the internal agency
code.

(2) <u>Activity description</u>.  Describe the work to be
performed or services provided with the incremental
resources specified in the package.  This section should
include a discussion and evaluation of significant

accomplishments planned and the results of benefit/cost and other analyses and evaluations that will contribute to the justification of that level.

(3) Resource requirements. Include appropriate information, such as obligations, offsetting collections, budget authority or outlays, and employment (full-time permanent and total), for the past, current, and budget years for the upcoming budget. The increment associated with each package should be listed, along with the cumulative totals for each measure used in that package, plus all higher ranked packages for that decision unit. At an appropriate level in the process, budget authority and outlay amounts for the four years beyond the budget year should also be included, in accordance with criteria in OMB Circular No. A-11.

(4) Short-term objective. State the short-term objectives (usually achievable within one year), that will be accomplished and the benefits that will result with the increment specified and the cumulative resources shown in the package. The expected results of the work performed or services provided should be identified to the maximum extent possible through the use of quantitative measures.

(5) Impact on major objective(s). Describe the impact on the major objective(s) or goals of both the incremental and the cumulative resources shown in the package.

(6) Other information. Include other information that aids in evaluating the decision package. This should include:

-- explanations of any legislation needed in connection with the package;

-- the impact or consequences of not approving the package;

-- for the minimum level package, the effects of zero-funding for the decision unit;

-- for packages below the current level, an explanation of what now is being accomplished that will not be accomplished at the lower level; and

-- the relationship of the decision unit to other decision units, including the coordination that is required.

c. Ranking sheet. Each review level will prepare a ranking sheet to submit to the next higher review level. This ranking sheet should generally contain the information shown in Exhibit 4 for the budget year.

In instances (e.g., revolving funds) where budget authority and net outlays are not a factor in reflecting the appropriate or priority level of performance, managers should use other measures (e.g. total obligations, employment).

8.  OMB review and consultation.  As an important element of
initiating zero-base budgeting, agencies are required this
year to submit for OMB and Presidential review their
proposals for:

    -- the program, activity, or organizational level to be
the basis of the (consolidated) decision packages that  will
form the agency budget submission to OMB;

    -- current and/or budget year  issues  that  should  be
highlighted  through either particular decision packages or,
when decision packages are not  appropriate,  through  issue
papers  that  ultimately  tie  in to one or several decision
packages; and

    -- longer-range issues for which agencies will  initiate
extensive evaluations.

This identification of issues will play an integral role  in
OMB's  spring  review  of  agency  programs, activities, and
plans.  Policy guidance letters to  the  agencies  regarding
the  preparation of the fall budget submission will be based
in part on this information.

OMB representatives will contact the  agencies  shortly  and
request these proposals.

9.  Inquiries.  Should additional discussion  be  necessary,
agencies should contact their OMB budget examiner.

Bert Lance
Director


Attachment

# DECISION PACKAGE RANKING AND CONSOLIDATION PROCESS ILLUSTRATED

BULLETIN NO. 77-9

Managers A, B, and C each rank packages for their units and send to Manager X

Manager X receives packages and evaluates and ranks them within each unit

Manager X ranks packages for units A, B, and C against each other, and sends to Manager R

Manager R evaluates packages from Managers X and Y, and then ranks them against each other

Manager R prepares some consolidated decision packages before submitting budget request to next higher level

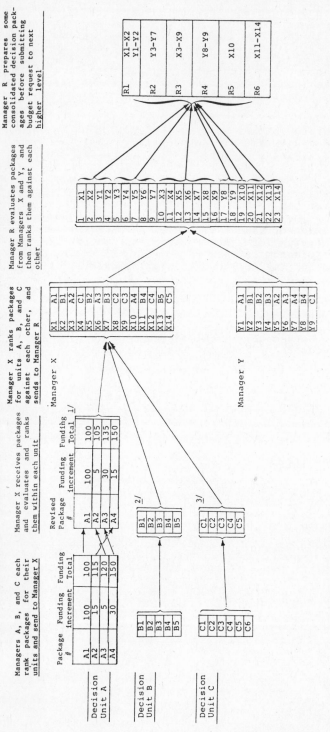

1/  Higher level manager reorders the proposed priorities of the subordinate decision unit managers.  The packages may be revised by either the initial decision unit manager or the higher level manager.

2/  Higher level manager accepts proposed priorities of the subordinate manager.

3/  Higher level manager accepts proposed priorities of the subordinate manager, but chooses not to propose funding of lowest priority package.

Bulletin No. 77-9
Exhibit 2

DECISION UNIT OVERVIEW
Department of Health, Education, and Welfare
Mental Health Administration
Federal Support of Community Mental Health Services
Mental Health:  75-0001-0-1-550

Goal.

To ensure needy citizens access to community based mental health services, regardless of ability to pay. Services should be of high quality, provided in the least restrictive environment, and in a manner assuring patients' rights and dignity.

Major objective.

To assist in the establishment and operation of a nationwide network of 1,200 qualified community mental health centers (CMHCs) by 1984 to ensure availability and accessibility of services to residents of each mental health catchment area.

Current method of accomplishing the major objectives.

Grants are made to public and nonprofit entities to plan and operate community mental health center programs. The planning grants are one-time grants, not to exceed $75,000 each. The operating grants are for eight-year periods with a declining Federal matching rate.

Alternatives.

1. Consolidate Federal funding for community mental health services and other categorical health service programs into a single formula grant to the States.

2. Consolidate Federal funding for community mental health services and other community-based inpatient and outpatient services—as well as institutionally based short-term acute and long-term care services—for the mentally ill and mentally retarded.

These alternatives are not being pursued because the States thus far have not been able to ensure that funds will be targeted into high priority areas. The Secretary believes the Federal Government must have the ability to control the funding.

3. Provide for mental health services coverage through the national health insurance proposal. This alternative is not presently viable because passage of the national health insurance act is not near. Intensive study is now being directed toward this alternative for possible consideration next year.

Accomplishments.

Since the establishment of the CMHC program in the mid-1960's, 670 CMHC's have received Federal funding of nearly $2.0 billion. In 1977, nearly 600 centers were operational, covering 45% of the population (90 million people) and providing treatment services to 2 million individuals annually.

In 1977, 450 centers received Federal grant support and 100 centers completed the eight-year Federal grant cycle. To qualify for an operational grant, P.L. 100-63, requires centers to provide the following services on a 24 hour a day, seven day a week basis:

1.  Inpatient hospitalization;
2.  Outpatient treatment and counseling;
3.  Partial hospitalization as an alternative to full-time hospitalization;
4.  24-hour emergency services by telephone or on a walk-in basis;
5.  Consultation and education services;
6.  Services to children;
7.  Services to the elderly;
8.  Screening services to the courts and other agencies;
9.  Follow-up care for former full-time patients from a mental health facility;
10. Transitional services for same;
11. Alcoholism and alcohol abuse program and drug addiction and abuse program.

Bulletin No. 77-9
Exhibit 3

Package 1 of 4 (minimum level)

DECISION PACKAGE
Department of Health, Education and Welfare
Mental Health Administration
Federal Support of Community Mental Health Services
Mental Health: 75-0001-0-1-550

Activity Description:

Continue grants only to the 450 CMHC's currently receiving Federal support, until each CMHC's eight-year grant cycle is completed.

Resource Requirements: Dollars (in thousands)

| | 1977 | 1978 | 1979 This Package | Cumulative Total |
|---|---|---|---|---|
| Planning grants ($) | 1,000 | 1,000 | 0 | 0 |
| Operating grants ($) | 97,000 | 147,000 | 120,000 | 120,000 |
| Total obligations | 98,000 | 148,000 | 120,000 | 120,000 |
| Budget authority | 98,000 | 148,000 | 120,000 | 120,000 |
| Outlays | 97,000 | 145,000 | 119,000 | 119,000 |

| Five-year estimates | 1979 | 1980 | 1981 | 1982 | 1983 |
|---|---|---|---|---|---|
| Budget authority | 120,000 | 100,000 | 80,000 | 60,000 | 40,000 |
| Outlays | 119,000 | 98,000 | 79,000 | 59,000 | 40,000 |

Short-term objective:

To ensure in 1979 access to qualified comprehensive mental health services to 45% of the population (this results in treatment of about 2 million patients).

Impact on major objectives:

The major objective of 1200 qualified CMHC's by 1988 would not be met if this short term objective were continued. It is unlikely that any net increase in qualified CMHC's would result at this level because few communities have the resources to develop a qualified program. It is estimated that for each community that would develop a qualified CMHC, an existing qualified CMHC would cease to qualify because of cutbacks in service provided due to tight funds. The impact of continuing this level objective follows:

|  | 1977 | 1978 | 1979 | 1980 | 1981 | 1982 | 1983 | 1984 |
|---|---|---|---|---|---|---|---|---|
| Number of public and non-profit CMHC's | 700 | 710 | 720 | 730 | 740 | 750 | 760 | 770 |
| Number of CMHC's providing comprehensive services, as now defined | 550 | 600 | 600 | 600 | 600 | 600 | 600 | 600 |
| Number of CMHC's receiving grants | 400 | 450 | 400 | 350 | 300 | 250 | 200 | 150 |
| Percent of population covered | 43 | 45 | 45 | 45 | 45 | 45 | 45 | 45 |
| Percent of probable patients covered | 45 | 50 | 50 | 50 | 50 | 50 | 50 | 50 |

Other Information:

Continuing grants to the 450 CMHC's currently receiving Federal support until each CMHC's eight-year cycle is completed is the minimum level because (a) the government has an eight-year contract with each CMHC, and (b) no new CMHC's will receive any grants. If zero-funded, the government would be subject to legal action brought by CMHC's.

This level would cease to encourage communities to develop CMHC's because of the (a) lack of planning grant funds and (b) lack of operational grant funds, thus negating the potential growth in the number of qualified CMHC's.

Only 57% of the high priority catchment areas would receive qualified CMHC coverage.

Bulletin No. 77-9
Exhibit 3

Package 2 of 4

DECISION PACKAGE
Department of Health, Education, and Welfare
Mental Health Administration
Federal Support of Community Mental Health Services
Mental Health: 75-0001-0-1-550

## Activity Description

Continue grants to a total of 450 Currently funded CMHC reaches the end of its eight-year cycle for eligibility, provide an eight-year grant to a newly qualified CMHC.

## Resource Requirements: Dollars in thousands.

|  | 1977 | 1978 | This Package | 1979 Cumulative Total |
|---|---|---|---|---|
| Planning grants ($) | 1,000 | 1,000 | 0 | 0 |
| Operating grants ($) | 97,000 | 147,000 | -20,000 | 140,000 |
| Total obligations | 98,000 | 148,000 | -20,000 | 140,000 |
| Budget authority | 98,000 | .000 | 20,000 | 140,000 |
| Outlays | 97,000 | 145,000 | 19,000 | 138,000 |

|  | 1979 | 1980 | 1981 | 1982 | 1983 |
|---|---|---|---|---|---|
| Five year estimates |  |  |  |  |  |
| Budget authority | 140,000 | 142,000 | 143,000 | 145,000 | 146,000 |
| Outlays | 138,000 | 141,000 | 142,000 | 144,000 | 145,000 |

## Short-term objective.

To ensure in 1979 access to qualified comprehensive mental health services to 49% of the population (this results in treatment of about 2.1 million patients).

## Impact on major objectives.

Even without the planning grants, many communities will be encouraged to develop CMHCs because of the possibility of receiving the operating grants. However, the major objective would not be met at this level of funding. It would take until about 1990 to establish 1200 qualified CMHCs. The impact of continuing this level follows:

|  | 1977 | 1978 | This Package | 1979 cumulative | 1980 | 1981 | 1982 | 1983 | 1984 |
|---|---|---|---|---|---|---|---|---|---|
| Number of public and nonprofit CMHCs | 700 | 710 | 40 | 750 | 800 | 850 | 900 | 950 | 1,000 |
| Number of CMHCs providing comprehensive services, as now defined | 550 | 600 | 50 | 650 | 700 | 750 | 800 | 850 | 900 |
| Number of CMHCs receiving grants | 400 | 450 | 50 | 450 | 450 | 450 | 450 | 450 | 450 |
| Percent of population covered | 43 | 45 | 4 | 49 | 58 | 65 | 75 | 80 | 85 |
| Percent of probable patients covered | 45 | 50 | 4 | 54 | 64 | 69 | 80 | 84 | 88 |

## Other information.

By 1982, 70% of the high priority catchment areas will have a qualified CMHC. Assuming the objective of CMHCs is desirable even by 1990, stretching out the program past the major objective date of 1984 will increase total program costs from $3.6 billion to $4.3 billion due to estimated increases in service costs.

Bulletin No. 77-9
Exhibit 3

Package 3 of 4 (Current level)

DECISION PACKAGE
Department of Health, Education, and Welfare
Mental Health Administration
Federal Support of Community Mental Health Services
Mental Health: 75-0001-0-1-550

Activity Description:

Fund 50% more newly qualifying CMHC's. That is, for every two CMHC's whose eight-year eligibility period ends, fund three newly qualifying CMHC's.

Resource Requirements: (Dollars in thousands)

|  | 1977 | 1978 | 1979 This Package | 1979 Cumulative Total |
|---|---|---|---|---|
| Planning grants ($) | 1,000 | 1,000 | 0 | 0 |
| Operating grants ($) | 97,000 | 147,000 | 10,000 | 150,000 |
| Total obligations | 98,000 | 148,000 | 10,000 | 150,000 |
| Budget authority | 98,000 | 148,000 | 10,000 | 150,000 |
| Outlays | 97,000 | 145,000 | 10,000 | 148,000 |

| Five year estimates | 1979 | 1980 | 1981 | 1982 | 1983 |
|---|---|---|---|---|---|
| Budget authority | 150,000 | 162,000 | 172,000 | 183,000 | 194,000 |
| Outlays | 148,000 | 161,000 | 171,000 | 182,000 | 193,000 |

Short-term Objective:

To ensure in 1979 access to qualified comprehensive mental health services to 51% of the population (this results in treatement of about 2.2 million patients).

Impact on Major Objectives:

|  | 1977 | 1978 | this Pkg. | 1979 Cum. | 1980 | 1981 | 1982 | 1983 | 1984 |
|---|---|---|---|---|---|---|---|---|---|
| Number of public and non-profit CMHC's | 700 | 710 | 25 | 775 | 850 | 925 | 1,000 | 1,075 | 1,150 |
| Number of CMHC's providing comprehensive services, as now defined | 550 | 600 | 25 | 675 | 750 | 825 | 900 | 975 | 1,050 |
| Number of CMHC's receiving grants | 400 | 450 | 25 | 475 | 500 | 525 | 550 | 575 | 600 |
| Percent of population covered | 43 | 45 | 6 | 51 | 65 | 75 | 80 | 85 | 90 |
| Percent of probable patients covered | 45 | 50 | 6 | 56 | 66 | 77 | 83 | 87 | 90 |

Other information:

By 1982 95% of the high priority catchment areas will have a qualified CMHC. If stretched out from 1984 to 1986, total program costs for establishing 1200 CMHC's will increase from $3.6 billion to about $3.8 billion.

Bulletin No. 77-9
Exhibit 3

Package 4 of 4

DECISION PACKAGE
Department of Health, Education, and Welfare
Mental Health Administration
Federal Support of Community Mental Health Services
Mental Health: 75-0001-0-1-550

Activity Description:

For every CMHC whose eight year eligibility periods ends, fund two newly qualifying CMHC's.

Resource Requirements: Dollars in thousands

| | 1977 | 1978 | This Package (1979) | Cumulative Total (1979) |
|---|---|---|---|---|
| Planning grants ($) | 1,000 | 1,000 | 0 | 0 |
| Operating grants ($) | 97,000 | 147,000 | 10,000 | 160,000 |
| Total obligations | 98,000 | 148,000 | 10,000 | 160,000 |
| Budget authority | 98,000 | 148,000 | 10,000 | 160,000 |
| Outlays | 97,000 | 145,000 | 10,000 | 158,000 |

| Five year estimates | 1979 | 1980 | 1981 | 1982 | 1983 |
|---|---|---|---|---|---|
| Budget authority | 160,000 | 172,000 | 133,000 | 193,000 | 204,000 |
| Outlays | 158,000 | 170,000 | 182,000 | 192,000 | 203,000 |

Short-term Objectives

To ensure in 1979 access to qualified comprehensive mental health services to 53% of the population (this results in treatment of about 2.3 million patients).

Impact on Major Objectives

| | 1977 | 1978 | this pkg. | 1979 cum. | 1980 | 1981 | 1982 | 1983 | 1984 |
|---|---|---|---|---|---|---|---|---|---|
| Number of public and non-profit CMHC's | 700 | 710 | 25 | 800 | 900 | 1,000 | 1,100 | 1,200 | 1,300 |
| Number of CMHC;s providing comprehensive services, as now defined | 550 | 600 | 25 | 700 | 800 | 900 | 1,000 | 1,100 | 1,200 |
| Number of CMHC's receiving grants | 400 | 450 | 25 | 500 | 550 | 600 | 650 | 700 | 750 |
| Percent of population covered | 43 | 45 | 2 | 53 | 75 | 80 | 84 | 93 | 100 |
| Percent of probable patients covered | 45 | 50 | 2 | 58 | 77 | 82 | 85 | 93 | 100 |

The major objective will be met at this level of funding.

Other Information

By 1982 100% of the high priority catchment areas will have a qualified CMHC. Total program cost by 1984 will be $3.6 billion.

BULLETIN NO. 77-9
EXHIBIT 4

RANKING SHEET

Department of Government
Fiscal year 1979

Date: July 17, 1977

(Other identifying information)

| Rank | Decision Package | BA | Outlays | Cumulative BA | Cumulative Outlays |
|---|---|---|---|---|---|
| 1 | A1 | 924 | 901 | 924 | 901 |
| 2 | B1 | 800 | 785 | 1,724 | 1,686 |
| 3 | A2 | 121 | 121 | 1,845 | 1,807 |
| 4 | C1 | 0 | 0 | 1,845 | 1,807 |
| 5 | B2 | 30 | 30 | 1,875 | 1,837 |
| 6 | A3 | 0 | 0 | 1,875 | 1,837 |
| 7 | B3 | 30 | 30 | 1,905 | 1,867 |
| 8 | C2 | 0 | 0 | 1,905 | 1,867 |
| 9 | C3 | 0 | 0 | 1,905 | 1,867 |
| 10 | A4 | 22 | 22 | 1,927 | 1,889 |
| 11 | B4 | 11 | 11 | 1,938 | 1,900 |
| 12 | C4 | 0 | 0 | 1,938 | 1,900 |
| 13 | B5 | 30 | 30 | 1,968 | 1,930 |
| 14 | C5 | 0 | 0 | 1,968 | 1,930 |
| 15 | C6 | 0 | 0 | 1,968 | 1,930 |

# BIBLIOGRAPHY

Arkansas, Little Rock Dept. of Finance and Administration, "1977-79 Biennium Budget Procedures," April 30, 1976.

Axelrod, Donald, "Post-Burkhead: The state of the art or science of budgeting," *Public Administration Review,* Nov.-Dec. 1973, v. 33, pp. 576.

Anderson, Donald N., "Zero-based Budgeting: How to get rid of Corporate Crabgrass," *Management Review,* pp. 4-16.

Anderson, Donald N., "Zero-based Budgets Offer Data, Spending Control," *Industry Week,* Jan. 12, 1976, p. 49.

Anderson, Donald N., "Zero-based Budgeting: Weeding out Corporate Crabgrass," *Manager's Forum,* May 1976.

Anthony, Robert N., "Zero-base Budgeting is a Fraud," *Wall Street Journal,* April 27, 1977.

Anthony, Robert N. and Regina Herzlinger, *Management Control in Non-Profit Organizations,* 1975 (Richard D. Irwin, Inc.), pp. 213, 245, and 344.

Betts, Ernest C., Jr. and Miller, Richard E., "More about the Impact of the Congressional Budget and Impoundment Act," *The Bureaucrat.*

Broder, David S., "A Closer Look at Zero Base Budgeting," *Washington Post,* August 8, 1976, Sec. 3, p. 7.

Broder, David S., "The Carterization of the Federal Government," *Washington Post,* April 10, 1977, p. 1.

Broadnax, Walter D., "Zero-Base Budgeting: New Directions for the Bureaucracy?," *The Bureaucrat.*

Budget and Program Newsletter, February 11, 1977.

Carter, Jimmy, "Jimmy Carter tells why he will use Zero-Base Budgeting," *Nation's Business,* January 1977, pp. 24-26.

Carter, Jimmy, "Start from Zero," Chapter 11, *Why Not the Best?, 1975.*

Cheek, Logan M., "Cost Effectiveness Comes to the Personnel Function," *Harvard Business Review,* May-June 1973, pp. 96-105.

Cheek, Logan M., *Zero-Base Budgeting Comes of Age,* AMACOM, 1977.

Cole, Robert J., "Rising Interest in Zero Base Budgeting," *New York Times,* August 27, 1976, p. D1.

Drucker, Peter, "Managing the Public Sector," *The Public Interest,* Fall 1973, pp. 43-60.

Dunn, Ronald E., "Zero-Base Budgeting at Commercial Credit Company," *Cash Management Forum,* Atlanta, Georgia, v. 2, no. 1, March 1976, p. 4.

Environmental Protection Agency, *Zero Base Budgeting For ADP,* Washington, D.C., June 1976.

Executive Office of the President, Office of Management and Budget, "Preparation and submission of budget estimates," OMB Circular A-11, July 1977.

Executive Office of the President, Office of Management and Budget, *Zero-Base Budgeting,* Bulletin 77-9, April 19, 1977.

Executive Office of the President, Office of Management and Budget, "Evaluation management: a background paper," May 1975.

Gardner, Judy, " 'Sunset' bills: an eye on big government?," *Congressional Quarterly,* April 24, 1976, pp. 955-956.

Georgia, State of, Office of Planning and Development, *General budget preparation procedures, fiscal year 1978 budget development,* July 1976.

Granof, Michael H. and Kinzel, Dale A., "Zero-base budgeting: modest proposal for reform," *Federal Accountant,* December 1974, pp. 50-56.

Halverson, Guy, "Zero Base Budgeting gaining acceptance in the U.S.," *The Christian Science Monitor,* October 28, 1976.

Havemann, Joel, "Congress tries to break ground zero in evaluating Federal programs," *National Journal,* May 25, 1976, pp. 706-713.

Hogan, Roy L., *Zero-base budgeting: a rationalistic attempt to improve the Texas budget system,* 1975. (University of Texas, Austin)

Huntington, Eugent, "Implementation of the Priority Budgeting System," State of Montana, March 1977.

Idaho Division of the Budget, Policy Planning and Coordination, *Program Management and Budget Development Manual,* May 1976.

Idaho, State of, *Considerations on Zero-Base Budgeting: An evaluation of Idaho's Experience and Recommendations for the Future,* Division of Budget, Policy Planning and Coordination, February 17, 1977, 15 p.

Idaho, State of, *ZBB Program Management and Budget Development Manual,* Division of Budget, Policy Planning and Coordination, April 11, 1977.

Illinois Bureau of the Budget, *Instructions to Agencies on Preparation and Submission of Annual Budget Estimates,* September 1, 1975.

Knighton, Dr. Lennis M., "Accounting for the Benefits of Public Programs," *The Federal Accountant,* v. XXI, no. 1, March 1972.

LaFaver, John D., "Zero-base budgeting in New Mexico," *State Government,* Spring 1974, p. 108.

Leininger, David L. and Wong, Ronald C., "Zero-base budgeting in Garland, Texas," *Management Information Report,* v. 8, no. 4a, April 1976.

Leone, Richard C., "How to Ride Herd on the Budget," *The Nation,* May 22, 1976.

Leone, Richard C., "Zero-base system in New Jersey," testimony delivered before the Subcommittee on Intergovernmental Operations of the Senate Committee on Government Operations, Washington, D.C., May 25, 1976.

Louisiana, State of, *Zero-base Budget Instructions – 1977-1978,* Division of Administration, Office of Budget and Management, September 1976.

Lynch, Thomas D., "A Context for zero-base Budgeting," *The Bureaucrat.*

McGinnis, James F., "Pluses and minuses of zero-base budgeting," *Administrative Management,* September 1976, pp. 22-23.

Merewitz, Leonard and Sosnick, Stephen, *The budget's new clothes: a critique of planning-programming-budgeting and benefit-cost analysis,* 1971. (Markham Publishing Company, Chicago)

Miller, Karl A., "Zero budgeting in Yonkers, N.Y." *Government Executive,* January 1977.

Miller, Richard E., "Zero-base budgets, or What's new in budgeting of Violated Environments," *The Bureaucrat,* January 1977.

Minmier, George S., *An evaluation of the zero base budgeting systems in governmental institutions,* 1975. (Research monograph – Georgia State University, School of Business Administration)

Minmier, George S. and Hermanson, Roger H., "A look at zero-base budgeting – the Georgia experience," *Government Accountants Journal,* winter 1976-77.

Montana Office of Budget and Program Planning, *Priority Budgeting System – 1977-79 Biennium – Instructions and Procedures,* June 1976.

Montana, State of, *A Review of the Priority Budgeting System,* Budget and Program Planning, Office of the Governor, 14 p.

Morrisey, George L., *Management by Objectives and Results in the Public Sector,* 1976. (Addison-Wesley Publishing Company)

Murray, Thomas H., "The Tough Job of Zero Budgeting," *Dun's Review,* October 1974, pp. 71-72.

National Governor's Conference, Innovations in State Governments; messages from the Governors (Washington, 1974), "Planning a budget from zero," by Jimmy Carter; reprinted in Congressional Record, February 25, 1976.

Noel, Philip W., Zero-base Budgeting, Memorandum to all Department Directors and Agency Heads, State of Rhode Island, July 27, 1973.

Peirce, Neal R., "The sunset demand for bureaucratic justification," *Washington Post,* March 25, 1976.

Porter, Fred and Ms. Rita Henry, "Presentation Materials on the Arkansas Base Level/Priority Budget System," prepared for ZBB-ZBR Symposium by the Association of Government Accountants, Washington, D.C., June 1977, 11 p.

Pyhrr, Peter A., "Critique of Zero-base Budgeting," *The Bureaucrat.*

Pyhrr, Peter A., "Zero-base Budgeting," *Harvard Business Review,* Nov.-Dec. 1970, pp. 111-121.

Pyhrr, Peter A., *Zero-base Budgeting, A Practical Management Tool for Evaluating Expenses,* 1973. (John Wiley and Sons, Inc.)

Pyhrr, Peter A., "Zero-base Budgeting: Where to Use It and How to Begin," *Advanced Management Journal,* Summer 1976.

Pyhrr, Peter A., "The Zero-Base Approach to Government Budgeting," *Public Administration Review,* Jan.-Feb. 1977, pp. 1-8.

Rhode Island, State of, "Introduction to Zero-base Budgeting," memo from Philip W. Noel, Governor, July 27, 1973, 17 p.

Sarant, Peter, "ZBB — Impact on Poor, Federal aid and grants to State and Local Programs," Focus, Joint Center for Political Studies, Washington, D.C., May 1977.

Sarant, Peter, *Zero-Base Budgeting in the Public Sector — A Pragmatic Approach,* September 1977, 225 pp. (Addison-Wesley Publishing Company, Reading, Mass.)

Sarant, Peter, "Is PPB Dead?," *Journal of Accountancy,* Malaysia, May 1973. (U.S. Civil Service Library)

Sarsfield, E. William, "Zero-base Budgeting: The Pros and Cons," *Federal Times,* November 8, 1976.

Sawyer, Kathy, "Zero-based Budget ABCs," *Washington Post,* April 18, 1977.

Schick, Allen and Keith, Robert, "Zero-base Budgeting," August 31, 1976. (Congressional Research Service)

Schick, Allen, "Zero-base Budgeting and Sunset: Redundancy or Symbiosis?," *The Bureaucrat.*

Schultz, Charles I., *The Politics and Economics of Public Spending,* 1968. (The Brookings Institution)

Singleton, David W., et al., "Zero-based budgeting in Wilmington, Delaware," *Government Finance,* August 1976, pp. 20-29.

Smith, Linda L., "The Congressional Budget Process: Why it Worked This Time," *The Bureaucrat.*

Stonich, Paul J., "Zero-base Planning — A Management Tool," *Managerial Planning*, July-August 1976, pp. 1-4.

Stonich, Paul J. and Steeves, William H., "Zero-base Planning and Budgeting for Utilities," *Public Utilities Fortnightly*, September 9, 1976, pp. 24-29.

Stonich, Paul J., "Zero-Base Planning and Budgeting: Improved Cost Control and Resource Allocation." Chicago: Dow Jones-Irwin, 1977.

Taylor, Graeme M., "Introduction to Zero-base Budgeting," *The Bureaucrat*, Spring 1977.

Texas, State of, Legislative Budget Office, *Detailed Instructions for Preparing and Submitting Requests for Legislative Appropriations for the Biennium*, beginning September 1, 1977.

Texas, State of, *Instruction for Preparing Budget Requests for Fiscal Years 1978 and 1979*, Governor's Budgeting and Planning Office, Austin, Texas.

Texas, State of, *Budget Manual — Needs, Objectives and Measures for the 1978-1979 Biennium*, Governor's Budget and Planning Office, Austin, Texas.

Tufty, Hal, "Zero-base Budgeting and Value Engineering," *Value Digest*, December 1976, pp. 2-4.

U.S. Congress, Senate. Subcommittee on Intergovernmental Relations of Committee on Government Operations, *Government Economy and Spending Act of 1976, Hearings*, 1976, 539 pp. (Government Printing Office)

U.S. Congress, Senate, Committee on Rules and Administration, *Government economy and spending act of 1976*, 1976, 114 pp. (Government Printing Office)

U.S. Congress, Senate, Committee on Government Operation, *Compendium of Materials on zero-base budgeting in the states*, January 1976, 363 pp. (Government Printing Office)

U.S. Congress, "Reorganization Act of 1977," April 1977.

U.S. Congress, House of Representatives, Zero-base Budget Legislation, Hearings before the Task Force on Budget Process, 1976, 149 pp. (Government Printing Office)

U.S. Department of Health, Education, and Welfare, *Zero-Base Budgeting for the Public Health Service*, Washington, D.C., April 1977.

U.S. Department of Labor, ZBB Instructions for FY 1979, Office of Assistant Secretary for Administration and Management, 1977.

"Ways to make Uncle Sam spend more wisely," *Nation's Business*, August 1972, pp. 26-28.

Wildavsky, Aaron, *Budgeting: A Comparative Theory of Budgeting Processes of Boston*, 1975, pp. 278-296. (Little, Brown, and Company, Boston)

Wildavsky, Aaron, "The Annual Expenditure Increment: How Congress can regain control of the Budget," *The Public Interest*, Fall 1973, p. 84.

Wildavsky, Aaron and Hamman, Arthur, "Comprehensive versus Incremental Budgeting in the Department of Agriculture," In Lyden, Fremont, Jr. and Miller, Ernest G. et al., *Planning, Programming, Budgeting: A Systems Approach to Management*, 1968, p. 153. (Markham Company, Chicago)

Wildavsky, Aaron, *The Politics of the Budgetary Process*, 1964. (Little, Brown, and Company, Boston)

Wright, Chester and Tate, Michael D., *Economics and Systems Analysis*, 1973. (Addison-Wesley Publishing Company)

Wright, Norman H., Jr., "Zero-base budgeting and planning — the ranking process," *Management World*, February 1977, pp. 31-33.

Wilson, Charles H. Representative, "Zero-Base Budgeting: Will it Work or is it Another Buzzword?," *Congressional Record — House*, January 31, 1977, pp. 627-633.

"Zero-base budgeting for the fiscal year 1979 budget," The President's memorandum for the heads of executive agencies and departments, *Weekly Compilation of Presidential Documents*, February 21, 1977, p. 197.

"Zero-base Budgeting Made Simple," *Federal Times*, April 4, 1977.

"Zero-based budgeting — A way to cut Spending, or a Gimmick," *U.S. News and World Report*, September 20, 1976, pp. 79-82.

"Zero-base Budgeting: One Way to Erase Needless Government Programs," *Nation's Business*, November 1976, pp. 52-56.

Zero-Base Budgeting Digest, National Press Building, Washington, D.C. 20045.

Harvey, L. James, PhD, and Rusten, Allan C., *The ZBB Handbook for Local Governments*, Ireland Educational Corporation, Littleton, Connecticut, 1977.